Beyond Technology

Children's Learning in the Age of Digital Culture

DAVID BUCKINGHAM

polity

First published in 2007 by Polity Press

Polity Press
65 Bridge Street
Cambridge CB2 1UR, UK

Polity Press
350 Main Street
Malden, MA 02148, USA

ISBN-13: 978-07456-3880-5
ISBN-13: 978-07456-3881-2 (pb)

A catalogue record for this book is available from the British Library.

Typeset in 11.25 on 13 pt Dante
by SNP Best-set Typesetter Ltd., Hong Kong
Printed and bound in Great Britain by MPG Books Ltd, Bodmin, Cornwall

The publisher has used its best endeavours to ensure that the URLs for external websites referred to in this book are correct and active at the time of going to press. However, the publisher has no responsibility for the websites and can make no guarantee that a site will remain live or that the content is or will remain appropriate.

Every effort has been made to trace all copyright holders, but if any have been inadvertently overlooked the publisher will be pleased to include any necessary credits in any subsequent reprint or edition.

For further information on Polity, visit our website: www.polity.co.uk

Contents

Preface

It is now more than a quarter of a century since the first microcomputers began arriving in British schools. I can personally recall the appearance of one such large black metal box – a Research Machines 380Z – in the North London comprehensive school where I was working in the late 1970s; and I can also remember very well the computer program that was demonstrated to the English Department – a simple but genuinely thought-provoking package called 'Developing Tray', a kind of 'hangman' game in which a poem gradually emerged like a photographic image in a developing tray.[1] I also recall, a couple of years later, being involved in a research project called 'Telesoftware', run from Brighton Polytechnic, where educational software was (amazingly to us at the time) sent over the telephone line and recorded onto little cassette tapes. Actually, very few of the other teachers were interested in the software that was being delivered, but the students in my media studies class were quick to commandeer the equipment to make animated title and credit sequences for their scratch-edited video productions.

Around the same time, the American technology guru Seymour Papert was telling us that computers would fundamentally transform education – and ultimately make the school itself redundant. 'Computers', he wrote in a book published in 1980, 'will gradually return to the individual the power to determine the patterns of education. Education will become more of a private act' (Papert, 1980: 37). Four years later, he told readers even more bluntly, 'There won't be schools in the future. The computer will blow up the school' (Papert, 1984: 38). He was not alone. Steve Jobs, the founder of Apple Computers, then pitching relentlessly to capture the education market in the US, was another passionate advocate of the revolutionary potential of educational computing; and he was later joined by an enthusiastic cohort of visionary marketers, such as Bill Gates of Microsoft, who were keen to use schools as a springboard into the much more valuable home market. Indeed, ten years earlier, the radical theorist Ivan Illich was creating a vision of a 'deschooled society', in which computers would permit the creation of informal, 'convivial' networks of learners, and schools and teachers would simply wither away (Illich, 1971).

Such predictions about the transformative potential of technology have a very long history, not just in education, and in retrospect it is easy to show that they have largely failed to come true. The wholesale revolution Papert and others were predicting patently has not taken place: for better or worse, the school as an institution is still very much with us, and most of the teaching and learning that happens there has remained completely untouched by the influence of technology. And yet, over the same period, electronic technology has become an increasingly significant dimension of most young people's lives. Digital media – the internet, mobile phones, computer games, interactive television – are now an indispensable aspect of children's and young people's leisure-time experiences. Young people's relationship with digital technology is no longer formed primarily in the context of the school – as it was during the 1980s, and even into the 1990s – but in the domain of popular culture. This raises the fundamental question that I want to address in this book. How should schools be responding to the role of digital media in young people's lives? Should they simply ignore them – as they largely appear to do at the present time? Should they enlist these media for the purpose of delivering the established curriculum? Or can they find ways of engaging with them more critically and creatively?

More than twenty-five years after my first encounters with computers in the classroom, my university research centre was relocated to a new facility, the London Knowledge Lab. Although it is situated in the heart of London's historic Bloomsbury district, the Knowledge Lab looks to the future: its strapline is 'exploring the future of learning with digital technologies'. In the process, a small team of us who are concerned with children, young people and media have come into closer contact with advocates of information and communication technologies (ICTs) in schools, and with advanced computer scientists. In some respects, it is this encounter – and the much broader changes in media, technology and education that it represents – that has prompted me to write this book.

My perspective is not that of a technology or computer specialist. Most of my research and teaching has been about *media* – and particularly about moving image media such as television and film. I have explored how these media are produced, the characteristics of media 'texts', and how children and young people use and interpret them. I have also considered how teachers in schools might teach about these media, and what happens when they do so. Inevitably, in recent years, this focus has expanded to encompass new media such as computer games and the internet. However, I continue to regard these things as *media* rather than as *technologies*. I see them as ways of representing the world, and of communicating – and I seek to understand these phenomena as social and cultural processes, rather than primarily as technical ones. Technologies – or machines – are obviously part of the story. But technologies should not be seen as simply a set of neutral devices. On the contrary, they are shaped in particular ways by the social interests and motivations of the people who produce and use them.

Likewise, I would challenge the notion of *information* technology – as though these devices were simply a means of storing and delivering an inert body of facts or data (Burbules and Callister, 2000). The term 'information' somehow implies that the content of communication is neutral – and that, like technology, it is independent of human interests. There is also an implication here – particularly in the discourse of policy-makers – that delivering 'information' will somehow automatically lead to knowledge and learning. In practice, this approach inevitably sanctions an instrumental use of technology in education – a view of technology as a kind of teaching aid. Adding 'communication' – and widening the term to 'ICT' – is a step in the right direction. But, ultimately, we need to acknowledge that computers and other digital media are technologies of *representation*: they are social and cultural technologies that cannot be considered merely as neutral tools for learning.

Like many media educators, I have been both excited and dismayed by the contemporary enthusiasm for digital technology in education. I am excited, because I feel there is considerable potential here for students to take control of the 'means of production' – to use this technology to communicate, to become creative producers of media, and to represent their perspectives and concerns. I also believe that it is vital for schools to address the cultural experiences that young people have outside the classroom – and many of these experiences are now intimately connected with digital media. Yet I am dismayed, because so many uses of technology in education seem to me to be unimaginative, functional and misguided. The critical questions that media educators have been concerned with for many years – questions about who controls communications media, and about how those media represent the world – have been marginalized in favour of a superficial infatuation with technology for its own sake. Ultimately, I believe that we need to be teaching *about* technologies, not just *with* or *through* them.

Yet, in questioning the use of technology in education, it is not my intention to support those who would seek to abandon it in favour of a return to 'basics' – whatever they may be. Many critics of technology in education are inclined to fall back on claims about the 'authentic' and 'natural' ways of learning which have supposedly been displaced by technology, and they also rely on assertions about the 'dehumanizing' effects of particular media that are, to say the least, highly contentious. A great deal of learning involves technology of one form or another (if we grant that the printing press or even the pen are forms of technology); and a great deal of learning is inevitably mediated (again, if we grant that the book – or indeed the curriculum itself – is a medium, a means of representing the world, just like television or the internet). We cannot simply abandon media and technology in education and return to a simpler, more natural time.

This book begins at the heart of the action, with a visit to London's BETT Show, a major UK educational technology marketing event. It moves on, in chapter 2, to consider the changing assumptions that have informed British government policy-making in this field and, in chapter 3, to explore the broader arguments that have been mounted both for and against the use of technology in schools. Chapter 4 shifts from rhetoric to reality, reviewing how technology is actually being used in education, and the evidence for its effectiveness. In chapter 5, we leave the classroom, to look at the changing role of digital media in young people's lives and the widening gap that exists between their use of technology outside school and what is happening in education. How, then, are schools to respond to this situation? Chapters 6 and 7 consider two approaches to using technology in education that I believe are fundamentally misguided: chapter 6 looks at the debate about computer games and learning, while chapter 7 explores the phenomenon of 'edutainment', focusing particularly on the home market. In chapter 8, I outline what I regard as a more rigorous, and more productive, approach to teaching with and about digital media, within a 'media literacy' framework. Finally, chapter 9 returns to some of the questions raised above about the future of the school: if schools are unlikely to disappear, how can we rethink their role in the age of digital culture?

Acknowledgements

Parts of this book draw on other writing and research I have undertaken over the past ten years or so, some of which has been published in books such as *After the Death of Childhood: Growing Up in the Age of Electronic Media* (Polity, 2000), *Education, Entertainment and Learning in the Home* (co-authored with Margaret Scanlon, Open University Press, 2003) and *Media Education: Literacy, Learning and Contemporary Culture* (Polity, 2003), as well as in a range of journal articles and papers. An early version of the overall argument was presented in a professorial lecture at the Institute of Education in London in November 2005, and published as *Schooling the Digital Generation: New Media, Popular Culture and the Future of Education* (Institute of Education, 2005). I would like to thank my colleague Michael Young for his thoughtful response to this lecture. All of this material has been very substantially reworked and updated for this context.

I would like to thank the researchers who have worked with me on various of the empirical projects that have informed this book, particularly Margaret Scanlon; and my other colleagues and collaborators with whom I have discussed some of these issues at length, notably Shakuntala Banaji, Liesbeth de Block, Andrew Burn, Diane Carr, Sue Cranmer, Caroline Pelletier, Julian Sefton-Green and Rebekah Willett. Thanks to Andrew and Diane for their comments on the manuscript. I would also like to acknowledge the scholars and researchers whose work has challenged me to think more deeply and critically about these issues, particularly Larry Cuban, Simon Egenfeldt-Nielsen, Jane Kenway, Sonia Livingstone, Ellen Seiter and Neil Selwyn.

1

Selling Technology Solutions
The Marketing of Educational Technology

The BETT (British Education, Training and Technology) Show[1] is reputed to be the largest educational trade fair in the world. Held annually in the cavernous Victorian arena of London's Olympia exhibition centre, it provides a startling indication of the growing importance of technology companies within the education marketplace. The main exhibition area is populated with stands from many major national and international corporations – Microsoft, Apple, RM, Oracle, BT, Dell – as well as broadcasters and other media companies with an interest in this field, such as the BBC, Channel 4 and Granada. More specialized mid-range software and hardware companies – TAG, Immersive, Harcourt, Promethean – also compete for attention, while around the fringes of the hall a wide range of smaller exhibitors ply their trade.

First established in 1984, the BETT Show is organized by EMAP Education, part of EMAP Business Communications, a leading UK media company. In addition to organizing exhibitions – particularly 'business-to-business' events – EMAP runs radio stations, and publishes trade papers and consumer magazines ranging from *Therapy Weekly* and *Steam Railway* right through to market-leading titles such as *FHM, More!* and *Heat*. Its annual turnover in 2005 was over £1 billion.[2] The BETT Show is sponsored by BESA (the British Educational Suppliers Association) and the magazine *Educational Computing and Technology*, and is run in association with the *Times Educational Supplement*, the government's Department for Education and Skills (DfES) and Educational Events Limited.

BESA is the leading partner in this alliance. Founded in 1933, it is the trade association for the educational supply industry, claiming a membership of over 250 manufacturers and distributors. These companies produce a range of ICT hardware and software, as well as more traditional teaching aids, furniture and other materials designed for use in educational settings ranging from pre-school to university. Some of these older products – wallcharts, stationery, worksheets, even books – continue to feature on the fringes of BETT, well away from the main site of the action.

Almost 30,000 visitors attended over four days in 2006, most leaving the exhibition with large bags emblazoned with logos and stuffed with lavishly produced handouts, catalogues and free software samples.[3] Attending BETT is a gruelling experience. The noise level in the hall makes it difficult to carry on a conversation, and it is almost impossible to find a place to sit down. The wide range of stands – reaching almost 650 in 2006 – can prove bewildering and disorientating. The 168-page official show guide contains advice on planning your visit; and it is now possible to subscribe to 'BETT mobbing', a service that sends alerts to your mobile phone about 'cool things to see'.

BETT has grown significantly in recent years, registering steady annual increases in the number of attendees and the number of stands. Those who visit are mainly UK teachers: according to BESA, around one-third of UK schools send teachers to the show each year. The organizers also promote the show through information sent to schools and through more practical means, such as arranging transport: in the past they have even collaborated with local education authorities to charter a train (dubbed the 'Education Express'), with the dual objective of providing transport to the show and ICT training on board. However, the attendance figures have also seen particular increases both in the proportion of business personnel and 'consultants', and in the number of international visitors. Each year, the British government sponsors more than sixty overseas education ministers to attend the show – and to enjoy the facilities of its 'international lounge' – suggesting that the UK is now playing a leading role in the global marketing of educational technology.

Sales pitches

The sales pitches adopted at BETT vary from the minimalist to the hyperactive, although the latter are much in evidence. Some of the larger exhibits are the most understated, suggesting that the central aim is one of branding rather than direct selling of products. Others use glossy images taken from the companies' CD-ROMs, web pages or books, often emphasizing primary colours in a style characteristic of children's publishing. Most of the larger stands include several terminals at which participants can try out the products on offer, as well as a presentation area with seating and a large whiteboard screen. Several run timetabled demonstrations and 'seminars' at which new products are showcased, and uniformed representatives are on hand to provide additional persuasion. Many exhibits include endorsements from reviewers or key figures in education, while others have large television screens showing promotional videos, often featuring fast-moving excerpts from their productions set to music. For technology companies, this is highly labour-intensive work: RM, for example, claimed in 2006 to have 100 staff working on its two stands, with fifty separate presentations in its two 'theatres'. The overall cost of the show to exhibitors is reputed to be more than £6 million.[4]

In some instances, the sales techniques are more assertive. Several exhibitors offer quizzes and competitions, or the chance to win a free lunch. Others provide gifts, in the form of pens, yoyos, badges and chocolate bars; the BBC launched its digital curriculum, with its new street-credible title 'BBC Jam', by offering free pots of jam. Several stands have salespeople in costume: in 2006, William Shakespeare was on hand, along with a large cuddly bear, a nineteenth-century aristocrat, a robot and various medieval peasants. In previous years, Lara Croft lookalikes have roamed the halls, while in 2006 'booth babes' dressed in white mini-skirts with company names emblazoned on their backsides attempted to entice the visitor to purchase the latest educational software solution.

While some of the presenters have a vaguely educational gravitas, most are more akin to market traders or 'barkers' at a funfair. They are fast-moving, amplified, 'punchy' and humorous, using repetition and rhetorical questions in the style of a department store salesman extolling the virtues of carpet shampoo. Prominent among them is Russell Prue, a self-styled 'independent ICT Evangelist', who presented at five different stands in 2006, in each case wearing different braces carrying the relevant company slogan along with his trademark glittering red bow tie. Formerly employed by the UK computer hardware company RM as 'Chief Product Evangelist', Prue is the author of *The Science of Evangelism*, and is frequently engaged by the Department for Education and Skills to promote its policies.[5]

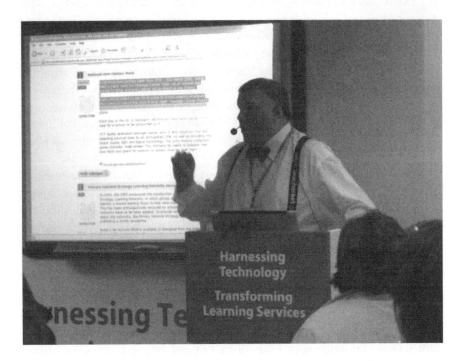

The view of technology promoted at BETT is relentlessly upbeat. In the words of the show's 2006 slogan, technology is 'Engaging – Enriching – Empowering'. It will motivate, inspire and stimulate teachers and students, and transform the learning experience:

> BETT . . . bringing together the global teaching and learning community for four days of innovations and inspirations. BETT is the place to see exciting ideas, the latest technology, practical solutions that can have an immediate impact, and new ways to put ICT at the heart of learning. (BESA website)

The straplines of individual exhibitors reinforce this almost mystical message: 'lighting the flame of learning' (Promethean); 'inspiring creativity in the classroom' (Smoothwall); 'share knowledge, spark brilliance' (Adobe); 'transforming the future' (RM). Even the DfES partakes of the same rhetoric, albeit in slightly more muted terms: technology is about 'creating opportunities, realizing potential, achieving excellence'. Learning via technology, it is repeatedly asserted, is 'fun', exciting and motivating for young people in a way that more traditional methods are not.

While the BETT Show is almost exclusively targeted at schools, several key exhibitors also have significant interests in the domestic market. This interest in out-of-school learning is reflected in the straplines: 'Extending the classroom into the home: Knowledge through your television' (NTL); 'Non Stop Learning – Non Stop Managed Services' (Compaq); 'Portable Learning' (ACER). Likewise, the Microsoft presentations speak of 'anytime, anywhere learning' and 'learners without limits', and claim that their products are 'bridging the gap between learning in and beyond the classroom'; part of the pitch of 'BBC Jam' is the ability of students to access it at home, 'or as a continuation of their learning at school', finding that 'almost without knowing it, they are actually learning all the time'.

One of the recurrent themes that emerges here is the idea that technology represents a 'solution' – although it is never quite clear what problems it solves. There are no problems at BETT, only solutions – 'solutions for schools', 'solutions that delight you', 'flexible solutions', 'solution providers', 'portable, hand-held solutions', 'integrated education ICT solutions', 'end-to-end solutions', and many more. Some companies promoting managed learning environments claim that they can cater for *all* ICT requirements and thereby provide the 'total solution' for every need. In some cases, the term 'solution' appears to take the place of the material object – the hardware or software – that is actually on sale. In this formulation, the technology seems to move beyond being a mere consumer product, and to assume an almost metaphysical dimension; and, in the process, it is endowed with a magical ability to stimulate and transform teaching and learning.

Another broad theme here is the view of technology as empowering and emancipating: 'What ever you want to do, YOU CAN!' (Microsoft); 'Release your time – release your potential' (Capita). Teachers, it is implied, have been held back in some unspecified way, but can now be freed by technology. In this utopian vein, BT (British Telecom) even promises to take consumers to 'educational ICT heaven':

> [Through technology] we are able to develop best-of-breed solutions that empower teachers, delight learners and enable everyone to realise their full potential.

According to this kind of futuristic rhetoric, 'the digital age' is a 'new era': it offers 'new horizons in education' and an opportunity to 'build your future'. Such assertions are frequently accompanied by images of outer space, the earth, the sun and the solar system.

Yet while they are keen to reassure teachers that technology is about freedom, and that its use is natural and intuitive, these promotional texts also give them cause for concern about their own role in this technological age. They draw attention to the dangers of being 'left behind', and the responsibility that teachers have to keep up to date, to implement government policy, and to use their ICT funding wisely. In a context of increasing investment in ICT, teachers *need* guidance; and this is precisely what the industry, by means of BETT, purports to provide. ICT, it is argued, is no longer a matter of choice: all teachers, regardless of their curriculum area, will need to be familiar with it. As Kevin Robins and Frank Webster (1999) have noted, debates around information technology have often been characterized by a rhetoric of 'inevitability'. In these formulations, this is allied with one of professionalism: just as the 'good parent' invests in technology in order that their child does not fall behind, so too does the professional teacher.

The underlying anxiety here – and it is one that (as we shall see) is borne out by research – is that teachers are not in fact integrating this technology in their teaching, and indeed that many remain uncertain about its value. Despite massive government funding for ICTs in schools, the fear of policy-makers and of companies is that technology is not becoming sufficiently 'embedded' in classroom practice. The director general of BESA, Dominic Savage, addresses this directly in his 'Welcome' to the 2006 official show guide. He recognizes that the 'transformation of learning' sought by government has yet to occur: harnessing the benefits of technology in schools, he argues, requires a new focus on 'the learning experience' and on developing teacher confidence. The need for more 'embedding' is also a theme strongly echoed in the government's own publicity materials, and in the speeches of ministers who are typically enlisted to open the show. By implication, they draw attention to the contrary possibility, that technology may in fact be making only a very superficial impact on schools.

Furthermore, the uplifting rhetoric of inspiration and empowerment often sits rather awkwardly with the more bureaucratic claims that are also made here. As Neil Selwyn (2005) has noted, digital learning is often presented in such contexts *both* as 'futuristic, exotic and endless' *and* as 'a set of benign tools which fit seamlessly into the daily drudgery of the classroom'. Software in particular needs to be sold, not only on the basis that it will transform learning or provide endless pleasure and fun, but also in terms of its ability to deliver specific assessment objectives, as defined by the government through the National Curriculum and measured through standardized examinations. 'Unleashing creativity' is all very well, but only if it improves test scores. Compared with the promise of technological utopia, these concerns about meeting the requirements of Key Stages and

SAT tests appear strangely mundane; yet marketers know that they are bound to be the major preoccupation for teachers. The use of technology may be innovative and transformative, but we also need to be assured that it will deliver efficiency, ensure improved performance and raise standards. Technology may offer freedom, but it often seems to be merely the freedom to do what you are told.

The political economy of educational technology

Educational technology is self-evidently big business; yet it has also been significantly promoted by government intervention in the marketplace. According to a 2005 survey report commissioned by BESA, the number of computers in UK schools doubled between 2001 and 2005, to just over 2 million. The number of 'client units' for networks also doubled, while the provision of internet-connected computers increased by a factor of 2.5. According to the DfES, the ratio of computers to students in 2005 rose to 1:6.7 in primary schools and 1:4.1 in secondaries. Total ICT budgets in schools rose from £336 million in 2001 to £551 million in 2005, and these figures exclude the substantial amount of ring-fenced funding from government (such as 'e-learning credits', of which more below). BESA estimates that total direct government investment on technology in education rose from £102 million in 1998 to £640 million in 2005. (Interestingly, the same report suggests that, despite this significant growth in investment, teacher confidence and competence in using technology have actually declined over the past three years.)[6]

A key factor in the growth of the sector was the move towards a 'free market' in education, via the introduction of Local Management of Schools (LMS), which was part of the Education Reform Act of 1988. Before this, most purchasing decisions in education were taken by local education authorities (LEAs). By virtue of their large budgets, the LEAs wielded a significant degree of power in negotiating with potential providers of products and services, although from the point of view of many schools they were often unnecessarily bureaucratic. LMS passed much of the control over purchasing decisions to individual schools; in the process, teachers became a significant new consumer market – albeit one that was not necessarily very well informed or well supported in its purchasing decisions.

Much of the support for the development of educational technology has come directly from government in the form of ring-fenced funding. Initially, most of this was directed towards hardware, as in the case of the ICT in Schools grant provided from the government's Standards Fund. Other key initiatives have included the National Grid for Learning, which acts as a portal for government-approved resources, and the New Opportunities Fund, which provided basic training for teachers. Both initiatives have been widely seen – even by advocates of ICT in education – as less than successful (see Conlon, 2004; Galanouli et al., 2004; and Ofsted, 2004).

More recently, the government has sought to 'pump-prime' the educational software industry through an initiative known as 'e-learning credits' (see Scanlon and Buckingham, 2003). The government's decision to engage the BBC to produce a £150 million Digital Curriculum (the new initiative, renamed 'BBC Jam', was ultimately launched in early 2006) generated a considerable amount of protest from the commercial software industry. It was argued that the BBC had obtained unfair advantage, and that the choice available to schools would be significantly reduced. BESA, among other organizations, argued that the government should be seeking to establish 'a competitive level playing field in education supply'.[7] The government ultimately responded by introducing e-learning credits, which are given directly to schools to spend on educational software. While there has been concern that not all the money made available in this way is being spent, the initiative has undoubtedly provided significant support for the software industry – and perhaps particularly for small and medium-sized companies. Since its commencement in 2002, the government has provided more than £100 million per year for schools to spend, albeit only on DfES-approved products and services.

For technology companies, this funding has obviously represented a considerable commercial opportunity. While some of the major companies have seen education as somewhat of a marginal concern – albeit a lucrative one – many smaller companies have sought to create particular 'niche markets'. As the number of teachers leaving the profession has grown, and as employment in the media industries has been increasingly casualized, educational technology has become an attractive opportunity for potential entrepreneurs; and the growth in the numbers of 'consultants' and other industry personnel attending the BETT Show might be taken as one indication of this.

Even so, educational credibility is a crucial selling point here. As the trade association, BESA has a code of practice designed 'to give confidence to schools that they would be satisfied with any product or service bought from a BESA member', and it is keen to promote its role in providing support and training to teachers through events like BETT. Crucially, BESA purports to mediate between public and private interests. 'Partnership' is the key term here, as its chief executive explains:

> The interdependency which is occurring between schools, commercial suppliers and their local support structure is the way forward for ICT in education and the consortium approach is to be welcomed where individual contributions are on the basis of specialist knowledge in a particular area. Whether to provide training for teachers or curriculum content, opportunities for partnerships exist and BESA is here to help.[8]

This kind of relationship between business and public services, fostered by central government, is typical of New Labour policy more generally. The promotion of ICT in education represents a form of 'public–private partnership', although it is arguably one in which the private is significantly more powerful than the public. While the state acts as a facilitator of the market (not least, in this instance, through forms of financial 'pump-priming'), it is ultimately assumed that the market will provide.

The marketing of educational technology is only one example of the growing incursion of market forces in education. While this phenomenon is particularly well advanced in the United States, it is now widespread in most developed countries (see Bridges and Mclaughlin, 1994; Kenway and Bullen, 2001; Molnar and Garcia, 2005). To some extent, this is simply a matter of schools being used as vehicles for marketing: direct advertising, sponsored classroom materials, branded vending machines, incentive programmes (such as voucher schemes), and the use of schools as venues for market research are all on the rise. However, in recent years we have also seen the privatization of several key aspects of schooling, ranging from the provision of school meals to school buildings themselves (via the Private Finance Initiative). Assessment is also a private concern: in the US, the Educational Testing Service (ETS), which runs the national SAT tests, is a private company, while in the UK, examination boards are also profit-making enterprises (one of the largest, EdExcel, is owned by the multinational media corporation Pearson – who not coincidentally claim to sell one in four of the textbooks in use around the world (Seiter, 2005: 7)). Private companies are also increasingly involved in the sponsorship, and in some cases direct management and governance, of schools – a trend the government has sought to encourage through its promotion of 'trust' schools, 'city academies' and specialist schools, which are required to involve commercial partners. These kinds of activities are often presented as a form of philanthropy, or through a rhetoric of 'partnership'; yet they are essentially a matter of generating profit and of building future markets. Indeed, education could be seen to provide a kind of alibi for companies seeking to create a positive brand identity within the broader marketplace – as in the case of the leading British supermarket chain Tesco, which has run a voucher scheme for computers in schools for many years.

Meanwhile, the provision of education itself has been progressively 'marketized'. The emphasis on 'parental choice' has led to a situation in which schools compete for customers much like any other business; and, inevitably, some customers are in a much stronger position than others to manipulate the market to their own advantage (see Gewirtz et al., 1995; Gorard et al., 2003). One consequence of this is that there is a widening gap between 'winners' and 'losers' in the education market, and this has significant implications in terms of widening social segregation. The drive towards 'customer choice' is most apparent in proposals to introduce voucher schemes, which are steadily gaining political credibility in many countries (Cohn, 1997). In this competitive climate, schools have increasingly been obliged to market themselves, through the production of elaborate publicity materials and public relations activities of various kinds. As Kenway and Bullen (2001) point out, the existence of lavishly appointed computer suites is often regarded as a key selling point in this respect.

In this broader context, the provision of educational technology has played a key role in opening up schools to the influence of business. Amid a volatile and rapidly changing economy, education has provided a relatively stable market for technology corporations eager to sustain their profit margins, and it has also been widely seen as a springboard into the lucrative domestic market. Meanwhile, as Bettina Fabos (2004) has pointed out, the internet has become increasingly commercialized – albeit often in ways that are invisible to many of its users. In this respect, she suggests, schools' reliance on commercial search engines represents another intrusion of business into the classroom, and public and non-profit sites are becoming more and more difficult to find amid the welter of advertising and commercially sponsored content. Furthermore, the internet is also being used as a means of gathering market research information on young people, as they are encouraged and required to provide personal information online (Burbules and Callister, 2000; Seiter, 2005). The internet is now essentially an unregulated commercial medium; while this does not in itself automatically undermine its educational value, it does mean that it can no longer be seen merely as a neutral conduit for 'information'.

This is not necessarily to imply that the market has no place in education, or indeed that a non-commercial, Eden-like world of teaching and learning pre-existed the serpent of ICT. Nor is it to imply that students – or indeed teachers – are merely passive victims of the manipulations of evil marketeers. In a mixed economy, state and public institutions are perhaps bound to function as a kind of market. However, the traditional pattern of market regulation in education has changed, and there has been an alignment between the education market and the wider consumer market. In this new dispensation, teachers have become individual consumers, and can no longer rely on the bargaining power – and, to some extent, the expertise – of local education authorities. Meanwhile, schools have become an increasingly important means for commercial companies to target young people – a market that is traditionally seen as volatile and difficult to reach. This raises significant new questions about the role of education, and about the need for teachers and students to develop more critical approaches to using technology.

Conclusion

The BETT Show represents a prime example of what we might call the 'educational–technological complex' in action. While not quite as conspiratorial as the military–industrial one, this complex represents a powerful alliance between public and private interests – journalists, educationalists, researchers, marketeers, commercial corporations and (crucially) government departments. It is a complex that, in the UK, includes a number of high-profile research centres, weekly publications such as the *Times Educational Supplement* and *Guardian Education*, groups of teacher advisers and teacher trainers, as well as companies such as Microsoft, Apple, RM and BT. This work is largely sustained through government funding, and via successive initiatives deriving from the technology directorate and the so-called innovation unit of the DfES, and from BECTA (the British Educational Communications and Technology Agency), a government-funded body charged with advising on the implementation of its ICT strategy.

Thus, the sales pitches I have described, and the discourses they invoke, are routinely recycled in the advertising pages and 'online supplements' of the educational press, and in the publicity material that pours into schools on a daily basis. There is, to say the least, a blurring of the distinctions here between public and private interests. As Daniel Menchik (2004: 197) has observed, 'the line that separates benevolent, authentic concern for student learning enrichment from self-interested entrepreneurship [is] difficult to ascertain'. Indeed, as we shall see in subsequent chapters, academic and political proponents of technology in education have often traded in precisely the kind of inflated claims that typify the sales pitches of the major corporations.

Of course, there are considerable grounds for questioning the claim that the products on sale at BETT are as genuinely 'innovative' as the marketeers claim. Digital encyclopaedias, multiple-choice online quizzes, copy art packages and even so-called interactive storybooks are, for the most part, only superficially different from their non-technological counterparts. The 'interactive' whiteboard often appears to be merely a means of reasserting traditional, teacher-centred whole-class teaching in the manner of its prehistoric predecessor, the blackboard – just as tablet PCs bear a striking resemblance to slate and chalk (albeit with added possibilities for teacher assessment and control). Certainly, much of the educational content made available via these new media is far from novel: much of it is little more than a repackaging of the traditional curriculum.

Nevertheless, for some commentators, it is the technology itself that makes all the difference. Technology is believed to motivate learners in and of itself – particularly 'disaffected' learners, who in contemporary debates are almost always implicitly identified as boys. Technology is seen to provide guaranteed pleasure and 'fun' in a way that older methods simply fail to do; and, it is argued, it can even make the most painful aspects of education (such as testing) engaging and exciting. As we shall see in subsequent chapters, such claims rest on assumptions about young people's relationship with technology that are, to say the least, somewhat questionable.

For all the excesses of its marketing, the BETT Show is a telling indication of broader tendencies in the educational use of technology. It represents a coming together of public and private interests, and a concentration of discourses that are symptomatic of the field much more broadly. Technology is presented here as a source of innovation, of empowerment and liberation, and of authentic educational practice. Yet, in much less celebratory terms, it is also part of a broader move towards bureaucratization, regulation and surveillance. These discourses define the roles of the student and the teacher in diverse ways, and they also invoke much broader assumptions about the nature of learning. My aim in this book is to pick apart some of these contradictory discourses about technology in education, to puncture some of the inflated claims (both positive and negative) that are often made about it, and to provide some indications of a practice that I believe is genuinely new and challenging.

Ultimately, however, I do not believe that it is possible to stand outside these developments. I attended the BETT Show in 2006 not only to gather material for this chapter but also to participate in a seminar myself, presenting some of the research conducted at my university, in collaboration with a commercial software company. I also saw some products that I believe are genuinely innovative, useful and even creative. My criticism of the dominant use of technology in education is not motivated by a desire to reassert the supposedly more authentic methods of an earlier era. On the contrary, I believe we need to move the discussion forwards, beyond the superficial fascination with technology for its own sake, towards a more critical engagement with questions of learning, communication and culture.

2

Making Technology Policy

ICTs and the New Discourses of Learning

As we have seen, the drive to insert digital technology into education has been led not only by commercial companies, but also by government – and, indeed, by a range of alliances between them. The government has provided ring-fenced funding, set targets and standards for acceptable practice, and reinforced these through a punitive regime of school inspections. It has supported the broader privatization of schooling, removing obstacles to commercial involvement; yet in some instances it has also acted as a 'developmental state', directly supporting particular sectors of business and providing significant incentives for commercial activity.

To some extent, however, the assumptions that have informed government policy on technology in education have shifted over time. In this chapter, I look at the changing character of policy discourse in this field in the UK, focusing particularly on the ten years since the election of the first New Labour administration in 1997. I explore the shift from broader economic arguments about the need to respond to the 'information society' to ones that focus more specifically on learning. The chapter uses examples from government publications, but it also considers material produced by other government-funded organizations, ranging from BECTA (the body responsible for advising on ICT policy) through to Futurelab (a technology research lab) and Demos (a centre-left 'think tank' that has been particularly influential in policy circles).

New Labour, new technology

The drive to insert computers in UK schools dates back to the mid-1970s, although it began to appear more prominently on the political agenda during the 1980s. As Neil Selwyn (2002) has shown, the construction of the computer as an 'educational' device was by no means natural or inevitable: on the contrary, it arose through a complex combination of political, economic and social imperatives. For politicians, a focus on technology appeared to provide a means of addressing concerns about Britain's international competitiveness and the need for a well-disciplined work-force. As Selwyn demonstrates, media representations of computing – not least in programmes such as the BBC's popular science show *Tomorrow's World* – played a significant part in this 'educational mythologizing' of information technology. Yet, for technology companies, this discursive construction of computing provided a useful means of fulfilling their longer-term aim of targeting the domestic market: if the educational cred-ibility of computers could be established via schools, this would in turn place increasing pressure on parents to invest in technology in order to secure their children's educational success.

The interest in educational technology among policy-makers has signifi-cantly gathered pace since the election of the first New Labour govern-ment in 1997. While education policy under the last years of the former Conservative administration had resorted to a kind of threadbare tradition-alism, New Labour was keen to present itself as a modernizing party, ori-ented towards the future (see Jones, 2002). A key element of this approach was its response to the new challenges of the so-called knowledge economy. If Britain was to compete in global markets, it would need a workforce equipped with the appropriate 'skills'. This to some extent accounts for the overall prominence of education in New Labour policy-making. The eco-nomic basis of this emphasis was clearly evident in the 1998 Green Paper *The Learning Age: A Renaissance for a New Britain*, where education and employment secretary David Blunkett proclaimed that 'investment in human capital will be the foundation of success in the knowledge-based economy of the twenty-first century.'

The use of information and communication technology in education was seen as central to this process of 'upskilling' the future workforce and ensuring its employability – and in this respect the UK government was broadly in line with international trends (Selwyn and Brown, 2000). Announcing the establishment of the National Grid for Learning (NGfL) in the consultation document *Connecting the Learning Society* (DEE, 1997), Tony Blair asserted: 'Technology has revolutionised the way we work and is now set to transform education. Children cannot be effective in tomor-row's world if they are trained in yesterday's skills.' Meanwhile, in the symptomatically entitled document outlining the government's plans, *National Grid for Learning: Open for Learning, Open for Business* (1998), he argued that 'Britain's international competitiveness' would depend upon the adoption of technology, both in education and in industry.

From this perspective, then, the use of technology in education is a direct response to the demands of the modern economy. The 'post-industrial' or 'post-Fordist' economy is seen to require what Blunkett (1997) termed a 'computer literate workforce'; although, as Facer et al. (2001) point out, technology is also being used here to create new markets – and technological skill is regarded as an essential prerequisite for a person's effective functioning as a *consumer* of information and digital products. Those who fail to acquire such skills are seen to be at risk, not merely of unemployment, but also of a kind of disenfranchisement, as they will be unable to participate fully in the future 'information society'. As Neil Selwyn (1999) has shown, these arguments were particularly prominent in the marketing of Britain's version of the 'information superhighway', the NGfL during New Labour's first term in office. The grid was a grandiose project that was seen to have the capacity 'to consume and reproduce all the knowledge that had gone before it, rendering all previous incarnations of information obsolete' (1999: 58). Funded both by government and by large private companies, it would move the education system into the twenty-first century, and help to create the 'connected society' of the future (Blunkett, 1997: 11).

This discourse of technological 'skill' thus proposes a particular articulation – a joining together – of education, the commercial market and the future worker/consumer. In their analysis of *Connecting the Learning Society*, Jo Moran-Ellis and Geoff Cooper (2000) identify several discursive moves that are symptomatic of New Labour policy more broadly. Technology, they argue, is presented as an unquestioned benefit, and the task of government is to remove any potential barriers to its adoption. Behind those barriers, it is assumed, is 'a homogenous set of ready-made consumers who are eager to make use of the information on offer', and the ability to access information is held to be a kind of 'vaccine' against future unemployment (which of course might itself be technologically induced). In this sense, technology is presented both as the primary driver of social and economic change and as the solution to any problems that it might cause. The issue then becomes not *why* or *whether* to adopt technology, but *how*: there is a 'discourse of inevitability' (Robins and Webster, 1999), from which it is impossible to dissent – unless, of course, one wishes to be labelled as a hopeless 'dinosaur'.

Nevertheless, the place of the learner is somewhat paradoxical here. As Keri Facer et al. suggest, the discourse of the 'information society' (or the 'knowledge economy') constructs the child as a future worker, but also as a consumer of information – and indeed as 'a testbed market for software manufacturers' (2001: 96). To be sure, there is some rhetorical recognition here of the 'techno-savvy child' – the notion of children as a 'digital generation' that is somehow spontaneously competent in its rela-tionships with technology. However, this image is generally played down in favour of a view of the child as essentially *incompetent*, and hence in need of technological training. Childhood is constructed here as a matter of 'becoming' rather than 'being' (cf. Lee, 2001): there is very little atten-tion to children's existing uses of technology in their leisure time, let alone to the possibility that they might become producers of 'information' rather than simply consumers.

Underlying this broadly economistic discourse are some quite specific alliances between education and business. The role of schools is to train future workers in the skills that business requires, while business provides the software and hardware that makes this possible (Moran-Ellis and Cooper, 2000). Behind this is the more local aim of stimulating the UK software industry – which, as we have seen, was the specific aim of funding initiatives such as the NGfL and subsequently e-learning credits (see Scanlon and Buckingham, 2003; Selwyn, 2005). In the words of *Connecting the Learning Society*, this strategy is seen to be 'good for our children and for our companies'. As Roger Dale et al. (2004) suggest, the implementa-tion of such strategies, and the advice and guidance that has accompanied them, has been essentially driven from the supply side, rather than arising in response to demands on the part of educators.

Yet part of the function of this discourse is precisely to obscure the com-mercial and political interests of those involved. As Neil Selwyn (1999) and others have argued, commercial companies tend to feature here in a highly altruistic role; and, in this respect, the approach is clearly symptomatic of broader discourses of the 'information society' (or the 'knowledge economy'), which tend to disassociate 'information' (or 'knowledge') from the vested interests of those who produce and distribute it. From this perspective, technology itself is seen to create change, rather than the social actors who own and promote it (and who may well stand to gain the most from it).

These discourses clearly embody a form of *technological determinism* (see Robins and Webster, 1999; Webster, 1995; Williams, 1974). From this perspective, technology is seen to emerge from a neutral process of scien-tific research and development, rather than from the interplay of complex social, economic and political forces. Technology is then seen to have effects – to bring about social and psychological changes – irrespective of the ways in which it is used, and of the social contexts and processes into which it enters. Like the printing press, television and other new technolo-gies that preceded it, the computer is seen as an autonomous force that is somehow independent of human society, and acts upon it from outside. In the case of education, this often takes the form of what might be called 'information determinism'. Information is seen as a neutral good, which appears as if from nowhere. Learning often seems to be equated simply with access to information; and, in providing this access, technology is seen to perform an essentially beneficial function.

This 'transcendent' view of technology and of information has been widely challenged. Robins and Webster, for example, argue that it leads to a 'desocialized' view of technology, which ignores its social history, and sees it as somehow 'influencing society yet beyond the influence of society' (1999: 74). More broadly, many researchers have contested the claim that the 'information society' represents a new mode of social organization, in which established forms of economic, political and social activity are being fundamentally altered – and the assumption that any such change is somehow an inevitable consequence of technology (Garnham, 2000; May, 2002; Webster, 1995).

Furthermore, notions of the 'information society' and the 'knowledge economy' involve some highly debatable assumptions about the changing nature of employment, and about the 'skills' that workers will need in order to function effectively in the new economic and technological order. For example, the notion that industry is now 'demanding' flexible, technologically skilled workers, and that those without such skills will be unemployable, is very questionable: what employers actually say they want is workers with good communication skills, literacy and numeracy, and other attributes that are often associated with a traditional liberal education (Hockey and Wellington, 1994). When it comes to technology, employers prefer to train workers 'on the job'; and, in any case, much of the skills training students receive in school is likely to prove obsolete by the time they reach the workplace.

However, critics of technological determinism also point to the dangers of an opposite view – the notion that technology is somehow entirely shaped by existing social relations (an approach Raymond Williams (1974) defines as 'determined technology'). Crudely, this approach sees technology as simply a matter of what people choose to make of it: it has no inherent qualities, and is regarded as essentially value-free. Williams and others favour a more dialectical approach, in which technology is both socially shaped and socially shaping. In other words, its role and impact are partly determined by the uses to which it is put; but it also contains inherent constraints and possibilities which limit the ways in which it can be used. This approach thus challenges the assumptions of so much government policy in this field – the notion of technology as a simple 'cause' of social change (on the one hand) and as an easy 'fix' for complex social problems (on the other).

Changing times

To some extent, the policy discourse surrounding educational technology has shifted as new products have become available, and as the use of technology in schools has evolved. Tracing the arguments adopted by successive British education ministers in their keynote presentations at the BETT Show,[1] it is clear that the relentlessly forward-looking impetus must be sustained at all costs. There is much talk here of 'transformation', 'taking things forward' and 'opening up the waters of reform'. Despite its enthusiasm for public–private partnerships, government needs to appear intent on achieving value for money from educational technology – and that value is measured primarily in terms of its ability to 'raise standards', as reflected in test scores in national examinations. Thus, ministers speak of using technology to 'lever up attainment' or 'drive up standards' and of 'squeezing every ounce of innovation from new and emerging technology'.

In this context, ministers are generally extremely upbeat about the positive effects of technology on students' learning. In 2003, for example, education minister Charles Clarke spoke of ICT as 'a massive addition to teaching and learning': 'technology', he asserted, 'has a huge impact on pupils' performances. It can empower learners, improve self-esteem and help motivation, thinking skills and concentration.' As we shall see in chapter 4, the evidence for such claims is certainly dubious; but one striking feature of these presentations is their tendency to misrepresent research on such matters. For example, in 2001 Michael Wills (minister for learning and technology) referred to a BECTA report on ICT in schools, claiming that 'the weight of evidence on ICT in the classroom, boosted by the report published today, sends a clear message that ICT raises standards.' In 2003, Charles Clarke cited another BECTA report as evidence of 'the positive effect sustained use of ICT can have on pupil performance and educational standards', while in 2004 he referred to early findings from government-funded research at Lancaster University that apparently demonstrated 'how this technology is really working'. In fact, none of this research supports the claims being made for it by ministers. The work cited by Clarke in 2003, for example, found 'no consistent relationship between the average amount of ICT use reported for any subject at a given Key Stage and its apparent effectiveness in raising standards' (BECTA, 2003: 1), and the 2004 study found learning gains only in specialist ICT classes and not in other subjects (Passey and Rogers, 2004).

Nevertheless, amid such tough policy talk, it is also possible to detect a degree of uncertainty. Bold proclamations of statistics on the steadily increasing number of computers and internet connections, or the growing levels of government funding, are apparently no longer sufficient. In 2004, for example, Charles Clarke spoke of the need to have not just 'the kit', but also 'teachers who are trained and confident in using the kit', as well as the need 'to understand how to use each particular bit of kit in a way which focuses on particular educational standards'. More recently, his successor Ruth Kelly emphasized that technology should not be seen merely as an 'add-on', but as something that should be 'embedded' in classroom practice.

Recent policy documents have also tended to play down the economistic discourse, with its emphasis on 'skills' for employment. *Harnessing Technology: Transforming Children's and Learning Services*, published by the DfES in 2005, maintains the focus on 'standards', but leavens this with a new emphasis on 'personalization' – which will be discussed in more detail below. Thus, education minister Ruth Kelly's preface speaks of the need to 'put learners, young people – and their parents – in the driving seat, shaping the opportunities open to all learners to fit around their particular needs and preferences'. Personalization, as the report defines it, entails 'anytime, anywhere learning', 'extending the variety of places where people can learn'.

As this suggests, the home is increasingly being defined here as an important site of learning. Education, it is implied, cannot cease once children walk out of the classroom door: with internet connectivity and mobile technologies, 'learning can come to the learner'. Personalization in this form will depend upon enlisting parents, not least as an additional market for educational goods and services. As long ago as 1997, *Connecting the Learning Society* proposed the development of business consortia 'to develop home learning centres (packages of equipment, connectivity, software, services and support which would be marketed to parents and individuals as compatible with the Grid)' (DEE, 1997); and, as we shall see below, these packages are currently being promoted as 'learning platforms' and 'e-portfolios'. This attempt to extend the reach of the school into the home appears to have gathered pace in recent years, although there is little sense here that parents may have needs or imperatives that differ from those of teachers or government policy-makers.

A further key emphasis in this latest report is on the 'excitement' and 'motivation' that apparently derive from the use of digital technology, particularly for learners who are identified as 'hard to reach'. As Liz Beastall (2006) has put it, technology is seen to have the power to 'enchant the disenchanted child'; and, as we shall see in chapter 6, there is a particular interest here in exploiting the popularity of computer games. *Harnessing Technology* contains several glowing testimonials to the 'massive impact' of ICT, for example through transforming vocabulary tests into 'fun learning activities' via the use of 'interactive quizzes'. Such 'compelling learning experiences' will, it is argued, 're-engage the unmotivated learner' (DfES, 2005: 9–10) and entice those adults who have abandoned education back into the system.

By contrast, while the need for 'partnership' with industry and the discourse of the 'information society' is still present in the document, it is much less prominent than it was in the discourse surrounding the National Grid for Learning, discussed above. 'The skills needed for twenty-first century employment' remain an issue, but the primary focus now appears to be on producing well-regulated, self-motivating learners with 'clear personal goals' – who, among other things, will be able to access the range of government services that will increasingly be available online. If anything, the focus has shifted from the child as future worker to the child as future citizen.

Broadly speaking, then, it would seem that discourses of the 'information society' have now begun to give way to discourses that are more centrally concerned with *learning*. A fuller account of these new discourses will have to wait for another time: my aim in what follows is simply to flag up some of the difficulties and questions they pose. In particular, I want to address three key concepts: personalization, multiple intelligences and informal learning. While these ideas have been circulated much more widely, they have enjoyed a particular prominence among advocates of digital technology in education.

Getting personal

The notion of personalization has been a key emphasis in recent policy-making – albeit one that fits awkwardly alongside the continuing preoccupation with 'standards'. The focus on personalization is part of a broader argument about the reform of public services, and it has been debated in relation to health and welfare, social services and public safety as well as education. At least on the face of it, it offers a model in which individuals assess their own needs and become involved in managing the services they use, and in which service providers are required to be much more flexible and responsive to the diversity of their clients. This is a discourse that emphasizes dialogue, participation, consultation and the 'voice' of users; and it describes a world of perpetual change, in which everything is forever 'new'. In some respects, personalization represents a Blairite 'third way' solution, which moves away from the centralized provision of the old-style welfare state but also claims to refuse the neo-liberal 'consumer choice' approach.

However, Charles Leadbeater (2004), the author of a key report published by one of New Labour's favoured 'think-tanks', Demos, questions the extent of government commitment to this approach. He favours what he calls 'deep' personalization: rather than merely making services more 'user-friendly', this involves empowering individuals to become 'co-producers' of public goods, and to be centrally involved in organizing the delivery of services. Yet he also recognizes that this more radical version is potentially 'disruptive'. In the case of education, for example, the notion that learners might be setting their own targets, selecting and devising their own ways to learn, and assessing their own progress clearly flies in the face of centralizing government initiatives such as standardized testing and the National Literacy and Numeracy Strategies (Leadbeater, 2004: 70). Indeed, it is notable that, in his preface to Leadbeater's publication, the (then) minister for school standards David Miliband argues that the call for personalization needs to be balanced against a continuing insistence on the 'basics' and on accountability (Miliband, 2004: 12–13). Furthermore, users seem to be primarily defined here not as children but as parents; and, in this respect, personalization fits well with the government's emphasis on parental choice, as defined in the highly contentious 2006 Education Act.

A subsequent – and significantly more glossy – publication, by NESTA Futurelab[2] (Green et al., 2005), argues that digital technologies have an important role to play in delivering personalization in education. According to these authors, the 'essence' of personalization is one in which 'the [education] system conforms to the learner, rather than the learner to the system': the system provides 'bespoke support for each individual that recognises and builds upon their diverse strengths, interests and abilities and needs' (ibid.: 4). Personalization will 'enable the learner's voice to be heard more powerfully in shaping the curriculum, contexts and practices of their learning, both in and out of school' (ibid.: 7).

Digital technology is seen to assist in this process in four main ways. It can enable learners to access information and guidance – and hence to make informed choices – about where, how and what to learn. It can assist learners in 'co-designing' their learning, recognizing their diverse skills and knowledge, and giving them greater control over the content, pace and process of learning. It can help to create more diverse learning environments, not just by 'extending' schools but also by providing 'anytime, anywhere opportunities for collaborative learning', for example through mobile technology (Green et al., 2005: 20). And it can assist in developing 'learner-focused' assessment and feedback, for example through the use of e-portfolios and virtual learning environments.

There are many questions that might be raised about this approach. To what extent is personalization possible in a system that is still essentially premised on the 'mass' delivery of public services? For all the protests to the contrary, personalization comes very close to the consumer market approach, in which individuals seek to satisfy their needs by choosing between competing providers; and this is readily apparent when we begin to consider how such a system might be funded (by vouchers, perhaps?). Personalization conceives of the individual as a self-regulating citizen who is responsible for their own welfare, yet this neglects the very real material difficulties people might face in exercising their responsibilities. As Leadbeater (2004: 74–5) is bound to acknowledge, different social groups have different potential in terms of their ability to take advantage of 'personalized' opportunities – and this is a matter not just of economic capital, but of educational and cultural capital as well. Leadbeater responds by asserting that the resources for making best use of 'individualized, home-based learning' need to be made equally available to all – but this is clearly easier said than done. Futurelab's 'Learners' Charter', for example, makes several specific suggestions about how technology might be used here; but these assume very high levels of access to technology, and extremely well-developed skills in using it – as well as an already established motivation to want to acquire such skills.

New styles of learning

The Futurelab publication in particular illustrates the connections between personalization and two other key terms in these new discourses of learning: multiple intelligences and informal learning. In the case of the former, it stresses the notion that learners have different 'learning styles', and that technology can help both in identifying and in catering for these. The notion of 'multiple intelligences' derives from the well-known work of the US psychologist Howard Gardner. Essentially, Gardner challenges the notion that there is a singular form of intelligence, as is typically assessed in the form of 'IQ' (intelligence quotient) tests. Gardner adds to the logico-mathematical and linguistic forms of intelligence generally favoured by schools several further varieties, including spatial, bodily/kinaesthetic, musical, intrapersonal, interpersonal, naturalist and existential (Gardner, 1993, 1999). Drawing on evidence from 'brain science', anthropology and developmental psychology, Gardner claims that these forms are universal aspects of the human mind.

Gardner's theory has been widely taken up in schools in many parts of the world. In the UK, for example, students may be given questionnaires to profile their intelligences, and some may even be provided with 'smart cards' inscribed with their preferred intelligences (White, 2004: 1). Students are routinely divided into 'auditory', 'visual' or 'kinaesthetic' learners, and allocated different tasks accordingly. These ideas have also become commonplace in discussions of technology in education. For example, both Seymour Papert (1996: 86) and Nicholas Negroponte (1995: 198) argue that the computer makes it easier to accommodate children with different 'learning and cognitive styles', while others have directly linked multiple intelligences theory to the notion of personalization or 'mass customization' made possible through ICTs (e.g. Freund, 2004).

However, multiple intelligences theory has been criticized on several grounds. John White (2004), for example, disputes Gardner's claim that there are eight or nine distinct intelligences: he argues that the basis on which these distinctions are made, and the criteria that are used to define them, are philosophically incoherent and insufficiently supported by the evidence. Most importantly in this context, White argues that the theory supports an *individualized* approach to learning, which is also implicit in current moves towards increasing selection, specialization and assessment in schools. Ultimately, it also divides up knowledge in a manner that resembles the traditional curriculum, with its discrete disciplines. In these respects, the apparently liberalizing approach of the theory may belie its fundamental conservatism – or at least the ease with which it can be accommodated within traditional conceptions of education.

The final key term in this nexus of ideas is 'informal learning'. The popularity of this idea reflects a growing recognition that learning can occur in a range of settings, not merely in institutions such as schools, and that it does not necessarily have to involve 'formal' definitions, either of content or of the pedagogic relationships between teachers and learners. Thus, many kinds of everyday leisure activities may involve learning, even if this is not explicitly identified (or indeed assessed); and many kinds of people – including parents and peers – may act as 'teachers', even if they are not identified as such. As Julian Sefton-Green (2003) points out, this idea has gained currency as a result of the growing emphasis on 'lifelong learning' and the notion of the 'learning society': in this context, 'informality' is typically seen as a characteristic of the new kinds of 'networked' learning taking place in more entrepreneurial or innovative businesses (Coffield, 2000).

Here again, technology is seen to have a key role to play in providing pedagogic structures and support; and, as we shall see in more detail in chapter 3, it is often connected with 'constructivist' theories that emphasize self-directed learning, play and exploration. Thus, Futurelab aligns informal learning and personalization, seeing both as key features of young people's out-of-school experiences with technology: 'many learners today are *already* creating personalised learning environments for themselves outside school using digital resources' – even if this remains 'unacknowledged by their formal school experiences' (Green et al., 2005: 5). Likewise, Sefton-Green (in another Futurelab report, 2004) focuses on the varieties of informal learning taking place, not merely in out-of-school settings like museums, galleries and science centres, but also in young people's everyday uses of computer games, production software and other digital media.

However, there are significant problems in defining informal learning – not least because it often appears to be discussed in terms of (assumptions about) what it is *not*. As Sefton-Green (2003) points out, it is not always entirely clear whether 'formality' refers to the *setting* (for example, in school or outside school), the *social roles* (that is, the pedagogic relationships between 'teachers' and 'learners') or the *cognitive processes*, or 'learning styles', that are involved (such as the emphasis on factors like experimentation and play). Obviously, there may be a great deal of 'informal' learning happening in schools, and a great deal of 'formal' learning happening outside schools – not least in online communities, or in relation to computer games (Kent and Facer, 2004: 454). As Sefton-Green argues, we need to take account of the interaction between the form, content and style of learning, each of which may be more or less 'formal'; and, as we push the term to its limits, it may be difficult to see the difference between informal learning and socialization, or indeed 'life in general' (2003: 48).

On the face of it, all the ideas I have discussed here embody an implied critique of traditional notions of education: they challenge uniform and 'impersonal' approaches, the notion of a singular intelligence, and the 'formality' of conventional schooling. As such, they fit awkwardly with the dominant imperatives in educational policy-making. The focus on high-stakes testing, the imposition of a prescribed curriculum, the emphasis on managerialism and accountability in schools, and the broader culture of 'performativity' all seem to point in the opposite direction, towards uniformity, centralized control and a rigidly normative approach to learning. To this extent, one might well argue that official support for these new discourses of learning (for example on the part of government ministers) is no more than empty rhetoric – or indeed a kind of alibi for the broader standardization of teaching and learning that is characteristic of the 'new fundamentalism' of contemporary education policy.

Yet, if only at the level of rhetoric, these new discourses also gesture towards a rather different – and perhaps more 'modern' – conception of the learner. They offer a definition of learning that purports to be more attuned to the demands of what is (often equally rhetorically) defined as the 'knowledge economy' or the 'network society'. Perhaps taking their cue from arguments about the change towards a 'post-Fordist' economy, these discourses imagine a more flexible notion of the human subject, and a view of learning as something that can be customized to the needs of the learner, and supplied 'just in time' when required. They imply that individuals are now in charge of their own fate – that, through constant learning, it is their responsibility to fashion themselves into adaptable workers and self-regulating 'good citizens'. This approach is reinforced by the emphasis on *individualization* that is particularly implicit in the notions of personalization and of multiple intelligences. Aligning these discourses with technology (which, as we have seen, embodies all sorts of other political values and imperatives) provides a powerful way of being seen to respond to the challenges of modernity – albeit in ways that can ultimately be regarded as rather superficial.

Learning platforms: online community or educational panopticon?

The ambivalent and sometimes quite contradictory ways in which these discourses are employed – and the ways in which they are taken up by commercial companies – can be briefly illustrated by a particular case study. Among the most significant new products on sale at BETT in 2006 were *learning platforms* – sometimes referred to as 'managed learning environments' or 'virtual learning environments' (VLEs). Learning platforms have already been widely used in higher education for some years, in the form of well-known packages such as 'Blackboard' and 'Web CT', but have only recently been taken up by schools. New government funding ring-fenced specifically for learning platforms came on stream in 2006 – thereby providing a further boost to a developing sector of the ICT industry.

Essentially, learning platforms provide an online means for teachers, students and parents to share educational resources and curriculum materials; to undertake automated assessment and profiling; to gather performance data and monitor progress; and to communicate with each other. Learning platforms typically interface with schools' management information systems, which are used for monitoring attendance and test scores as well as facilitating automated report writing and communication with parents. Crucially, however, they can be accessed by children and parents from home, assuming they have internet connections.

Promoted very strongly in the DfES's publicity materials, and in the appeals of key companies such as Granada and BT, learning platforms usefully combine several key aspects of the new discourses I have been identifying. They are seen to bridge the gap between home and school; to offer a 'personalized' form of learning; and to accommodate different learning styles. Yet, in line with the continuing insistence on 'standards', they also afford greater regulation and surveillance both of teachers and of students. These emphases also coincide with the interests of commercial companies, thus providing further grounds for the development of new markets.

The call to bridge the gap between home and school illustrates some of the ambivalence of these ideas. To some extent, this is seen as a matter of the school building on the kinds of 'informal learning' that occur more or less spontaneously in the home; yet it is also about the colonization of the home by practices designed to support and extend the authority of the school. By and large, it is the latter, regulatory emphasis that has been key to New Labour's education policy: developing parental involvement, the extension of school hours and the renewed emphasis on homework have all been key themes in recent legislation. Yet, as we shall see in more detail in chapter 7, the home market also represents an increasingly important target for educational technology and media companies. Although more volatile and less predictable than the schools market (which is ultimately regulated through the influence of government policy), it is also potentially much more lucrative. In this respect, products such as learning platforms, that allow companies to address both markets simultaneously, have self-evident appeal.

Meanwhile, learning platforms also promise to reflect learners' individual 'learning styles' and hence to deliver 'personalization'. Learning platforms typically incorporate extensive resources for psychological profiling, such as the 'myself as a learner scale' and the 'profile of learning styles', the results of which can be collected together in 'e-portfolios'. As we have seen, personalization can be aligned with the more liberationist emphases of some educational technology rhetoric – the notion of the computer as facilitating a more natural, authentic style of learning that grows from within rather than being imposed from without. However, these ideas fit uneasily alongside the government's insistence on extending national testing, reintroducing the ability of schools to select students and initiatives such as its imposition of a National Curriculum for under-fives (in 2005).

In this respect, however, learning platforms seem to provide a useful means of 'squaring the circle'. A DfES booklet on learning platforms, subtitled 'Making IT Personal', provides a symptomatic instance of this.[3] The booklet lays out a new ICT target, that 'all pupils will be able to access a personalised online workspace, capable of supporting an e-portfolio, by 2007–8'. Amid pictures of enthused, smiling children – almost invariably in school uniform – the booklet proclaims the value of 'anytime, anywhere learning', which can enable students to 'extend their learning and develop their interests and aptitudes through extra support and tuition beyond the school day'. It also proclaims the value of parents being able to look at their children's work and their performance 'data', and thereby 'become more closely involved in the pupil's development': all are part of 'a learning community'. Similar arguments were propounded by the then education minister Ruth Kelly in her opening addresses at BETT in 2005 and 2006. On the one hand, ICTs – and particularly learning platforms – were described as a means of 'empowering individuals to take more control of their own learning', and 'to learn at their preferred pace and time'; yet, on the other, they were seen as a means of improving data management, enabling parents to 'check' on how their children are performing and ensure they do their homework correctly.

The fundamental ambivalence of these ideas relates to broader strains in popular discourse about educational technology. On the one hand, technology is widely regarded as a force for liberation and empowerment, and the utopian rhetoric on this theme that often characterizes discussions of 'online community' and 'interactivity' is very readily carried over into education. On the other hand, there is the potential use of technology as a means of surveillance, and the use of learning platforms is typically integrated with systems of data-logging, web-tracking and other methods of managing student (and teacher) performance. Learning platforms, and the discourses that surround and define them, seem to address both perspectives. On the one hand, they recognize the potential of out-of-school learning and offer opportunities for students to control and extend their own learning, yet, on the other, they offer increased potential for regulation and control on the part of parents and schools.

Conclusion

Policy is both productive and coercive: it constrains the kinds of activity that can be carried out, but it also brings new practices into being. However, we should beware of assuming that it is necessarily coherent or automatically successful. As Stephen Ball (e.g. 2005) has argued, the making of policy involves serendipity and compromise as well as calculation and, as a result, it may be incoherent, contradictory or simply confused. Furthermore, policy does not always translate into practice in straightforward or easily controllable ways: it may be resisted, and it is always interpreted and negotiated in light of the everyday realities of schools and classrooms. In the case of educational technology, a great deal of policy appears to be invented 'on the hoof': technological innovations arrive on the market, offering solutions to problems that have yet to be adequately identified. Lavishly funded initiatives are launched with inflated claims about their educational value, and then quietly abandoned in favour of new ones, often with little evaluation of their success or failure.

Nevertheless, it would be false to assume that individuals – teachers, parents or children, for example – necessarily accept these claims unquestioningly. They may well find that the imperatives of policy – to acquire 'skills', or more generally to 'catch up' with the modern world, through using technology – do not coincide with their own needs or desires. To be sure, they may give qualified assent to the arguments. For example, Dale et al. (2004) found that teachers were not convinced that the use of ICTs had made much difference to their *own* students' learning, and some rejected it as merely 'a waste of money'; yet they remained persuaded by longer-term arguments about the need for schools to adjust to the demands of the 'information society'. Likewise, Facer et al. (2001) found that parents were somewhat ambivalent about the benefits of home computers: they struggled to justify their educational value, while recognizing that their children often appropriated them for 'non-educational' purposes. Here too, there was a 'discourse of inevitability':

despite their misgivings, people did not wish to feel that they (or their children) had been 'left behind'.

Yet however much they may assent to dominant discourses, the ways in which teachers, parents and children actually use these technologies are more complex than such discourses tend to allow. As we shall see, they may use technology in ways that are not foreseen or sanctioned by policy-makers or companies; they may use it only in superficial ways that do not alter their established priorities and preferences; and some may positively refuse to engage with it at all. There is frequently a significant gap between the imagination of policy-makers – and (as we shall see in the following chapter) of more academic accounts of educational technology – and the realities of teaching and learning.

3

Techno-Topias

Constructing Childhood, Learning and Technology

The idea that digital technology will fundamentally transform education is obviously part of a bigger story. Technology is frequently held to be changing social relationships, the economy, and vast areas of public and private life. Such arguments are routinely recycled in popular debates, in advertising and publicity materials, and indeed in academic contexts as well.

As Carolyn Marvin (1988) has indicated, such assertions have a long history. She shows how the introduction of electricity and telecommunications in the late nineteenth and early twentieth centuries was both promoted and challenged by discourses that attributed enormous power to technology. On the one hand, these technologies were accompanied by forms of expert 'boosterism', which glorified the opportunities they presented; yet on the other, there were frequent claims about the ways in which technology might destroy established social relationships. The telephone, for example, was celebrated for the way in which it could make business more efficient, and facilitate more democratic forms of social life; yet it was also condemned for its disruption of intimate relationships and its unsettling of established social hierarchies.

Needless to say, there are striking similarities between these debates almost a century ago and those that currently surround the use of digital technology. Popular discussions of the internet, for example, veer between celebration and paranoia: on the one hand, the technology is seen to create new forms of community and civic life, and to offer immense resources for personal liberation and empowerment; on the other, it is seen to pose dangers to privacy, to create new forms of inequality and commercial exploitation, as well as leaving the individual prey to addiction and pornography. On the one hand, the technology is seen to liberate the individual from constraint, and from narrowly hierarchical ways of working, while on the other, it is regarded as a false substitute for the supposedly authentic values it is seen to be replacing.

As we shall see in this chapter, the debate about technology in education has been similarly polarized. On the one hand, there are forms of technological 'boosterism' that attribute enormous power to technology to equip, to empower and even to liberate young people. Yet, as we shall see, such claims have been systematically challenged by those who see technology as positively harmful, or at least as merely an inauthentic substitute for 'real' learning. Both perspectives rest on a series of assumptions – about young people, about learning, and about the role of technology in society more broadly. My aim in this chapter is to compare and contrast some of these assumptions, and to identify some of their most important limitations.

Just another day in Edutopia

The use of computers in education has often been justified in terms of increasing 'efficiency' and providing students with 'skills' for employment; but it has also frequently been aligned with a much broader 'liberatory' discourse. Technology, it is argued, will free students to follow their own individual interests and learning paths and free teachers from the routine tasks of assessment and management, allowing them to engage with students in a more natural and authentic way.

One of the earliest prophets of educational computing was the behavioural psychologist B. F. Skinner. In a series of articles published in the mid-1950s, he proposed the use of 'teaching machines', based on equipment originally designed in the 1920s by Sidney L. Pressey for testing intelligence (Skinner, 1954, 1958). These pre-electronic machines involved 'frames' containing prompts or questions, which were stored on paper disks, cards or tapes and presented to the user one at a time. Users recorded their responses using a kind of hole punch, and the machine provided instant feedback. Skinner describes in great detail how these machines were to be 'programmed' – for example, how specialized technical terms were to be gradually introduced to the student, and how instruction would move from telling to eliciting.

Skinner's behaviourist theory is a long way from the 'constructivism' favoured by most contemporary advocates of educational computing. However, there are some striking similarities here. Skinner's broader aim is to apply a logical/mathematical approach (developed in his earlier laboratory research) to cognition: he aims to 'analyze the behaviour called "thinking" and produce it according to specifications' (1958: 976), through structured sequences of stimulus, response and reinforcement. However, he also argues that this technology allows for an *individualized* (if not yet 'personalized') approach, in which the student is able 'to play an active role' (ibid.: 970). This more 'efficient' approach also frees teachers from the routine task of 'presenting' material, and enables them to focus on their interaction with the students. Interestingly, Skinner saw the machine as having possibilities for 'home instruction' as well. While the 'teaching machine' had much in common with today's drill-and-practise software, it is also worth noting that it was not based on fixed-response multiple-choice questions: it allowed users to input responses in their own words, and to evaluate them. In today's jargon, Skinner's device was 'interactive', allowing considerable opportunities for 'scaffolding' and 'feedback' to learners.

These emphases – on mathematical approaches to cognition, on 'active' and individualized learning, and on redefining the role of teachers – find many echoes in contemporary arguments for computers in education. Bill Gates, the founder and former CEO of Microsoft, makes some very similar arguments in his book *The Road Ahead* (1995). Gates argues that computers will allow greater productivity and efficiency in education, just as they have (apparently) done in 'forward-thinking' businesses. They take over the traditional role of teachers in providing information, freeing them from 'tedious paperwork' and allowing them to concentrate on what they do best, which is interacting with students. Just as they do in business, computers also permit 'mass customization' of learning, allowing the creation of 'personalized lesson plans' that are attuned to individual students' 'varied thinking and learning modes'; and, like Skinner's teaching machine, they enable students to 'quiz themselves anytime without risk'. For Gates, 'information' is the key: computers, like education, are 'devoted to information', and delivering 'good information' apparently guarantees educational success.

Similar arguments are made by another technology guru, Nicholas Negroponte (1995). Here again, computers are seen to make it much easier to reach children 'with different learning and cognitive styles'; they make 'learning by doing . . . the rule rather than the exception', as well as providing automatic benefits to reading and writing. However, these authors add a further key emphasis, which does not appear in Skinner. This is to do with *childhood*. Children, Gates argues, 'just naturally love computers': 'kids and computers get along just great, because kids aren't invested in established ways of doing things' (1995: 212). For Negroponte, the 'dominant forces' in society are now generational: 'the control bits of [the] digital future are now more than ever before in the hands of the young' (1995: 231). Children are seen here to have a natural affinity with computers; and the use of computers will have lasting effects on their motivation and willingness to learn.

A more recent publication from the George Lucas Educational Foundation encapsulates several of these themes. *Edutopia: Success Stories for Learning in the Digital Age* (Chen and Armstrong, 2002) is a large-format glossy publication with an accompanying CD-ROM and website displaying numerous examples of technologically driven educational innovation. The book contains heart-warming stories of the 'pioneers' and 'unsung heroes' introducing computers in their schools, and of reluctant students transformed through technology. Amid these testimonials to the 'passionate', 'inspiring' and 'life-changing' consequences of technology, the book is illustrated with glossy colour photographs of smiling students staring enraptured into computer screens, and images of cute kids that would not be out of place in a Gap commercial. Sidebars proclaim: 'this is about as exciting as education can get'; 'they're engaged, they want to be here'; and 'it's harder to teach this way, but a hundred times more rewarding'. In the world of *Edutopia*, both students and teachers are endlessly energized, excited and empowered by technology.

In this account, the child has effectively merged with the computer – albeit in a rather benign version of the science-fiction cyborg. Children, we are told, are 'born wired to learn'. One middle-school student in a laptop school (one where all students are provided with individual laptops) is quoted as saying, 'It's a part of my brain. Why would I want to leave it behind in a computer lab?' Teachers, meanwhile, have also been liberated: they are free to focus on developing the 'emotional intelligence' of their students through new 'emotional learning programs'.

To be sure, technology is seen here as merely part of a broader process of educational reform. Much of the book is given over to (equally glowing) accounts of innovations in assessment, parental involvement, and business partnerships. However, technology is strongly aligned with a particular progressivist theory of learning, variously defined as 'constructivism' and 'project-based learning'. Thus, technology apparently allows students to become 'actively involved in the learning process rather than passively receiving information' (Chen and Armstrong, 2002: 30); it permits personalization that will enable the 'capabilities of each student' to be realized; and it creates a more authentic mode of learning that connects students to the real world beyond the classroom. In *Edutopia*, technology has fundamentally transformed the power-relationships between teachers and students: students are now 'teaching assistants', and teachers have become learners. Likewise, as the 'Industrial Age' has apparently given way to the

'Digital Age', the 'artificial barriers between school and community' are being dismantled, as both join together in new virtual networks (ibid.: 117).

The emancipated child

The most influential exponent of this 'Edutopian' discourse is undoubtedly Seymour Papert, Lego Professor of Learning Research at the Massachusetts Institute of Technology. Since the publication of his first book, *Mindstorms*, in 1980, Papert has enjoyed (and indeed cultivated) a guru-like status in the field of educational technology. Yet, as we shall see, his argument for the use of computers rests on a very specific set of assumptions about the nature of learning, and of childhood. It is important to recognize that Papert is primarily a mathematician, and that the main focus of his empirical research is on children learning to *program* computers. The key question is how far this very specific focus can be generalized to support much broader arguments about the value of technology in education.

Mindstorms is driven by a mission to combat what Papert calls 'mathphobia' – and, more broadly, 'the culture that makes science and technology alien to the vast majority of people' (Papert, 1980: 4). Seeking to bridge the gap between 'the two cultures' of the sciences and the humanities, he proposes that computers will create a new relationship with mathematics that is both more 'humanistic' and more 'humane'. According to Papert, programming in LOGO and using the Turtle (either as an on-screen cursor or as a kind of motorized robot) provides a more motivating and exciting way of teaching specific areas of science and mathematics: his examples include differential equations and the Newtonian laws of motion. However, it also teaches a form of *procedural thinking* – a way of breaking a given activity down into constituent elements and 'debugging' and removing any potential problems. Using this approach, the world is divided into a series of 'microworlds' that can be analysed separately, and then recombined according to consistent principles. Thus, he argues, it is possible to apply this form of 'epistemological modularity' to teach an apparently 'intuitive' activity such as juggling. The activity of programming with LOGO thereby allows the child to become an 'epistemologist', to understand more about their own thinking and learning processes – and hence to control them more effectively.

Papert is clear that this form of procedural thinking is not necessarily appropriate in all situations. 'Thinking like a computer' is 'a powerful intellectual tool', although it does not have to be applied all the time (Papert,

1980: 155). Nevertheless, he constantly seeks to broaden his argument from the learning of mathematics to learning in general. He declares that his interest is not merely in mathematics, but in 'mathetics' – that is, learning 'in a general sense' (ibid.: 39). Likewise, 'mathphobia' is generalized to a broader phobia about learning itself. In this way, Papert seeks to extend the findings of his work on children learning LOGO to a much more broad-ranging argument about computers and learning.

Papert was a student of the developmental psychologist Jean Piaget, although his work provides a rather ambivalent reinterpretation of Piaget's legacy. On the one hand, he clearly accepts the child-centred emphases of 'constructivism' – the notion of the child as an active processor of meaning, and the idea that learning is a spontaneous process that needs to proceed at its own pace. From this perspective, the role of the teacher is very much that of a facilitator or supporter of learning: the child needs to be free to learn without the intervention of deliberate teaching or of a prescribed curriculum. The emphasis is accordingly on individualized, 'self-directed' learning. Problems only arise, Papert argues, when parents, teachers and software designers seek to impose the old-fashioned assumptions and learning methods that derive from their own school days.

Papert clearly does not believe that technology will bring about change in itself: he has been critical of 'technocentrism', and in that sense cannot be accused of technological determinism. However, he does believe that the obstacles to what he terms 'Piagetian learning' can be overcome via the use of technology. Computers give people the tools to make far-reaching changes that were impossible in earlier times, and thus represent a kind of vindication or fulfilment of Piaget's theory.

Nevertheless, there are two major ways in which Papert's approach differs from that of Piaget. Where a strict Piagetian approach would assume that the child cannot learn until it is developmentally 'ready', and that it will do so only in a fixed sequence of stages, Papert suggests that the computer can accelerate this process. In *Mindstorms*, he argues that programming with LOGO can enable the child to develop more advanced intellectual structures – to move from the 'concrete' to the 'formal' phase, in Piaget's terms. However, in a later book, *The Children's Machine* (1993), he seems to make a contrary argument, emphasizing the inherent value of the 'concrete' stage – and implicitly taking it as a model for learning in general. At this point, Papert seeks to replace (or perhaps to supplement) 'constructivism' with what he calls 'constructionism' – an approach based on the making and handling of concrete objects, which he describes as a form of 'cybernetics for children' (1993: 182). He heralds a move towards what he calls a 'radically different theory of knowledge', based on the notion of 'learning-in-use'. Precisely what this theory entails is not fully clear: aside from 'giving yourself time' and 'opening oneself by freely talking about learning experiences', this approach apparently involves creating a 'personal connection' between new knowledge and existing knowledge.

A second break with Piaget derives from Papert's emphasis on the emotional and bodily aspects of learning with computers – aspects that barely feature in Piaget's essentially rationalistic model of child development. *Mindstorms* begins with a description of Papert's own childhood fascination with gears, and later waxes lyrical about 'mathematical pleasure' and 'mathematical beauty' – and even 'the mathematical unconscious'. Nevertheless, the kind of emotion Papert is describing is still very strongly focused on mathematics and technology: it is a delight in the power of numbers, and in the ability to control a mechanical device such as the Turtle. This emphasis on the emotional and aesthetic aspects of learning with computers becomes more prominent in Papert's work over time. As if to compensate for the mechanistic nature of his model of procedural thinking, Papert increasingly emphasizes the value of intuition, of 'childlike' thinking and the 'softer' aspects of computing. In *The Children's Machine*, for example, he explicitly rejects a scientistic approach to learning, although here, again, his examples of 'creative' activity involving computers are largely confined to drawings generated via LOGO programming. This argument also leads into the notion of 'learning styles', which (as we have seen) is an emerging emphasis in the discourse of 'personalization'. In *The Connected Family*, Papert proclaims the value of computers in accommodating diverse learning styles – or 'different strokes for different folks', as he puts it (Papert, 1996: 86). Here again, the use of computers could be seen as a vindication of the Piagetian (or constructivist) emphasis on the individual child as a unique developing consciousness.

As we have seen, Papert regards the school as an artificial, inefficient and hierarchical institution, and looks forward to a time in which education will become more of a 'private act'. School mathematics in particular is seen as a kind of reductive betrayal of the excitement that is afforded by real mathematics: it is a prime example of a form of 'disassociated learning' that is not connected with children's existing knowledge. By contrast, using LOGO permits a form of 'syntonic' learning that is more in tune with the child's bodily and cultural experience, and more rooted in 'personal knowing'. Likewise, both in *Mindstorms* and in subsequent books, Papert criticizes most classroom uses of computers, in the form of non-intuitive programming languages such as BASIC and mechanical drill-and-practise software. He is highly dismissive of the 'instructional', back-to-basics packages that are heavily promoted in the marketplace, particularly those which attempt to 'deceive' children into believing that they are simply playing a game. In the concluding chapter of *Mindstorms*, and again in *The Connected Family*, he calls for 'a social movement of people interested in personal computation' to lobby schools and to generate alternatives to traditional classrooms.

This critique of the school becomes somewhat more muted in Papert's subsequent work, although the opposition between school learning and 'natural' learning is sustained. In *The Children's Machine*, he remains optimistic that a new 'knowledge machine' (which clearly resembles the internet) will bring about a fundamental revolution in schooling. However, he argues that schools have resisted the more challenging aspects of computers, for example by locating them in specialized labs, confining them to a separate area of the curriculum, and failing to provide sufficient numbers of them to make a more radical transformation possible. *The Connected Family* shifts the focus to the home, setting up a polarization between 'home-style learning' ('sometimes called "natural learning" or "Piagetian learning" ': 1996: 41–2) and 'school-style learning'. According to Papert, home-style learning is self-directed, non-verbal, spontaneous and experiential – although this will depend upon the extent to which parents follow Papert's tips for using computers to foster a 'healthy home learning culture'.

The discourse of the 'digital generation' (which we have briefly identified above) also emerges much more strongly here. From this perspective, children are seen as innately competent in their dealings with computers: they are possessed of a natural 'technological fluency' and 'take to programming like ducks to water'. According to Papert, children all over the world are enjoying a 'passionate love affair' with computers that somehow transcends cultural differences and inequalities:

> Everywhere, with few exceptions, I see the same gleam in their eyes, the same desire to appropriate this thing. And more than wanting it, they seem to know that in a deep way it already belongs to them. They know that they can master it more easily than their parents. They know they are the computer generation. (Papert, 1996: 1)

There is, it appears, a kind of natural essence of childhood – an innate knowledge, a spontaneous fluency, a thirst for learning – that is somehow automatically released by this technology. Children, it would seem, just intuitively *know* how to use computers; and the computer's mode of operation magically coincides with their natural mode of learning.

By contrast, parents and teachers are represented as fearful and incompetent in their relations with computers, and yet reluctant to hand over control. However, Papert implies that this kind of resistance is bound to fade with the passing of time. In *The Connected Family*, for example, parents are urged to stop being 'cyberostriches', to abandon their outdated assumptions and join their children in the movement towards freedom in learning. When this happens, it would seem that only positive consequences can follow: reluctant learners are transformed into straight-A students, families become more caring and communicative, teachers discover new worlds of learning – all by virtue of their access to technology.

Papert's arguments are not always easy to pin down. As I have suggested, he shifts his ground on several key issues, and sometimes appears to contradict himself. Much of the evidence he presents to support his arguments is anecdotal – and, in some cases, what he calls his 'learning stories' seem to involve no small degree of poetic licence. There is also a strain of sentimentality in his work, which is particularly apparent in *The Connected Family*. Intended as a self-help text for parents, this book combines the homespun commonsense of popular advice literature with occasional Zen-like inspirational mottoes. Arguments that some readers might be forgiven for finding banal and patronizing are clearly intended to possess a child-like profundity. As Papert's colleague Nicholas Negroponte proclaims in his foreword to the book, 'Seymour is the emancipated child'.

As I have implied, one of the major difficulties with Papert's work is his tendency to generalize from the very specific experience of children learning to program to much broader arguments about computers in education. *The Connected Family*, for example, baldly asserts that 'everyone knows computers help children learn' (1996: 8); but most of the concrete examples are still taken from Papert's research with the programming package Microworlds (a successor to LOGO). Papert acknowledges that this work is unrepresentative of most uses of computers in education; and, while it might justify particular approaches to the teaching of mathematics, it is hard to see it as evidence for the broader arguments he is seeking to make.

Indeed, research on the use of LOGO provides far from unequivocal endorsement of its value and effectiveness. While LOGO may be a very effective way of inducting children into computer programming, there is very limited evidence that they are able to *transfer* the styles of procedural thinking apparently cultivated by this activity to other situations (Armstrong and Casement, 2000: 43–5). Joseph Weizenbaum, a former colleague of Papert, once responded to the claim that using computers would improve children's problem-solving skills as follows: 'If that were true, then computer professionals would lead better lives than the rest of the population. We know very well that isn't the case. There is, as far as I know, no more evidence programming is good for the mind than Latin is, as is sometimes claimed' (quoted in Cuban, 1986: 94).

In reality, it would seem that most teachers have used LOGO merely as a form of 'enrichment', or in whole-class instruction, rather than in the child-centred classroom environment Papert recommends; and students often find the approach frustrating and boring (Hativa and Lesgold, 1996: 138–40). Other research has found that children needed significantly more support and guidance than the MIT Logo Group felt was appropriate (Solomon, 1986). Advocates of LOGO would of course take this apparent failure as further proof of Papert's argument about the conservatism of schools. Using LOGO only in 'quick and shallow' ways, and incorporating it within existing curricula and assessment regimes, meant that the intentions of its pioneers were bound to be undermined. According to Agalianos et al. (2001), the radical promise of LOGO was ultimately defused by the ways in which it was implemented in mainstream schools – and, while this might have occurred in any case, it was probably hastened by the conservative drift within educational politics during the 1980s.

These issues of implementation will be addressed more fully in the following chapter. My aim here has simply been to draw attention to some of the basic assumptions of Papert's work – assumptions about learning, about childhood, about technology and about the institution of the school. These assumptions will be thrown into even starker relief as we now move on to consider the work of some prominent critics of the use of computers in schools.

Slaves to the machine

In recent years, these fantasies of 'Edutopia' have been challenged by some equally fervent condemnations of technology in education. Of course, there is a strain of apocalyptic criticism of technology that dates back at least to the Industrial Revolution. Anxieties about the impending destruction of culture and humanity by machines run through the work of many creative writers and social critics from the Romantics onwards. In the 1930s, for example, Lewis Mumford warned of the dehumanizing influence of technology, an argument that became even more far-reaching in his later work (Mumford, 1934, 1967, 1970). The Christian philosopher Jacques Ellul (1964) saw modern technology as a threat to human freedom, arguing that the scientific focus on rationality and efficiency would ultimately lead to the enslavement of humanity. Such authors typically define 'technology' in very inclusive terms, to include phenomena as diverse as electronic media, biotechnology and automobiles, as well as more broadly 'technocratic' modes of hierarchical, bureaucratic organization.

In time, the focus of this kind of criticism inevitably turned to computers. For example, Theodore Roszak (1986) argues that a computerized 'data glut' is steadily overwhelming the human capacity for critical thinking, as *ideas* are replaced by *information*. He sees the computer industry and the internet as being dominated by 'a predatory entrepreneurial sensibility', and argues that 'the computer contributes nothing essential to the life of the mind' (Roszak, 1999). Likewise, Neil Postman attacks what he calls 'technopoly' or 'totalitarian technocracy' – 'the submission of all forms of cultural life to the sovereignty of technique and technology' (1992: 52). Information, he argues, 'has become a form of garbage', and society has become controlled by a bureaucratic 'scientism'.

Again, both writers are very broad-ranging in their choice of targets, but both focus to some degree on education. Roszak (1986) acknowledges that computers may have some value as tools for storing and processing information, but they cannot address complex ideas; and as such, he argues, they should only be used by older students, and in strictly limited ways. Postman (1992) also sees the computer as undermining the traditional function of the school, which is to govern 'the ecology of information'. Schools, he argues, are caught in a 'media war', in which the discipline, objectivity and logic associated with print are being steadily undermined by the superficiality and 'quick emotional response' promoted by new media. Challenging the emphasis on computerized 'efficiency', Postman calls for a return to the traditional academic curriculum, placing a particular emphasis on the importance of history teaching.

Meanwhile, the educational philosopher C. A. Bowers (1988, 2000) has placed a 'New Age', ecological spin on these arguments. He asserts that the use of computers in education undermines environmental sustainability, not so much by virtue of the amount of physical waste they generate, but rather through the impersonal, decentred attitudes they are seen to cultivate. Computers replace authentic 'local knowledge', of the kind developed within pre-modern cultures, with decontextualized 'information'; and they encourage the view that the natural environment can be manipulated in an instrumental way, as though it were computerized data. Interestingly, Bowers also criticizes the constructivist approach espoused by Papert and others, asserting that it fosters a form of liberal individualism that neglects the importance of children being socialized into particular cultural traditions. Papert's approach, he argues, is based on an image of the individual as 'an autonomous self-directing being', and it leads to a view of learning as taking place in a kind of cultural vacuum. Bowers urges teachers to address issues such as the use of computers for surveillance and social control, and to critique the anti-environmental ideology of some educational software packages – although, in general, the implications of his argument for schools are rather vaguely defined.

These criticisms are obviously informed by a kind of technological determinism – albeit one that is the obverse of that of the 'Edutopians'. As in his work on television (Postman, 1983), Postman's analysis of computers is indebted to the 'medium theory' of Marshall McLuhan and Harold Innis. From this perspective, media or modes of communication are seen to have inherent 'biases' that inevitably result in particular styles of thinking or learning. A focus on media that Postman regards as more visual, such as television and computers, results in children being unable to understand or sustain logical arguments: they become 'handicapped learner[s] – slow to respond, far too detached, lacking in emotion, inadequate in creating mental pictures of reality' (1983: 17). By contrast, Bowers (2000) argues that the 'technicist mind-set' promoted by computers results in abstract and theoretical ways of thinking: LOGO, for example, is accused of breaking knowledge down into 'mind-sized bites' and hence of promoting linear, rationalistic thought. Unlike Postman, he also argues that computers privilege literacy over orality, thereby leading to a neglect of traditional wisdom. Yet while these assertions about the negative influence of computers appear almost diametrically opposed, they clearly share a belief in the power of technology to shape fundamental thought processes.

The children's crusade

In the last few years, these somewhat generalized criticisms of the use of computers in education have been joined by some much more focused attacks. Like the material considered above, they come from some quite diverse positions. Clifford Stoll's *High-Tech Heretic* (1999) contains the reflections of a self-professed 'computer contrarian' with many years' experience in the computer industry, while Jane Healy's *Failure to Connect* (1998) comes from the perspective of developmental psychology. Alison Armstrong and Charles Casement, in *The Child and the Machine* (2000), present a comprehensive critique, written primarily for parents. Todd Oppenheimer's *The Flickering Mind* (2003) is largely based on investigative journalism conducted in schools. I will be drawing on several of these in the account that follows, but my main focus will be on a report entitled *Fool's Gold: A Critical Look at Computers in Childhood* (Cordes and Miller, 2000) – not least because it provides a fairly thorough compendium of the main criticisms.

Fool's Gold was produced by an organization calling itself the Alliance for Childhood – a title with clear polemical intentions (dissenters would presumably have to subscribe to the Alliance against Childhood). It received widespread attention when it was published, and was clearly written with a view to promoting a broader public campaign. Its objections to the use of computers in education are probably best identified by reproducing one of its many bullet-pointed lists.

WARNING: Computers May Be Hazardous to a Child's Health

Emphasizing computers in childhood may expose children to the risk of a broad range of developmental setbacks. Potential hazards include the following:

Physical hazards

- Musculoskeletal injuries
- Visual strain and myopia
- Obesity and other complications of a sedentary lifestyle
- Possible side effects from toxic emissions and electromagnetic radiation

Emotional and social hazards

- Social isolation
- Weakened bonds with teachers
- Lack of self-discipline and self-motivation
- Emotional detachment from community
- Commercial exploitation

Intellectual hazards

- Lack of creativity
- Stunted imaginations
- Impoverished language and literacy skills

- Poor concentration, attention deficits
- Too little patience for the hard work of learning
- Plagiarism
- Distraction from meaning

Moral hazards

- Exposure to online violence, pornography, bigotry, and other inappropriate material
- Emphasis on information devoid of ethical and moral context
- Lack of purpose and irresponsibility in seeking and applying knowledge.

Cordes and Miller (2000: 39)

This litany of the manifold ways in which computers are 'bad for children' overlaps at several key points with discourses about the effects of 'older' media such as television; and, as is also the case in Neil Postman's (1992) account, arguments about the effects of television are frequently transferred wholesale. Like other electronic media, computers are accused of overstimulating children with flashy, sensationalized and superficial images that will undermine their capacity for imagination and critical thought, and encourage a dangerous form of escapism. Edutainment software is seen to emphasize 'speed and control . . . at the expense of thoughtfulness and understanding' (Armstrong and Casement, 2000: 12), while the 'fun' element of computing is believed to mislead children into regarding learning as a matter of instant reward (Healy, 1998). According to these critics, children are not 'intellectually, emotionally and morally mature enough' to withstand these effects: on the contrary, 'to be a child . . . is to have the right to be immature and to need adult guidance and adult protection' (Cordes and Miller, 2000: 32).

Some of these concerns are clearly impossible to deny: for example, the epidemic of computer-related injuries such as RSI cannot be ignored. However, several of these arguments are highly problematic. They tend to assume that children's use of the computer will wholly displace other activities (such as reading or 'hands-on' experience). Terms such as 'creativity' and 'imagination' are poorly defined, and almost impossible to measure in any meaningful way. Anyone who has witnessed children's intense – and often highly sociable – engagement in playing computer games would certainly question claims about the tendency of computers to lead to 'social isolation' and 'poor concentration'. As with earlier claims about the effects of television, the evidence for many of these assertions is extremely limited: the research quoted by such critics is often just as problematic (both methodologically and theoretically) as the more positive research they seek to challenge.

Yet underlying these arguments is a broader suspicion – shared by some of the more philosophical critics identified above – of the apparently 'dehumanizing' effects of technology: computers are deemed to promote forms of disembodied rationality and mechanistic, abstract thinking that are fundamentally at odds with human qualities such as emotion, imagination and creativity. They isolate children from their peers, parents and teachers, and hence prevent the development of fulfilling personal relationships, and they deprive them of essential sensory and physical experiences that are vital for their development. In this respect, computers are seen to be leading inevitably to much broader social problems – such as 'violence'.

These arguments are normative, in the sense that they implicitly contrast the use of computers with a more 'natural' or 'healthy' approach to child-rearing. In the Alliance for Childhood report, these norms are celebrated in terms that are frequently breathless and sentimental. We are invited to marvel at the child's 'incredible capacities for lifetime growth', her 'rich, unpredictable inner life' and her 'capacity for quiet wonder and reverence' – all of which are alleged to be at risk from the 'bombardment' of computers. Furthermore, computers are deemed to be a poor substitute for direct hands-on experiences and for the reading of books – another 'second-hand', potentially isolating experience which is somehow exempted from this criticism. These norms, or 'childhood essentials', are very directly stated in another list.

Childhood Essentials

1 Close loving relationships with responsible adults
2 Outdoor activity, nature exploration, gardening, and other direct encounters with nature
3 Time for unstructured play, especially make-believe play, as part of the core curriculum for young children
4 Music, drama, puppetry, dance, painting, and the other arts, offered both as separate classes and as a kind of yeast to bring the full range of other academic subjects to life
5 Hands-on lessons, handcrafts, and other physically engaging activities, which literally embody the most effective first lessons for young children in the sciences, mathematics, and technology

> 6   Conversation, poetry, storytelling, and books read aloud with beloved adults.
>
> Cordes and Miller (2000: 47)

As this implies, *Fool's Gold* clearly promotes a certain ideology of childhood. It offers a vision of a pre-technological childhood, in which children are supposedly closer to nature, and occupied with activities (such as play) that are deemed proper to their position as children. In this world of puppetry, gardening and handicrafts, children are believed to grow and learn at their own natural pace. By contrast, computers stifle qualities such as imagination and creativity that are deemed to be part of the condition of childhood. Children are perceived to have innate 'needs' that computers simply cannot meet.

Here, and in Healy's (1998) book – on which the report draws – there is a strong emphasis on normative models of child development, derived from Piaget and from psychologists such as David Elkind (1981). Thus, the authors argue that children need to be confined to activities that are 'appropriate' to their stage of development and, following Elkind, that childhood must not be 'hurried'. According to the Alliance report, 'the national drive to computerize schools . . . emphasizes only one of many human capacities, one that naturally develops quite late – analytic, abstract thinking – and aims to jump start it prematurely' (Cordes and Miller, 2000: 19). (There is also explicit criticism of Papert on these grounds: see Armstrong and Casement, 2000: chapter 3.) From this perspective, the developmental process seems to be regarded as extremely precarious: childhood, it appears, is under particular stress in the modern world, and it now requires special protection. Thus, Healy (1998) draws on Piaget to propose that children below the age of seven should not be exposed to computers, on the basis that this would disturb the dramatic shift in development that occurs prior to this stage.

The differences between this natural childhood and a technological childhood might be defined in terms of a set of binary oppositions:

Computerized Childhood	**Natural Childhood**
Machines	Human beings
Abstract intellect	Emotion
Programming	Interaction
Cognition	Bodily/kinaesthetic experience
Accelerated growth	Natural growth
Computation	Arts and crafts

Simulation	Real, hands-on experience
Logic	Intuition
Information processing	Imagination
Instruction	Play
Impersonality	Inner life
Destructive	Creative
Emotional detachment	Moral commitment

As this implies, the debate is defined here in absolutist, either/or terms. More of one automatically means less of the other. Furthermore, most of the key terms are poorly defined: qualities such as 'humanity', 'creativity' or 'inner life' are subject to an almost infinite range of interpretations. Much like the myths studied by the French anthropologist Claude Lévi-Strauss, the argument sets up a binary opposition between 'nature' and 'culture': it presumes, rhetorically, that there is a form of pure, 'natural' childhood that somehow pre-exists culture, and to which we will somehow be able to return once we abandon technology.

When it comes to schools, the Alliance authors challenge the idea that computers will result in a more 'child-centred' approach. On the contrary, they argue that they result merely in 'computer-centred education'. Computers lead teachers to place a 'premature' emphasis on cognitive skills, and to regard the child's mind as 'a machine that can and should be both powered up and programmed into adult levels of operation as quickly as possible' (Cordes and Miller, 2000: 6). Real, hands-on experiences are replaced by computerized simulations. The computer turns the classroom into something resembling a workplace, as children are distracted by the superficial interactivity of electronic books and numbed into 'information fatigue' by the world wide web. Any motivation that computers encourage is seen to be only temporary and superficial. Even where they seek to develop 'technology literacy', teachers are led to focus on the operation of mechanical tools at the expense of cultivating critical thinking.

Finally, the critics point out that there are 'hidden costs' in the rush to implement computers in schools (see Oppenheimer, 2003). In addition to the costs of equipment, training, maintenance and regular replacement, these include the costs of removing funding from other areas, such as teachers' salaries, school buildings and libraries, as well as from welfare provision (for example of food programmes or health prevention) that might be directed specifically at children living in poverty. Time spent on computers reduces the time available for more valuable activities such as the arts, and unstructured play, and this may be particularly significant for 'at-risk children in troubled neighbourhoods'. While they can see some specialized uses for computers with older children, the Alliance authors ultimately call for an 'immediate moratorium on the further introduction of computers in early childhood and elementary education' (Cordes and Miller, 2000: 98).

Several of these more specific criticisms of the use of computers in schools will be taken up in the following chapter. Here again, I have sought merely to explain some of the key points of the argument, and to identify some of the implicit assumptions on which it is based. One of the most obvious problems here is the all-encompassing nature of the criticism. These texts catalogue the dangers of technology at considerable length, but they seem unable to recognize any potential value in using it. It is as if they are denouncing an enormous act of deception that has been practised, somehow behind the backs of children, teachers and parents. Yet the Alliance report, and the other critical texts on which it draws, are clearly based on some very particular assumptions about childhood and child development, about learning, and ultimately about the nature of humanity. These assumptions are laid out as if they were commonly accepted facts; yet they are clearly open to question.

Conclusion

As we have seen, the debate about technology in education has often been conducted in quite absolutist terms. Either you are 'for' or you are 'against'. The urgency of the critics' case leads them to state these oppositions in particularly polarized terms, although the glowing enthusiasm of the 'Edutopians' is also premised on a set of absolute distinctions between good, child-centred uses of computers and bad, instructional ones. In a sense, each throws the other into relief and exposes some of their mutual limitations. Yet, ironically, there are also several underlying similarities here. Despite the differences between them, Papert's conception of child development, and his view of the essential nature of childhood, has a great deal in common with that of the Alliance for Childhood. Furthermore, both arguments rest on similar distinctions between reason and emotion, between authentic and artificial learning, and between humanity and technology – even if they seem to pose these distinctions in very different ways.

Nevertheless, there seems to be little opportunity here for more nuanced responses – or indeed for imagining alternative uses for technology in education. As I have implied, this polarization is symptomatic of popular discourse about the effects of technology much more broadly. While the 'boosters' have enthusiastically proclaimed the ability of technology to liberate and to empower, the critics have seen it as a fundamental assault on authentic modes of learning, and indeed on childhood itself. In some respects, the extreme polarization of this debate can be taken as an index of its immaturity. Those who question or challenge the uses of technology in education are all too easily condemned as prehistoric 'technophobes' or as 'Luddites', irrationally resisting 'progress',[1] while those who profess the benefits of technology are perhaps too easily stereotyped as naïve and unrealistic in their aspirations. In the process, fundamental questions about what teachers and students might want to use technology for, and about what we might need to *know* about technology, tend to be marginalized.

As I have suggested, both positions are problematic, both in terms of their implicit assumptions and in terms of their empirical claims. Yet this is not to imply that we should seek to arrive at a 'happy medium' between them. As Nicholas Burbules and Thomas Callister (2000) suggest, this is to assume that the 'costs' and 'benefits' of using technology can be separated – when in fact they are often intimately related. It also assumes that consequences can be easily foreseen – an impossible task given the current pace of technological change. As Burbules and Callister argue, the relationship between means and ends – or, in other words, what we want to use technology *for* – does not remain static; and there will always be 'unintended consequences'.

Several of the broader issues raised here will be taken up in much more detail in subsequent chapters. Chapter 5 looks at the notion of the 'digital generation', and the ways in which childhood is typically defined in relation to digital media. Chapter 6 addresses assumptions about how young people learn with digital technology, via a specific case study of computer games, while in chapter 7 I consider the place of educational technology in the home. Chapter 8 returns to the issue of 'skills', addressing questions about the competencies young people need to acquire in order to deal effectively with new media and technologies. In the following chapter, however, we need to make the move from rhetoric to reality. 'Edutopia' might be a nice place to live – but how far removed is it from the everyday situation of most schools? To what extent has the promise of technology in education been fulfilled? How far has technology been integrated within schools and classrooms, and what difference has it made to learning?

4

___

Waiting for the Revolution

The Unfulfilled Promise of
Technological Change

> I believe that the motion picture is destined to revolutionize our educational system, and that in a few years it will supplant largely, if not entirely, the use of textbooks . . . The education of the future will be conducted through the medium of the motion picture, a visualized education, where it should be possible to obtain one hundred percent efficiency.
>
> Thomas Edison, 1922[1]

Thomas Edison's vision of educational revolution is merely one in a long line of grandiose claims that have been made by technology marketeers and enthusiasts over the past century. Yet, in practice, these visions of technological utopia have largely failed to materialize. This chapter seeks to explain some of the reasons why this has been the case. It begins by tracking some of the claims that have been made about the educational potential of older technologies such as radio and television, and it then moves on to consider the current implementation of computers and ICTs in schools. To what extent are teachers making use of these new technologies? What appear to be the obstacles to the widespread use of ICTs? And what evidence do we have for the apparent benefits of using them?

A fickle romance?

The American educational historian Larry Cuban (1986) has written a valuable history of what he calls the 'fickle romance' between education and technology. Edison was by no means the only advocate of the revolutionary potential of the cinema; and, in the decades that followed, many similar claims were made about the medium of radio. Thirty years on, the same kind of rhetoric was arising around the new medium of television – and, as we entered the 1960s, hopes were again fixed on a new generation of 'teaching machines' in the form of programmed learning laboratories.

Cuban's history traces a recurring cycle of grand claims, followed by disillusion and recrimination. Foundation executives, educational administrators and marketeers repeatedly proclaimed that such technological advances would provide far-reaching solutions to the problems of schooling, making old media such as books, and in many cases also teachers, redundant. Academic studies followed, mostly purporting to demonstrate the effectiveness of these machines as compared with traditional teaching techniques. Nevertheless, there would be growing complaints about the difficulties of use, technical problems and incompatibilities; and surveys would subsequently show that teachers were using these tools only very infrequently. Administrators would then be blamed for leaving such expensive machines to gather dust, while teachers were rebuked for being narrow-minded or old-fashioned in failing to use such apparently effective new devices. And with each new technology, the cycle would be inexorably repeated.

Cuban explores several reasons for teachers' apparent indifference to technology. To some extent, he argues, the problems are logistical: technology often proves more difficult to use than its advocates suggest, and it is hard to secure convenient access given the constraints of school accommodation and timetables. Even if the hardware is available, there is often a limited supply of software that is appropriate for classroom use; and teachers may also not be given sufficient training, either in handling the equipment or in using the resources to support learning. Cuban suggests that older technologies, such as textbooks and chalkboards, have a degree of simplicity and flexibility that makes them much better suited to 'the complicated realities of classroom instruction'. He also argues that teachers value the face-to-face contact they have with students, and are reluctant for it to be replaced or interrupted by technology. Teachers, Cuban suggests, make 'situationally constrained' choices: they 'alter classroom behaviour selectively to the degree that technologies help them solve problems they define as important and avoid eroding their classroom authority', but they are likely to resist changes that they perceive as irrelevant, burdensome or undermining of their position (1986: 70–1).

Perhaps the most significant issue, however, is that the use of technology is often mandated from the top down: it is a decision made by administrators or other outsiders that is then imposed upon the teaching profession. These 'non-teaching reformers' often assume that change in schools is a straightforward technical matter that can be implemented with a kind of military precision. In a subsequent historical analysis, Tyack and Cuban (1995) argue that this is characteristic of attempts at educational reform much more broadly. Whether it comes to experimenting with the structure of the school day, the grouping and allocation of pupils or the content of the curriculum, reform is typically imposed by central authorities, and there is little attempt to enlist teachers as collaborators. As a result, they suggest, the utopian promises that are so frequently made are almost invariably disappointed: change, if it occurs at all, happens slowly and incrementally. Tyack and Cuban argue that the 'grammar' of schooling – the institutional character of the school, which (among other things) exists in order to process large numbers of students – tends to resist radical transformation, particularly when it comes from outside. It is certainly possible to think of many exceptions to this argument – the mandating of centralized curricula and testing regimes in the UK over the past two decades has certainly been more than a superficial passing phase – but it does apply with particular force to the use of technology in schools.

Bettina Fabos (2004) places a slightly different spin on this argument, suggesting that (at least in the US context) the successive commercialization of these media largely undermined their educational value. She traces how film, radio and television each appeared to promise radical solutions to the administrative problems of schools, as well as offering new ways of enhancing and enriching learning. The history of each medium is different, but in each case educational aims effectively gave way to commercial imperatives. Cheaply produced and poor quality content or advertising-sponsored 'infomercials' did not move teachers to embrace the medium; and teachers themselves were unable to get involved in, or to influence, the production of content that more effectively met their needs. Channel One, the US news-and-commercials channel that is now used by around 40 per cent of US schools, is one of the most recent manifestations of this: however valuable its news content may be, it serves primarily as a means of selling youth audiences to advertisers – and the incentives of free equipment in exchange for compulsory daily screenings have proven particularly enticing for schools in less wealthy neighbourhoods (see De Vaney, 1994).

Brave new media

Even so, the history of these technological developments takes a different form in different national contexts. In the case of the UK, for example, educational radio and television have been provided primarily as a dimension of public service broadcasting (on the part both of the BBC and of terrestrial commercial channels, which are also required by law to provide programming for schools). In this context, the rhetoric of 'efficiency' shared by Thomas Edison and B. F. Skinner has generally been subordinated to a much more 'child-centred' approach.

A couple of years after Edison's statement (quoted above), Mary Somerville, one of the pioneers of BBC radio for schools, described how she first heard a broadcast 'by accident' in a country schoolhouse. It was a talk on music by Sir Walford Davies, broadcast around Spring 1924 – not a schools programme, but . . .

> No matter, he was teaching, and he was making music, and the impact of his personality and of his music was tremendous. Things happened in all of us, in the children, in their music-loving teacher, and in me. The children's eyes were round with wonder. We grown-ups were exalted. Science, as Bridges later wrote, had 'outrun all magic, spiriting the dumb inane with the quick matter of life'. Beauty now could enter every home and every classroom! After the broadcast we made our own music, the children sang and their teacher played to us some of the themes we had heard on the air; and then, far into the night, she and I talked of what this brave new medium of communication might mean to the schools. (Quoted in Palmer, 1947: 9)

Somerville's story recurs in several later accounts of schools broadcasting in Britain (e.g. Bailey, 1957; Scupham, 1967; Fawdry, 1974); and it is clearly seen to possess a timeless relevance. These books – most of them published by the BBC itself – frequently wax lyrical about the power of this 'brave new medium' to transform the classroom. Bailey's *The Listening Schools* (1957), for example, is filled with testimonials from teachers, letters from child listeners and instances of poems and drawings produced in response to schools radio programmes. It describes a world in which teaching always magically succeeds, a world of infinite promise, enthusiasm and reward – a world that seems to exist despite the contemporary realities of teacher shortages, large classes and lack of resources. Likewise, John Scupham, controller of schools broadcasting at the BBC in the 1960s, enthuses about the ability of radio and television to promote 'romance in learning' and the 'delighted awareness of new worlds' (Scupham, 1967). And Kenneth Fawdry (1974) paints a picture of children as infinitely inquisitive, their attention 'glued to the screen' in complete acceptance: a mimic in one comprehensive school is roundly silenced by his classmates, while even the 'difficult' boys are 'with the broadcast all right'.

As Mark Pegg (1983) suggests, early press coverage of educational broadcasting also saw it as a powerful force for good:

> Contemporary press comment invariably referred to this service in the most glowing terms. Newspapers seemed to lapse into reams of rhetorical

excess. In its educational role, radio was seen as a 'social revolution', 'a great force for enlightenment' and 'the most important essential of an educated democracy'. (Pegg, 1983: 165–6)

Throughout its early history, educational broadcasting was persistently linked to what were seen as progressive forces in education – and particularly to the ideology of constructivism. Rather than providing direct instruction, it was seen to offer a form of 'experience'. Thus, Palmer (1947: 30) argues that a broadcast is 'not a *lesson*, prefabricated or mass-produced. It is an *experience* for the children on which the teacher can build.' Likewise, Bailey (1957) argues that radio can open up 'wide and rich fields of experience': drama can allow us to 'eavesdrop' on distant times and places, while radio talks allow us to feel that the speaker is '*in* the classroom in full reality'. Broadcasting is seen to offer experiences that are no different in kind from direct encounters with reality: it 'opens the doors of the classroom to let interesting visitors in, and to take the children out on journeys into time and space' (Moir, 1967: 48–9). Good broadcasting, according to these authors, is characterized by its vividness and immediacy: it provides a 'window on the world', and any sense that what we are seeing or hearing has been constructed must be suppressed for fear that it may destroy the illusion of transparency. From this perspective, learning comes to be seen as a natural, organic process, a matter of simply *learning from experience*: it is 'a mystery akin to art and before it one must stand with something like awe' (Bailey, 1957: 127).

Like computers, educational broadcasting was also seen to have the power to 'enchant the disenchanted child' (Beastall, 2006). As we have seen, early books on schools broadcasting frequently described children as being transfixed by its magical power, completely absorbed in wonder and delight. Historically, schools broadcasting in Britain was targeted primarily at secondary modern schools – that is, at educational 'underachievers'; and it was noted that grammar schools were often reluctant to release classes from examination studies in order to view programmes (Schools Broadcasting Council, 1962). Pupils who were deemed 'difficult to stimulate by traditional teaching methods' were seen to 'respond more readily to what they have actually experienced than to the consideration of generalisations and abstract ideas' (Moir, 1967: 51). Television, as a 'visual medium', was seen to permit a form of 'directness and immediacy in communication' that was particularly suited to such learners. In the work of John Scupham (1964, 1967), this view of the inherent characteristics of television is clearly aligned with a deficit model of the working-class child. Television is most appropriate, he argues, not for the 'academically gifted', but for 'those who accept and understand life most readily in concrete terms . . . and who perhaps will never move easily into the realm of generalisation and abstraction' (Scupham, 1964: 8). The 'visual immediacy' of television, with its focus on 'striking particulars', is seen to compensate for such innate limitations in intellectual ability (ibid.: 10).

Reading between the lines of these euphoric accounts of schools broadcasting, however, it is possible to discern a frustration that this material was not in fact being widely used. Charles Curran, a director general of the BBC in the 1970s, notes that broadcasts were 'not used as widely and effectively as they should be' (Curran, 1972: 6). He argues that the BBC's work in educational broadcasting has been 'left unsupported' and implicitly calls for increased government funding. Likewise, Moir (1967) expresses dismay at teachers' hostility and suspicion towards the 'honest handiwork freely offered' by broadcasters at successive conferences; and there is a sense from other accounts (e.g. Robinson, 1982) that teachers are simply being 'old-fashioned' in their apparent resistance to educational television.

In fact, there is only limited evidence about the use of educational broadcasting. Within the broadcasting organizations, the line between research and public relations has often been blurred; and there has been a marked reluctance to support independent evaluation. The Annan Report, for example, noted that there was little evidence on 'the reality, as distinct from the aspirations, of educational broadcasting', and that broadcasters were suspicious of research, preferring instead to rely on 'the subjective appraisal of those involved' (Home Office, 1977; see also Bates, 1984: 194). It also appears that educational programmes were steadily pushed to the margins within the BBC itself. Kenneth Fawdry, in a BBC publication, even suggests that educational broadcasting 'seems a foreign body in the BBC's eye': while it values the 'good name' of its educational services, 'it sometimes treats them as if they were hardly a part of itself, but rather the embodiment of a problem imposed on it by this powerful and appallingly respectable pressure group' (1974: 184–5).

Ultimately, the problem here is one that can be seen as characteristic of public service broadcasting more broadly. While educational broadcasting is a legal requirement (identified, for example, in the BBC charter), broadcasters have historically remained very distant from those they purport to serve. Educational broadcasting is essentially a service 'delivered' to teachers from outside, rather than something that is produced by them or in collaboration with them. Broadcasters' judgements of 'quality' in broadcasting are thus largely derived not from an understanding of the educational *use* of programmes, but from the professional criteria that apply within mainstream broadcasting. As we have seen, these criteria typically define the 'inherent characteristics' of media in particular ways, and hence as particularly well suited to particular types of learner. They also sanction a particular epistemology – a view of broadcasting as a 'window on the world', a form of 'experience' that is somehow beyond question. In this sense, the institutional structures of broadcasting appear to have sanctioned a particular instrumental definition of what – and indeed who – educational broadcasting is for.

To what extent should we expect the use of computers to replicate this kind of history? Certainly, the far-reaching utopian claims that have been made about the potential of computers provide many echoes of earlier arguments about film, radio and television. Like previous technologically driven reforms, the use of computers in schools has primarily been mandated from the top down, and, like them, it has also been driven by commercial interests. Just as educational broadcasting has been seen as a means of delivering 'experience', so computers have been seen to deliver 'information' – a seemingly neutral resource that will automatically guarantee learning. And, as we shall see, teachers are likely to continue to make 'situationally constrained' choices that are in line with their own imperatives as regards classroom management, workload and curriculum priorities.

However, there are some significant differences. The scale of investment in ICTs – not least on the part of government – is significantly greater than was the case with older media. Computers are arguably penetrating a much wider range of areas of social life – including, crucially, many workplaces – even when compared with television, which has remained primarily a domestic, leisure technology. At least potentially, computers can be used in more individualized ways: they afford a degree of interactivity and 'personalization' that older media such as film and television do not. They also appear to have a much wider range of possible applications in the classroom. While it would not be unrealistic to expect more of the same, it is also not unreasonable to expect some more far-reaching, and more lasting, change.

Using computers in the classroom

To what extent are teachers using computers in their classrooms? The evidence from UK government statistics (quoted in chapter 1) clearly shows that there has been a significant increase in the amount of hardware in schools over the past decade. Yet research also suggests that the use of this technology has been uneven and piecemeal – and, in general, distinctly limited.

For example, a major cross-national survey published by the Organization for Economic Co-operation and Development (OECD) in 2004 found that the educational use of computers was 'sporadic' across all the fourteen countries surveyed. On average, only around 20 per cent of teachers were reported to be using computers 'a lot' as a source of additional instruction or to allow students to work at their own pace. According to school principals, only a minority of teachers regularly use standard computer applications (such as word processors), and only in Denmark, Sweden and Korea did the proportions who do so reach 60 per cent. The most common reasons cited for this underuse were difficulties in integrating ICT into classroom instruction, problems in scheduling enough computer time for classes, and teachers' lack of ICT skills and knowledge. In addition, principals reported that obtaining ICT teachers was by far the most difficult recruitment problem that they faced across all school subjects (OECD, 2004: 74–80).

In the UK, a 2004 survey by the schools inspection agency, Ofsted, found that, while teachers' expressed levels of competence in using technology were rising, there was much diversity across the system, and that the use of computers was generally sporadic. The training provided for teaching staff (the national New Opportunities Fund scheme) was judged to be disappointing, with an insufficient emphasis on classroom learning, and schools were not making realistic long-term financial plans for the provision of technology (Ofsted, 2004).

Meanwhile, the British Educational Communications and Technology Agency, which is charged with advising on the government's policy in this field, noted in a 2005 report that, while some significant change had occurred, the use of technology was generally not 'systemic' or 'embedded' in classroom practice. Teachers were finding it hard to locate appropriate resources: while a high proportion (over three-quarters) were using computers for management and administration, the proportion using them regularly in lessons was only 10 to 20 per cent. This report also found significant disparities across the system: while there were some instances of effective use, the general pattern was of fragmentation and underutilization. Here again, a key problem was the lack of effective financial planning. A high proportion of computers in schools were over three years old, and schools were finding it difficult to make provision for regular replacement. As the report concluded: 'a small minority of institutions display a high level of ICT maturity, but a large core are struggling to deal with issues of sustainability and effectiveness' (BECTA, 2005: 7).

These government reports are more than confirmed by independent academic research. Larry Cuban's own study, pithily entitled *Oversold and Underused: Computers in the Classroom* (2001), was conducted in extremely well-equipped, affluent schools in Silicon Valley, California. Cuban found that teachers and students enjoyed high levels of access to computers, both at home and in school, and there was little evidence of 'technophobia' or resistance to technology *per se*. Many teachers used computers for administrative tasks, preparing teaching materials, and communicating with parents. However, only a small proportion (less than 10 per cent) were using computers in the classroom more than once a week, and well over half were not using them at all. Even where students were using computers, this was often peripheral to their learning: only on rare occasions were computers a central aspect of their work. Furthermore, there was no clear evidence of students increasing their academic achievement as a result of doing so.

Tom Conlon and Mary Simpson (2003) compared Cuban's findings with those from a major Scottish report, *The Impact of ICT Initiatives in Scottish Schools* (Condie et al., 2002), a longitudinal study based on a much larger sample of schools. The findings are strikingly similar. Both teachers and students enjoyed high levels of access to computers, but there was very limited use in the classroom. There was some use of word processing and internet searches, but very limited use of simulations or multimedia authoring packages. In the upper secondary school, most use of computers was accounted for by technology-intensive subjects such as computing studies, business studies and graphic communication. While teachers were far from 'technophobic', high percentages of them said that they did not have time to find out about appropriate resources, and that their training needs had not been met. In general, there were few changes in these findings across the three-year period of the research. (These conclusions were also echoed in a further Scottish report, focusing specifically on early years education: Stephen and Plowman, 2003.)

The obstacle race

Of course, there are exceptions to this overall pattern: all these studies suggest that a small minority of teachers have changed their practice, and are integrating technology much more effectively into their classrooms. There are many examples of this, not just in the more predictable, technology-intensive areas such as science, maths or design and technology, but also in areas such as music, English and media studies; and, needless to say, they are frequently documented in the technology supplements of the educational press. I shall be considering some of the more creative uses of digital media in more detail in chapter 8. In general, however, it seems fair to conclude that classroom teaching and learning have been far from transformed through the advent of technology.

What are the reasons for this? In general, advocates of technology tend to blame teachers, arguing that they are simply too old-fashioned or lazy to adapt – or alternatively too threatened by such an apparently fundamental challenge to their authority. In the discourse of Ofsted and BECTA, the failure to use technology is frequently identified as a 'weakness' – although here the weakness is often seen to be on the part of senior managers rather than teachers themselves. Nevertheless, the studies quoted above suggest that most teachers are quite ready to use computers at home and in other areas of their professional lives: they tend to 'resist' only when it comes to using them in the classroom.

Clearly, there will be differences between teachers – differences of attitude, confidence level and even emotional or cognitive 'style' – that will influence their willingness to engage with technology. There will also be social differences – for example of gender or social class background – that may result in different levels or types of use. However, there are also several professional concerns and difficulties that teachers are likely to share.

Some of these are broadly structural or logistical. Several of the reports quoted above draw attention to the complexity of financial planning, which – despite the extensive provision of 'pump-priming' funds from central government – is now largely devolved to individual schools in the UK. Equipment purchasing and supply, administration, and maintenance represent significant new challenges for school managers that are on a different scale from those they have faced before – particularly as school funding itself appears to be increasingly insecure. The introduction of computers involves several 'below-the-line' infrastructural costs – subscriptions, networks, upgrades, specialist furniture, as well as training – that may prove hard to predict (Westbrook and Kerr, 1996). The use of technology – particularly desktop computers – requires larger classrooms, although it seems likely that class sizes will rise as a growing proportion of school budgets is spent on technology. One further consequence of this situation is that schools are bound to rely more heavily on corporate sponsorship of various kinds, not least from technology companies that are keen to build 'brand loyalty'.

These difficulties are particularly apparent in a situation that amounts to 'planned obsolescence'. For example, computers that are over three years old (as are almost half the computers in UK primary schools: BECTA, 2005) are unlikely to be able to make best use of the latest software programs. The cost of maintenance and replacement is one that many schools have found particularly hard to predict and control, given the rapid pace of technological development. Software is now routinely sold in a 'beta' form, as purchasers are expected to identify bugs and then pay for 'upgrades'. As a result, technology failures – system crashes, incompatible formats, lost data – are extremely common in schools; and, as Dale et al. (2004) indicate, technical faults (or the expectation of technical faults) have been identified as a significant factor affecting teachers' confidence in using ICT. These are not problems that will simply disappear once technology reaches a certain stage of development: on the contrary, they are endemic.

Training is clearly crucial to the implementation of technology in schools, and yet the proportion of funding spent on training is consistently lower than most educational planners see as necessary (Cordes and Miller, 2000: 78). Furthermore, much of the available training has tended to focus on the operation of the technology, rather than how it might be used in the classroom (Lawson and Comber, 2000a). Even government reports (e.g. Ofsted, 2004) have pointed to the limitations of current training provision, and this has been reinforced by several academic studies. Both Galanouli et al. (2004) and Conlon (2004) found that teachers were overwhelmingly negative about the New Opportunities Fund training, which to date has been the major UK government initiative in this area (costing £230 million). Conlon argues that the most significant problem here derived from what he calls the 'delivery' or 'empty vessel' model, 'in which the teacher is positioned as the uncritical implementer of outside policies' (Conlon, 2004: 119). Like other top-down initiatives condemned by Tyack and Cuban (1995), this approach does not fully account for the complexity of teachers' professional development, or their attempts to meet the needs of learners. The scheme failed to build on teachers' existing ICT skills and lacked relevance to individual curriculum subjects, and as such, there is little evidence that it brought about lasting change.

These difficulties may intensify as teachers struggle to keep up with the accelerating pace of technological change. As Hativa and Lesgold (1996) point out, the drive to implement computer technology in schools has involved successive waves of innovation: from BASIC and LOGO programming in the early 1980s, through CAI and integrated learning systems, the use of generic programs (such as word processors and spreadsheets), multimedia authoring and telecommunication via the internet, to the electronic whiteboards, educational games and learning platforms currently dominating the marketplace, there has been an ever-changing succession of apparently essential, ground-breaking new devices, each of which has raised new expectations. Deryn Watson (2001) estimates that the UK has seen at least thirty major hardware and software initiatives in schools over the past two decades – and she notes that each new initiative is launched with little attempt to evaluate or analyse those that preceded it. Despite the emphasis on 'evidence-based policy', research tends to follow innovation rather than to inform it. In this situation, there is clearly a danger of 'technology fatigue', which may lead some teachers simply to abandon the struggle to 'keep up', not just with the equipment but also with the new educational theories that it appears to require. J. Michael Spector (2001) argues that the field has increasingly been dominated by a form of 'technification', in which the newest educational devices are usable only by 'a scarce cadre of technocrats' and the majority of teachers are reduced to mere consumers.

A further problem relates to the provision of software. In the UK, as in most other countries, government priorities with regard to ICT have traditionally been defined in terms of student-to-computer ratios (Dale et al., 2004). Only comparatively recently has the focus begun to shift to the provision of software, with some of the initiatives described in chapter 1 (Selwyn, 2005). Here again, government has placed the emphasis on stimulating commercial industry, rather than enabling teachers themselves to become involved in the design and production of appropriate software. As we shall see in more detail in chapter 7, this has resulted in a market that is dominated by what might be termed 'lowest common denominator' software – and, in particular, packages that are defined by the requirements of national testing. As we have seen, advocates of computers in education (such as Papert, 1996) routinely bemoan the dominance of 'drill-and-practise' software; yet more challenging or creative packages are still very hard to find.

There are also limitations here in terms of teachers' ability to obtain information about available software. Events such as BETT are scarcely reliable sources of independent evaluation; and the technology supplements of the educational press are rarely noted for their objective or incisive criticism (not least, perhaps, because the owners of such publications themselves have significant interests in the educational technology business).[2] According to BECTA (2004), the provision of educational 'content' in the UK is dominated by a small number of major suppliers: 61 per cent of spending goes to 2 per cent of the government-registered suppliers (ten companies), and 48 per cent to the most popular twenty products (which are primarily office applications, word processors, spreadsheets and testing software). Even if there is innovative software available, it is likely that few teachers will ever hear about it.

Going down slow

In this situation, it is perhaps unsurprising that teachers have appeared reluctant to use technology in the classroom. However, there are further reasons, to do with the organization of schools and with teachers' professional imperatives and commitments. What Tyack and Cuban (1995) call the 'grammar' of schooling is undoubtedly significant here. Educational reformers often complain about the rigid structure of school timetables and the inflexible organization of space in schools. Yet, to a large extent, these must be seen as inevitable consequences of the institutional function of the school, and of the large numbers of students it must accommodate. For example, in the case of computers, one of the ongoing debates has been to do with the location of equipment. Progressive educators often complain about the tendency to locate computers in 'labs', with classes timetabled for specific lessons: they argue that this restricts both the flexibility of use and the integration of computers with everyday learning activities (Watson, 2001). Yet the often mooted alternative – providing class sets of laptops – poses significant problems for teachers, who may spend much of their time setting up and troubleshooting. The use of centralized labs also facilitates routine maintenance, which (as we have seen) is often a major expense.

Constraints on teachers' time are another factor. Over the past two decades, teaching has steadily been infused by the 'audit culture': the requirements on teachers to monitor their own and their students' performance, and to report to senior managers and parents, have grown exponentially. What critics have termed 'the terrors of performativity' (Ball, 2003) mean that the professional work of teachers is now more intensively regulated – and indeed self-regulated – in terms of externally defined targets and indicators. Among other things, this inevitably affects their ability to respond to new technologies. In the Scottish survey reported by Conlon and Simpson (2003), for example, almost all teachers agreed with the statement that 'too many other priorities are competing for staff time and attention' and 'there is too little time to preview software'.

However, research also suggests that the use of technology may conflict with teachers' deep-seated beliefs and commitments. Some of these are broadly shared, while others may be specific to particular curriculum subjects. For example, Janet Schofield (1995) is relatively optimistic about the potential of computers to create a less teacher-centred classroom; yet she also argues that computers will be unable to replace the 'humanness' that is so important to teacher–student interaction – by which she means the use of one's own judgements and feelings, and one's understanding of others' feelings. Cuban (1986: 89–90) likewise argues that it is this 'human touch' that makes teaching such a demanding, but also potentially rewarding, occupation – although he is careful to warn against the dangers of sentimentality in this respect.

Research has repeatedly shown that most teachers adopt an 'incrementalist' view of technology: they use it to help them do what they are currently doing more easily, efficiently or effectively (Mumtaz, 2000; Schofield, 1995). They evaluate technology in terms of its 'fit' with ongoing classroom practices and the existing subject curriculum. The few enthusiasts who integrate technology into their teaching do so because it relates to their own philosophical beliefs about teaching or the nature of their subject; but the majority fail to do so not because of laziness or some imagined 'technophobia', but for sound professional reasons (Watson, 2001).

For example, in a series of empirical studies, Goodson et al. (2002) show how teachers tend to use computers as 'just another tool': they use technology to modify aspects of their existing practice, but tend to keep the basic structures and objectives unchanged. Likewise, Tony Lawson and Chris Comber (2000a) found that the implementation of the UK government's 'Superhighways Initiative' did not make much impact in terms of blurring the boundaries between subjects, as its advocates had initially claimed. Teachers recognized the value (in this case) of using the internet, but tended to use it as a means of 'delivering' the existing curriculum in a more efficient way, and of meeting examination requirements. Like Cuban (1986), these studies suggest that teachers generally 'make do': in a context of scarce resources, escalating workloads, and the pressures of ever-changing government initiatives, they seek merely to generate serviceable classroom strategies.

Other studies point to the ways in which teachers' use of technology – particularly in secondary schools – is mediated through their academic 'subject sub-cultures'. Sara Hennessy, Kenneth Ruthven and Sue Brindley (2005) provide extensive examples of this in the case of the core subjects of English, mathematics and science. In general, the teachers they interviewed were relatively 'open' in their views of technology and committed to using it, but they were also cautious, reflective and sometimes critical of what they saw as distracting or excessive use. They did not assume that the use of technology would automatically result in learning, and they resisted using it in mechanical or inappropriate ways. In general, they employed technology selectively in order to enhance – rather than transform – existing teaching and learning activities, and were keen to hold on to important aspects of their subject practice. Interestingly, they also saw the need for developing a 'critical literacy' among their students, stressing the need for interpretation and analysis of digital resources (an issue to be discussed in detail in chapter 8). While these authors do see signs of gradual evolution, they argue that teachers are maintaining the focus of attention on subject learning aims: rather than technology transforming subject learning, the 'subject sub-culture' effectively co-opts and colonizes the computer.

Whose revolution?

As we have seen, there are many 'local' reasons why technology has failed to transform learning in the manner that many of its advocates have envisaged. Yet perhaps the overriding one is to do with the centralized, top-down nature of the innovation itself. The pressure for change has come largely from government and from industry, rather than from teachers themselves. As in other centralized reforms – most notably the UK's national Numeracy and Literacy Strategies – change has largely been a matter of implementing government-produced lesson plans and government-endorsed resources. In this respect, it has much in common with the other kinds of educational reforms analysed by Tyack and Cuban (1995). Here again, reformers have largely ignored the institutional constraints of schooling, the professional imperatives of teachers, and the need to adapt change to local knowledge and needs. In the UK, as Hennessy et al. suggest, this coercive approach has contributed to 'a perception of eroded autonomy and a feeling of disempowerment in teachers' (2005: 170). In this situation, they maintain, teachers are unlikely to develop 'a sense of ownership' of ICT – or, one might add, of any centrally imposed innovation. Declining teacher morale, increased rates of retirement and mobility, and escalating stress are now characteristic of education systems in most developed countries; and in such a context, it may be quite unrealistic to expect far-reaching transformation of classroom practice.

Moreover, there have been several significant confusions of purpose in government policy. Policy sometimes appears to have been invented 'on the hoof', in response to inflated commercial claims about the value of new products. Like teachers, policy-makers have been persistently urged to 'catch up' with technology, and at times this pressure has resulted in misguided and inconsistent decisions. The apparent failure of major initiatives such as the UK's National Grid for Learning and the New Opportunities Fund training provides clear evidence of this (see Conlon, 2004; Galanouli et al., 2004; and Ofsted, 2004).

More broadly, there has been a fundamental confusion between the use of technology as a 'tool' for subject learning and technology as a separate subject in its own right. Deryn Watson (1998, 2001) argues that these two practices are typically disconnected from each other, not least in government policy. 'ICT' as a separate curriculum subject is generally justified in terms of its vocational relevance, and remains compulsory for all students in UK secondary schools. As Watson argues, it is typically based on the learning of relatively low-level skills, which are taught in isolation from any real or meaningful purpose that students may have. Students often have few opportunities to apply these skills in other curriculum areas. Yet 'ICT across the curriculum' also has its limitations. In this model, different subject departments typically take primary responsibility for different areas of ICT skill: English may take on word processing, geography or history may cover databases, while mathematics will deal with modelling. Yet specialist teachers in these areas may themselves be poorly trained in relevant skills and may experience other pressures on their time, and they often find it hard to combine the teaching of subject content with the teaching of generic computer skills.

Meanwhile, the drive to implement technology has often been at odds with other aspects of educational policy. As we have seen, advocates of computers in education frequently espouse a broadly 'constructivist' approach, which emphasizes student-centredness, open-ended enquiry and 'learning by doing'. Yet in the UK, as in many other countries, government policy over the past two decades has been characterized by a move 'back to basics' – or what Jane Kenway and Elizabeth Bullen (2001) call 'educational fundamentalism'. In the UK, for example, we have seen the imposition of a traditional subject-based curriculum, reinforced by an extensive apparatus of national testing; the implementation of centrally defined 'strategies' for literacy and numeracy, characterized by a return to much older teaching methods (such as synthetic phonics); the rise of a centralized inspection regime driven by inflexible, government-defined targets and indicators, and reinforced by a highly punitive approach to 'failing' schools; and the growth of a culture of 'performativity', where the measurement of success in education is defined primarily in terms of standardized test scores. This general shift is evident in many other English-speaking countries (see Goodson et al., 2002; Schofield, 1995). To say the least, these developments fit awkwardly when set against another official rhetoric that emphasizes 'personalization' and challenges a 'one size fits all curriculum'.

This gives rise to some significant contradictions in the teaching of particular subjects. As Sara Hennessy et al. (2005) point out, the English National Curriculum actually provides very few opportunities for the use of ICT, and the definition of ICT as a cross-curricular 'key skill' is at odds with its strongly subject-centred approach. Teachers are ceaselessly urged to use technology to enhance learning; yet there appears to be little reward for doing so in terms of traditional forms of assessment – and it is by the results of assessment that the work of teachers is increasingly judged. This is perhaps most evident in the case of mathematics, where there have been explicit bans on the use of electronic calculators. Ultimately, despite the government's rhetoric of 'modernization', the drive to 'raise standards' has maintained a view of academic capability that is still defined in terms of very traditional forms of knowledge and skill.

How change can happen

Despite the broad picture I have outlined, there are undoubtedly instances of teachers using technology both extensively and in innovative, creative and effective ways. They are exceptional, but nevertheless important. In general, it would seem that 'good practice' of this kind depends upon a number of positive factors – as well as the relative absence of some of the obstacles and constraints noted above. If teachers can perceive there to be a role for technology in furthering their own aims – whether these are related to pedagogy or to the content of the curriculum – they are much more likely to adopt it. And where teachers are strongly supported, for example by senior management, by university researchers, or by targeted government initiatives, and where there are clear incentives, some far-reaching change is undoubtedly possible.

Ros Sutherland et al. (2005), for example, describe a project that involved teachers collaborating with university researchers to integrate technology within a range of subject areas. Teachers worked collaboratively with researchers and teacher educators (at a ratio of around three teachers to one outsider) to design and implement new computer-based approaches. In this relatively luxurious context, a significant majority of teachers successfully used technology to enhance learning, and to build bridges between classroom work and students' uses of technology at home. However, it could be argued that much of the reason for the project's success was precisely the unusual nature of the collaboration and the additional support it offered to teachers (Triggs and John, 2004).

Likewise, Penni Tearle (2003) presents an in-depth case study of one 'model' school where technology had effectively permeated across the curriculum. A range of factors contributed to this: the quality of the school leadership, the collaborative and consultative approach to decision-making, and the general 'ethos' or 'learning culture' of the school. This was a successful and well-resourced school, on a number of dimensions, and it had managed to implement a range of other innovations very effectively. Yet even here, Tearle argues, 'there were few signs of radical alteration to existing structures and working practices, or even evidence of particularly innovative application of ICT to enhance and extend learning opportunities' (Tearle, 2003: 579). As she suggests, the 'revolution' envisaged by policy-makers may arrive eventually, but for the time being one should expect only 'incremental' change, even in such hospitable circumstances.

Of course, the danger of such studies is what researchers term the 'Hawthorne effect'. The sense of novelty and enthusiasm that attends any educational innovation may in itself be responsible for any benefits that it appears to bring about – and, in this sense, the positive gains that are sometimes traced to the influence of technology might well have occurred if a different form of innovation had been implemented in its place. Much of the research into 'cutting-edge' uses of technology is inevitably small-scale, and much of it involves a form of participatory 'action research'. Indeed, this could be seen as an occupational hazard in research on ICTs in education: since the technologies in question are rarely used, researchers have to introduce and support them in order to be able to study what they are looking for. The unanswered question is whether any such changes stand the test of time; and in this respect, the sheer pace of technological change makes it almost impossible to judge.

Ultimately, research suggests that – in education, as in other areas of social life – technology does not bring about change in and of itself. Where change occurs, it generally derives not so much from technology *per se* as from the changes in the social functioning of the classroom that tend to accompany it. In other words, change is mediated through the social milieu into which it enters (Schofield, 1995) and, as such, it is likely to prove gradual, piecemeal and uneven. Given the factors I have identified here, it is clearly inadequate to conceive of this situation as merely a consequence of 'teacher resistance' – particularly if that resistance is seen to derive merely from a pathological inability to adjust to change, or an irrational insistence on outmoded ways of operating. Such criticisms merely seem to reflect a lack of understanding of the nature of schools and of teachers' working lives.

Where's the difference?

Few teachers would dispute that computers have brought significant advantages in terms of the management and administration of schools – although some might argue that they have merely extended the bureaucratic 'audit culture' of contemporary education. Yet what is known about the benefits of computers in terms of students' learning? Even where computers are being extensively used, what difference do they make to students' motivation and achievement? And is the investment in computers actually worth the money in terms of improving teaching and learning, when compared with other possible ways in which that money might be spent?

Answering these questions is not as straightforward as it might appear. A great deal of the research on educational technology has been driven by the overriding optimism of the enthusiasts. Much of the evidence has been anecdotal: there have been few large-scale studies or rigorously controlled comparisons, no longitudinal research, and little sustained observation of the realities of learning in computerized classrooms. The broader social and cultural issues that typically arise in studies of the 'social shaping' of technology (see, for example, Lievrouw and Livingstone, 2002; Mackenzie and Wajcman, 1985; Woolgar, 2002) tend to be neglected in favour of a limited 'cause-and-effect' approach. As such, it is quite hard to find definitive evidence as to the positive value of using computers in schools – not to mention any unintended consequences they might have.

This is particularly problematic, not just in light of the scale of investment in technology, but also in terms of the ability to address popular criticisms. For example, the journalist Todd Oppenheimer (2003) suggests that the use of computers allows students extensive opportunities for distraction, for 'goofing off', e-mailing friends and playing games – as well as copying large amounts of material from the internet. He argues that much of the work students undertake with computers is superficial: in the case of writing, for example, there is a focus on external aspects of presentation at the expense of developing rigorous arguments or clear critical thinking.

Oppenheimer's assertions are based on journalistic observation rather than in-depth research, yet it is actually hard to find definitive evidence that might counter them.

To some extent, the difficulties here are symptomatic of educational research more broadly. As Hativa and Lesgold (1996) point out, classrooms pose unique conditions: the effects of any teaching strategy are bound to vary significantly depending upon the characteristics of the school, the individual teacher and the students themselves. As such, the consequences of using technology are unlikely to be unitary or consistent: they may well be very different from those planned for and expected, and there are almost bound to be unanticipated 'side-effects'. The role of the individual teacher is clearly crucial, yet this is extremely difficult to control in a sufficiently 'scientific' way. This is compounded by the fact that researchers in this field have tended to use very different methods for assessing effectiveness, and to measure very different things.

To be sure, government-funded studies in the UK have often claimed to find positive associations between the use of ICT and student attainment. BECTA's review of this area (Cox et al., 2004) finds some positive evidence, albeit only at some levels and in some subjects (most notably in secondary-school science). Even here, however, the authors draw attention to the limitations of the available evidence, and they suggest that the most significant influence derives from the teacher's pedagogical practice. BECTA's major *ImpaCT2* study (BECTA, 2003) also found some associations, and even sought to calculate these into predictions of test scores (claiming that using ICT would result in an increase of 0.37 of a grade in students' results in GCSE geography, for example). Elsewhere, however, the report notes that there is 'no consistent relationship' between the amount of ICT use and its apparent effectiveness in raising standards. Ultimately, one of the most significant limitations of these studies is that they find *associations* (that is, correlations) rather than *causal* relationships between the use of ICT and educational attainment. The *ImpaCT2* study, for example, found that students who were high ICT users outperformed low ICT users, but failed to control for other variables (most notably social class) that might have accounted for that difference. Despite its title, this study falls well short of providing definitive evidence of the *impact* of ICT.

Meanwhile, independent academic reviews of research in this field have frequently reached equivocal conclusions. Numerous studies have found only mixed evidence as to the value of computers as compared with other methods (e.g. Kerr, 1996; Kirkpatrick and Cuban, 1998; Stephen and Plowman, 2003). For instance, a comprehensive review undertaken for the British Educational Research Association (Higgins, 2003) found that ICT *could* make a difference, although the link between ICT and attainment was only 'weak' and not as strong as with other educational innovations. Even authors who are sympathetic to the use of technology tend to conclude that it is not technology itself that makes the difference. At best, it is an enabler of other changes in teaching method – and it is these other changes that tend to account for any gains that might be made. Christine Stephen and Lydia Plowman (2003), for example, conclude that there can be increases in achievement, but only if the use of technology is accompanied by changes in teaching practice. Nevertheless, it seems that the use of computers in itself does not necessarily inspire any radical rethinking of teaching practice – let alone any radical transformation in what students are doing when they are *not* using computers (Salomon and Perkins, 1996).

Over the past several years, the Evidence for Policy and Practice Information and Co-ordinating Centre at the Institute of Education in London has conducted a series of systematic reviews of research on the use of computers in teaching literacy (e.g. EPPI Centre, 2004). These are 'state-of-the-art' reviews that adopt an exceptionally rigorous approach to evaluating all existing research on a given topic. Aside from specialist ICT and technology courses, the use of computers in English teaching is generally much more common than in other school subjects – and it is here that government studies have tended to identify some evidence of increased attainment (BECTA, 2003). However, these reviews have repeatedly found that the evidence for the effectiveness of ICT is patchy and uneven. There have been hardly any randomized controlled trials, which these reviews regard as the most appropriate means of assessing effectiveness. In three meta-analyses of existing research, the reviews have found no evidence of benefit or harm in two, and only weak evidence in one (in this case with a very small sample) – and they suggest that even these conclusions may be 'overoptimistic', since studies that have negative findings are more likely to remain unpublished than those with positive ones. The reviews conclude that there is no evidence that non-ICT methods of instruction and non-ICT resources are inferior to the use of ICT – and that the existing evidence is far from being a sufficient basis on which to justify the vast scale of spending on ICT equipment, software and training.

Others have attempted to address the benefits of computers from an economic perspective. One extremely rigorous quantitative study, conducted by two economists (Angrist and Lavy, 2002), explored the effects of introducing computers into Israeli elementary and middle schools (an initiative that was funded by the state lottery). These authors found that teachers did become more aware of computer-aided instruction, and used it more, but that this did not result in improvements in students' test scores – indeed, the only statistically significant effects were negative ones. These findings have been echoed by other such quasi-experimental studies conducted by economists (e.g. Goolsbee and Guryan, 2002; Leuven et al., 2004). By contrast, a more recent UK study (Machin et al., 2005) found a positive impact of the use of ICT on English test scores at the end of primary school, although less for science and none for mathematics. However, this study compares 'winners' and 'losers' in the allocation of funding without taking account of other differences between them – not least the reasons why they might have been judged to be winners or losers in the first place.

Obviously, test scores are only one measure of effectiveness, and a limited one at that – although, as we have seen, much of the government's rationale for investing in computers is precisely in terms of their ability to 'raise standards', which are measured primarily in terms of examination results. There is other research that suggests that the use of computers contributes to raising pupils' *motivation*; and increased motivation might well lead to gains in learning and achievement, although the relationship is unlikely to be straightforward. Janet Schofield's (1995) research – which remains one of the few sustained qualitative studies in the field – suggests that students welcome the opportunity computers provide to work at their own pace, and they also believe that technological skills may be of value to them in their later working life. A more recent DfES-funded study by Passey et al. (2004) also found that the use of ICT led to positive motivational outcomes, particularly where students were engaging with it directly (rather than its use being controlled by teachers). However, neither these nor other studies adequately address the possibility that such motivation might prove to be a short-term novelty effect, or that it might arise simply because the use of ICT offers a welcome relief from more teacher-directed lessons (in which case, any such change of method might produce similar results). This work also needs to be set against studies (to be discussed in chapter 5) which indicate that many children find the use of computers in the classroom boring and frustrating, particularly when compared with the way they use them outside school.

None of this, of course, suggests that the use of computers in the classroom is positively harmful – and, to that extent, the claims of critics such as the Alliance for Childhood are no more securely based on the available evidence. However, these studies do not adequately address the *differential* effects of ICT on different types of students. Clearly, the use of computers may alienate students who cannot, or do not wish, to engage with them (Hativa and Lesgold, 1996). One significant aspect of this, which will be addressed in more detail in chapter 5, concerns the relationship between students' uses of computers outside school and their use in the classroom. Students who enjoy high levels of access to technology at home are likely to gain most from using it in school, because they will already have many of the skills and the understanding they need in order to do so. In Cuban's (2001) study, having a computer at home significantly affected students' competence and confidence in using them in school, while Selwyn (1998a) and Mumtaz (2001) also found that use at home led to significantly more positive experiences of use in school.

As such, there is a distinct risk that schools' use of technology will simply reinforce existing inequalities or 'digital divides', for example those based on social class or gender. Studies have repeatedly shown that children from working-class families are less likely to have computers at home, or to have access to the kind of 'cultural capital' that is required to use them (e.g. Livingstone and Bober, 2004; Roberts et al., 2003). These inequalities are also likely to be accentuated by the uneven funding of schools. In the US, where funding is tied to local property taxes, schools in more wealthy areas are obviously likely to have greater access to technology than those in poor neighbourhoods; and in the UK, this will apply to schools with commercial sponsorship, and of course to private schools. While there is some evidence that government initiatives to improve ICT access in underprivileged areas have been successful, schools in less wealthy areas also tend to be the least well resourced (Reynolds et al., 2003).

The gendered dimensions of this are discussed by several authors. Sue Clegg (2001) argues that 'gendered dynamics' in classrooms may serve to reproduce existing definitions of computing as a 'masculine domain', and hence discourage girls from further participation at higher levels. She notes that boys typically have greater access to computers in the home, and that computers are still marketed as 'a tool for male hobbyists'. While girls' achievement in education has risen dramatically relative to that of boys in recent decades, there is certainly evidence that gender inequalities persist in relation to technology. Schofield's study, conducted in the late 1980s, found that girls were systematically isolated and marginalized in computer-based classrooms, and often subjected to gender-linked teasing and harassment (Schofield, 1995). Fewer girls than boys chose optional computer classes, there were fewer female computer teachers, and course materials were often gender-stereotyped. It is depressing to encounter similar findings in much more recent studies, such as Sarah Holloway and Gill Valentine's (2003) work on UK schools and Joel Cooper and Kimberley Weaver's (2003) research in the US.

The one clear exception to these arguments relates to children with learning disabilities. Here, there is some good evidence that technology can be used to give such children access to learning opportunities that might otherwise be denied to them (Abbott, 2002). This is perhaps most apparent with children who have sensory impairments (Douglas, 2001). In general, however, there is good reason to doubt the idea that access to technology in school is likely to compensate for inequalities that obtain in the wider society – and some reason to argue that it may help to accentuate them.

Conclusion

Ultimately, it is impossible to generalize about the consequences of using technology in education. This is partly because there are so many diverse forms of technology, and so many ways in which they can possibly be used. Findings that apply to the use of multimedia authoring tools, for example, cannot simply be extended to the use of the internet or games or word processors. To this extent, generalized claims to the effect that 'everyone knows computers help children learn' (Papert, 1996: 8) – or indeed that computers *per se* are necessarily inimical to 'authentic' learning (Cordes and Miller, 2000) – are significantly wide of the mark.

Equally, it is clear that the impact of technology depends upon a wide range of contextual factors, which themselves interact in complex ways. These factors range from 'macro' factors such as social policy, commercial strategies and different forms of institutional provision, right through to 'micro' factors such as the physical placement of computers, the number available and the ways in which teachers and students can gain access to them. They include questions about different types of hardware and software, about teachers' and students' attitudes, and about the types of activities that are undertaken. The use of technology often involves a whole set of further changes (not all of which can be planned in advance), and it can entail a range of unanticipated consequences. Both technology and our understanding of its potential uses are also constantly evolving. Above all, however, it is clear that technology does not have 'effects' in and of itself: on the contrary, its impact – whether for good or ill – depends to a very great extent on the contexts in which it used, the motivations of those who use it, and what they attempt to use it for.

Nevertheless, it seems fair to conclude that the educational use of technology has so far largely failed to deliver on the promises that are so frequently made on its behalf. Technology has not transformed learning, nor has it revolutionized the institution of the school. It has yet to show a proven impact in increasing educational achievement or in promoting long-term motivation towards learning. In the face of this argument, advocates of technology typically claim that it is still early days, and that the real change is yet to come. But, as I have shown, computers have been in schools for more than thirty years, and it is possible to trace a history of failed technological innovation in education that dates back almost a century. It seems absurd to maintain – as some do – that the revolution is just around the corner, if only we had *more* computers, if only we could use *this* latest technological innovation, if only *all* teachers could use technology in the way we believe they should . . .

This is not in any sense to deny that there are individual teachers – and, indeed, professional networks of teachers – who are using technology in genuinely innovative, exciting and creative ways. Nor is it to deny the broader potential for change, or even the need for utopian thinking. Indeed, I would argue that taking the challenge of new media seriously requires a much more radical rethinking of what the school is for, and how it should operate. My primary concern is not so much to do with the *extent* to which technology is or is not being used – as if more would automatically mean better (or worse). On the contrary, my concern is with *how* it is used. As I shall argue, there is a widening gap in this respect between how technology is used in school and what children are doing with it outside school. By contrast with the opportunities available in their leisure time, many children find the uses of technology in classrooms to be narrowly defined, unimaginative and instrumental. It is to this issue that the following chapter is devoted.

5

Digital Childhoods?[1]

New Media and Children's Culture

If most schools have remained relatively unaffected by the advent of modern media technology, the same cannot be said of children's lives outside school. On the contrary, childhood is now permeated, even in some respects defined, by the modern media – by television, video, computer games, the internet, mobile phones and popular music, and by the enormous range of media-related commodities that make up contemporary consumer culture. In fact, this has long been the case. As early as the 1960s, it was apparent that children were spending more time watching television than they were in school. And while, with the advent of other screen-based media, children's television viewing has slightly declined in recent years, the overall picture is clear: children spend more time with media of various kinds than they do on any other activity apart from sleeping.

Digital technologies represent a relatively recent addition to this 'media-saturated' environment and, as we shall see, they are far from equally available to all young people. Yet the internet, computer games and mobile communication technologies are often seen to present unique opportunities – and indeed dangers – for the young. In these debates, the distinction between 'new' media and 'old' media is often drawn in stark and absolutist terms. As in education, the talk is of a fundamental transformation – a revolution – in young people's cultural experiences. We are warned of a 'digital generation gap' (Papert, 1996), as children who have grown up with digital media are apparently living in a different world from their parents, who grew up with television. Both socially and psychologically, the 'digital generation' is seen to operate in quite different ways from the generations that preceded it.

lacking imaginativeness

As I shall attempt to show in this chapter, the reality is both more prosaic and more complex. The optimistic view of young people as a 'digital generation' – as somehow automatically liberated and empowered through their experience of these new technologies – is little more than a form of wishful thinking. It neglects some fundamental continuities, as well as some important differences and inequalities, in young people's cultural experiences. Nevertheless, I do not wish to imply that nothing has changed. On the contrary, there have been some significant developments in the wider media landscape; and while these are partly technological in nature, they also reflect much broader shifts in contemporary consumer culture. These developments have led to a significant and growing divide between most young people's experience of technology outside school and the use of technology in the classroom. And it is this 'new digital divide' that educational policy and practice now urgently need to address.

Living the digital life?

On the face of it, young people's media experiences today appear very different from those of earlier generations. My own children have grown up with computers, video games and multi-channel television: they zap and surf with apparent ease and fluency from one medium to the next, creating digital music tracks, podcasts and web pages, downloading songs and movies, playing online games, e-mailing, chatting, texting and instant messaging. Compared with my own childhood, in which the arrival of a third television channel was the limit of technological innovation, theirs is a media world of infinite diversity and creative potential. Studying these experiences is a matter of following a rapidly moving target; and yet it is easy to be seduced into believing that everything has changed utterly and forever.

To be sure, the advent of digital technology has led to a massive proliferation of media channels and outlets and a considerable extension in young people's access to media. The domestic television screen has become the delivery point for an ever broader range of media and means of distribution. The number of channels has grown spectacularly with the advent of cable, satellite and digital TV, while the screen is also being used for video in various forms, as well as for computer games and the internet. Meanwhile, home computers are no longer seen as toys for the technologically oriented 'hobbyist', or indeed as merely devices for storing and retrieving information: they are increasingly being used for viewing television programmes, films and videos, playing games, listening to music, and communicating with other people.

Much of this technology is specifically targeted at children and young people, and many of the new cultural forms that have emerged (such as computer games) are at least primarily identified with them. Children have become an increasingly important 'niche' market, as is evident from the continuing expansion of specialist children's television channels (in the UK, there are currently twenty-two) and the growth of online provision. The take-up of satellite and cable television, video, digital cameras and home computers has been much higher in households with children than in those without. While mobile phones are fast approaching market saturation among teenagers, they are also being used by growing numbers of younger children. Likewise, much contemporary youth culture, and the forms of music, fashion and style that define it, is now mediated and defined through digital technology. (For a recent review of research and statistics on these areas, see Buckingham et al., 2005.)

Technology is also being used in more individualized ways. Thus, a majority of children in the UK now have televisions in their bedrooms, a significant proportion have VCRs or DVD players, and nearly three-quarters of them have mobile phones and personal computers for their own use. These tendencies towards individualization are encouraged by the general democratization of relationships within the family, although collective uses of media – 'family viewing' – are far from disappearing. As Sonia Livingstone (2002) has noted, children in the UK are increasingly enjoying a media-rich 'bedroom culture', which compensates at least partly for a decline in independent mobility outside the home. Meanwhile, mobile technologies – phones, iPods, PDAs (personal digital assistants) – accentuate this individualization: access is no longer tied to physical location, and the user can mentally escape from their immediate physical setting into another virtual or communicative environment.

At the same time, new technology also permits an intensification of interpersonal relationships and social networks among the peer group. With mobile phones, peer-to-peer interactions are less likely to be mediated by the family: with each family member having their own phone, young people are calling each other directly, bypassing any contact with other family members (Ito, 2004). However, teens are especially susceptible to peer pressure to be constantly available: a turned-off phone can be considered rude and as a social snub (Kasesniemi, 2003), and instant messaging typically requires instant response. Meanwhile, media such as chat, e-mail and instant messaging enable young people to form relationships with those whom they may never have met face to face.

Many of these new media forms are 'interactive', at least in the sense that they require an ongoing input on the part of the user. Computer games and the internet, for example, are sometimes referred to as 'pull' media, as distinct from older media such as television that 'push' content at the user. Many of these new media are also non-linear: they can be accessed at any point, and the user can navigate their own pathway through the material. Of course, much of this interactivity is relatively limited – a matter of selecting from pre-given content, or following routes that have already been laid down. However, some of these new media do allow young people new opportunities to communicate with each other, to become creative producers of media content in their own right, and to make contact with unknown or geographically distant 'audiences'. At the time of writing, for example, there has been a remarkable rise in so-called social networking sites on the internet, such as 'MySpace', which combine elements of home pages, blogs and message boards with facilities to post and distribute photographs, videos and music.

These are certainly significant developments, yet it would be a mistake to see them simply as a result of technological changes. As I shall argue in the sections that follow, contemporary children's culture is indeed changing; but those changes are a result of broader political changes (for example, in the relation between the state and the market), economic changes (for example, in the strategies of commercial companies) and social changes (for example, in the nature of family life, or the power-relationships between adults and children). These different 'levels' interact in complex and sometimes quite contradictory ways: there is no simple determinism in operation here. Furthermore, we also need to recognize the continuities and connections between these 'new' media and the 'older' media that continue to play an important role in children's lives.

Convergence

What used to be called 'information technology' is now more commonly referred to – at least in the world of education – as 'information and communication technology' (ICT). This slight shift in emphasis reflects something of the changing uses of digital technology. Yet it does not fully acknowledge the ways in which 'information' technologies are now converging with other technologies of representation – particularly visual media such as film and television – that schools have largely tended to ignore. In this context, these technologies are by no means simply purveyors of 'information': on the contrary, they carry images, narratives and fantasies that work on the imagination as much as on the intellect.

New media typically build upon existing forms of children's and youth culture, rather than eclipsing or displacing them, and, as such, it makes little sense to discuss 'new' media in isolation from 'older' media. The history of innovation suggests that new media do not necessarily replace older media so much as add to the range of options which are available. In the process they may alter the reasons why people use existing media, the kinds of people who use them, or the contexts in which they do so. But at least in the sphere of culture and communications, technologies typically complement each other in complex and sometimes unforeseen ways. Television, for example, has not replaced the book, just as the book did not replace earlier forms of oral storytelling or communication – even if the purposes for which people use these different media may have changed (Ong, 1982).

On present showing, it seems likely that the same will be true of digital technologies. Of course, there may be an element of displacement here: statistics show that children in homes with computers and game consoles do spend less time watching television, and there is a perceptible decline in overall viewing hours. In fact, however, this change has been far from dramatic. Likewise, despite the growing proliferation of electronic media, there is little evidence that children's reading of print has actually declined, although they may well be reading for different reasons, or in different ways (Neuman, 1995). As in the case of television and reading, what is notable is that children are increasingly able to combine different activities – to chat on the computer as they watch TV and listen to CDs and do their homework (or so they will frequently allege). While some see this as evidence of a form of postmodern distraction, others see it as a manifestation of children's ability to undertake 'multi-tasking' and 'parallel processing' using contemporary communications media (Prensky, 2001a).

As this implies, the current context is not so much one of displacement as of convergence. Thus, it is argued, we are witnessing a blurring of boundaries, a coming together of previously distinct technologies, cultural forms and practices, at the point both of production and of reception. To be sure, this convergence is partly a result of changes in technology. The possibility of 'digitizing' a whole range of different forms of communication (not just writing, but visual and moving images, music, sound and speech) transforms the computer into much more than a calculator or a typewriter with a memory. It becomes a means of delivering and producing not just written texts, but texts in a variety of media, and, as a result, the digital screen has become the focus of a whole range of entertainment, information and communication options.

However, this convergence of media is also driven by commercial imperatives. 'Integrated marketing' is more and more the rule: television programmes, for example, have become increasingly linked with movies, books, comics, computer games, toys, clothes, and other merchandise.

Children's media culture is rarely medium-specific: it crosses the boundaries between texts and between traditional media forms – most obviously in the case of phenomena such as 'Teenage Mutant Ninja Turtles', 'Mighty Morphin' Power Rangers' and, more recently, 'Pokémon'. In this process, the identity of the 'original' text is sometimes far from clear: these commodities are packaged and marketed as integrated phenomena, rather than the text coming first and the merchandising following on. And this development is not confined to the work of exclusively 'commercial' corporations – as is illustrated by the success of public service productions such as *Sesame Street* and the BBC's *Teletubbies*.

Such phenomena typically entail a high degree of 'interactivity', not just in the texts themselves (such as computer games) but also in the communication that takes place as children move between one cultural form and another, from the TV series to the trading card game to the books and the toys. In the process, the gathering of specialist knowledge – much of it impenetrable to adults – becomes inextricably entailed in the purchase and collecting of commodities (Buckingham and Sefton-Green, 2003). In this form of 'integrated marketing', each medium has become bound up with other media, in what Marsha Kinder (1991) has aptly called the 'supersystem' of 'transmedia intertextuality' – a development which, as she acknowledges, is fundamentally driven by profit.

At the same time, we can point to a convergence of forms of communication. The advent of video, desktop publishing and the internet has helped to break down the distinction between interpersonal communication and mass communication. At least potentially, such equipment enables 'consumers' to become 'producers', as it becomes possible to reproduce and to publish using technologies that were formerly the preserve of small elites. More and more teenagers have home computers in their bedrooms that can be used to create music, to manipulate images or to edit video to a relatively professional standard. These technologies also permit a highly conscious, and potentially subversive, reworking or remixing of commercially produced media texts, for example through sampling and editing found material, alongside 'original' creative production. Likewise, the internet is both a public and a private medium, which allows new forms of interpersonal communication as well as new forms of 'publishing'.

Even so, what remains striking about many of these new media technologies is how much they rely on the forms and conventions of old technologies. Just as a great deal of television is in some sense literary or theatrical, so many CD-ROMs and websites implicitly use the book as the model for structuring the ways in which readers get access to information;

and the internet, of course, is heavily reliant on written text and on conventional verbal literacy – as indeed are many computer games.

Nevertheless, this convergence of technologies and cultural forms has been greeted by many critics as reflecting a breakdown of established cultural and social hierarchies – including those that are based on age differences. Thus, it is argued, these new cultural forms both express and create new forms of social identity, in which hitherto marginalized groups come to be represented and to represent themselves. In the case of children and young people, these new forms undoubtedly do offer new possibilities for self-expression and communication. The internet, for example, provides *some* children with the opportunity for their voices to be heard, in ways that transcend hitherto insurmountable barriers of geographical distance or social difference. Even within the protected space of mainstream broadcasting, the paternalism which characterized the public service tradition has been steadily undermined and abandoned: to the distress of many adults, children's media culture is increasingly distinguished by a kind of pleasurable anarchy and sensuality which is very different from the sedate and often patronizing approach of earlier decades (Buckingham, 2002; Holland, 1996).

Commerce

However, there are several reasons to be more cautious about this broadly optimistic scenario. As I have noted, many of these developments are economically driven: they are part of a much more general move towards a market-led media system, in which the maximizing of profit takes precedence over any public service imperatives. These technological developments have helped to reinforce – and been reinforced by – fundamental institutional and economic changes in the media industries. The past two decades have been characterized by growing privatization. The media have been inextricably caught up in the broader commercialization of contemporary culture, in which fields such as politics, sport, health care – and indeed education itself – have increasingly been 'invaded' by commercial forces. Meanwhile, public sector provision – for example in broadcasting – has gradually been commercialized from within, and regulation to do with the social and cultural functions of the media is being abandoned in favour of a narrower concern with morality.

One inevitable consequence of this development has been the integration and globalization of the media industries. The media market is now dominated by a small number of multinational conglomerates, and global brands provide an international language or 'common culture', particularly among young people. For nationally based companies, success in the international market is increasingly necessary for survival. Significantly, most of these global corporations are cross-media empires: they integrate broadcasting, publishing, media and digital technology, and in many cases have interests in both hardware and software. Yet integration does not necessarily mean homogenization: growing competition has also resulted in the fragmentation of audiences and the rise of 'niche marketing'. Media are targeted to a greater extent towards specialized fractions of the mass audience, albeit on a global scale; new technologies also permit more decentralized communications, and the creation of 'communities' that transcend national boundaries.

Children have effectively been 'discovered' as a new target market only in the past few decades. In the case of commercial television, for example, children were not initially seen as an especially valuable audience. In the early decades of the US commercial system, programmes would only be provided for children at minimum cost, and at times when other audiences were not available to view (Melody, 1973); even in the UK, where the public service tradition has been very strong, children's television was for many years comparatively underfunded. Yet in the contemporary era of niche marketing, children have suddenly become much more valuable: they are seen to have significant influence on parents' purchasing decisions, as well as substantial disposable income of their own (McNeal, 1999). At least within the media industries, the vulnerable child in need of protection has increasingly given way to the child as 'sovereign consumer'.

In the 1980s, much of the debate here centred on the emergence of 'thirty minute commercials' – animated programmes produced or commissioned by toy manufacturers with the express intention of advertising toys and related merchandise (Engelhardt, 1986). While 'exploitation' of this kind can be traced back at least to the earliest days of Disney, the concern was that merchandising had begun to drive the production of media for children, rather than the other way round. Since that time, the boundaries between these different activities have become almost imperceptible: every text has become an advertisement for other texts. After watching the latest Disney movie, for example, it is now possible not only to buy the toys, the clothes, the books and the spin-off videos from the Disney shop in your local mall, or to watch further episodes on the Disney Channel, but also to visit the website, play the computer game and obtain the 'educational' CD-ROM.

While such tendencies have been more pronounced in the US, children's media in Britain – even in the public service sector – are rapidly moving in the same direction. Children's TV magazine shows, for example, construct a self-referential world where the guests are pop stars or actors from soaps, the games and the pop videos are ads for other commodities, and the prizes are other media artefacts (Wagg, 1992). Meanwhile, the programmes themselves are a kind of extended advertisement for a range of spin-off products, such as magazines and websites. Similar issues are now very apparent in relation to the internet. For all its potentially liberating decentralization, the internet provides advertisers with very accurate ways of reaching particular kinds of consumers and of gathering detailed information about their consumption habits and preferences. Not least in relation to children, it represents a highly effective means of 'niche marketing' (Seiter, 2005).

Of course, this is not to posit some kind of golden age where culture was somehow uncontaminated by commerce; nor indeed is it to imply that commercialism is somehow incompatible with creativity or with genuine communication. Discussion of these issues – particularly in relation to children – is often characterized by a form of puritanism, in which children's leisure time is expected to be occupied with activities which adults define as 'educational' and 'improving'. We also need to be wary of economic determinism here. It is far too easy to fall back on traditional notions of children as vulnerable to commercial exploitation or to the seductions of media imperialism. A large proportion of commercial products aimed at children simply fail to generate a profit: the market is highly competitive and uncertain. To this extent, there is some justification in producers' recurrent claim that children are a volatile, complex market which cannot easily be known and controlled.

Nevertheless, the fact remains that children's leisure activities are becoming steadily more privatized and commercialized. More of their time is spent in the home or in supervised activity of some kind; while the cultural goods and services they consume increasingly have to be paid for in hard cash. Family expenditure on entertainment media (both software and hardware) has been growing exponentially over the past decade, both as a global figure and as a proportion of household income. The public spaces of childhood – both the physical spaces of play and the virtual spaces of broadcasting – have progressively fallen into decline or been overcome by the commercial market.

One inevitable consequence of this is that children's social and media worlds are becoming increasingly unequal. The polarization between rich and poor is positively reinforced by the commercialization of the media and the decline in public sector provision. In the case of computers, just as in the early days of television, those with greater disposable income are the 'early adopters': they have newer and more powerful equipment and more opportunities to develop the skills that are needed to use it. Recent studies in the UK suggest that more than 20 per cent of children do not have internet access at home and, for those who do, access may well be limited (Livingstone and Bober, 2004; Cranmer, 2006). These inequalities are of course writ large when we examine access to technology on a global level (Warschauer, 2003).

Even so, the 'digital divide' is no longer simply a matter of access to equipment: it is also to do with the quality of the equipment (and of internet connections), and with the skills and 'cultural capital' that are required to use it (Angus et al., 2004; Warschauer, 2003). As Ellen Seiter (2005: 13–14) suggests, 'the children of elites and urban professionals experience new technologies in a qualitatively different way from poor children': far from levelling class differences, she argues, the internet has deepened social divisions along the lines of class, race and ethnicity, both within and between countries. Middle-class children are not only likely to have better quality computers and software; they are also likely to have much more informed support in using them from parents and other adults, and greater access to social networks which will provide them with a sense of motivation and purpose in using such technology in the first place – although (as I shall argue in more detail below) we should certainly beware of assuming that they necessarily have all the knowledge and expertise they need. By contrast, poorer children simply have less access to cultural goods and services: they live not just in different social worlds, but in different media worlds as well.

The child at risk

What are the implications of these developments for our understanding of contemporary childhood? As we have seen, definitions of childhood in the discourse surrounding educational technology are quite diverse. The child may be seen as already 'techno-savvy' and highly competent – as compared with the teacher, who urgently needs to 'catch up'. Yet the child may also be seen as a learner, or a future worker, who is in need of the 'skills' that teachers are required to provide. And, as we have seen, the child may also be defined as 'disenchanted' – and hence in need of the enchantment and motivation that technology is presumed to provide (see Facer et al., 2001;

Selwyn, 2002, 2003). When it comes to media outside the school, however, there is a striking polarization between two very different constructions of the child. On the one hand, we have the child at risk – as essentially vulnerable and in need of protection – while, on the other, we have a view of the child as liberated and empowered by technology.

To some extent, the view of the child at risk stems from adults' sense of *exclusion* from children's digital culture. Much of the media that is now available to children – and many of the ways in which they use media – have become more and more inaccessible to the majority of adults. The seemingly infinite worlds of contemporary computer games, the specialized language of texting and instant messaging, the arcane complexities of children's 'crazes' such as Pokémon and Yu-Gi-Oh, the wild pace of music videos and rap music – these are 'postmodern' media forms that seem almost deliberately designed to exclude adults. Yet children are also increasingly gaining access to material that was hitherto confined largely to adults – most obviously to 'sex and violence' (both of which are often very loosely defined). Even material produced specifically for a child audience is characterized by a degree of subversiveness and sensuality – and in some cases by a frank discussion of topics that were previously considered taboo – that is often shocking or incomprehensible for some of the adults who encounter it.

In this context, adults may experience a sense of losing control, and for understandable reasons. When compared with older technologies such as the cinema or broadcast television, digital media significantly undermine the potential for centralized control by national governments. With digital technology, it is now possible not only for material to be easily copied and circulated, but also for it to be sent across national boundaries on the telephone line. Via the internet, children can communicate much more easily with each other and with adults, without even having to identify themselves as children, while the use of mobile devices enables children to communicate independently, without the knowledge or mediation of parents. And, of course, the privacy and anonymity afforded by the internet particularly lends itself to the easy dissemination and sale of pornography.

As with older technologies, the argument here is that children are an especially vulnerable audience – easily influenced and exploited, at risk from all sorts of grubby commercial interests, and particularly from those who peddle violence and pornography. As we have seen, digital technology is being held responsible for the wholesale destruction of childhood as we know it, just as television used to be (Cordes and Miller, 2000). One of the boundaries that is being blurred here, we are told, is that between adults and children: the problem with these new technologies is that they give children access to things which used to be kept hidden from them, and which they really ought not to know.

This situation has led to growing calls for stricter regulation and censorship, and to the search for a 'technological fix' – for example in the form of filtering software – that will prevent children from gaining access to material that is deemed to be undesirable. Indeed, as Julie Frechette (2006) suggests, there is a sector of the technology industry currently generating significant profits from parental anxieties about 'inappropriate content' – although such software often defines what is 'inappropriate' in narrow (and sometimes quite bizarre) ways. Yet evidence of the effectiveness of such devices – not least in schools – is decidedly limited (Lawson and Comber, 2000b): policy-makers seem to accept that the producers of internet sites, or those who use them, will be able to find ways of defeating these technologies, and that ever more sophisticated measures will be required (Waltermann and Machill, 2000).

The notion that children are turning on their computers and being confronted by a barrage of graphic pornography is, to say the least, somewhat of an exaggeration, and much of the research that is cited in support of such claims is extremely problematic. Yet, here again, there appear to be much wider issues at stake. Current concerns about censorship and media regulation are merely part of a wider sense of crisis about the changing relationships of power and authority between adults and children. The debate around the James Bulger case in Britain in the early 1990s was perhaps the most obvious example of this process in recent times – and one which symptomatically came to focus on the media, as though (yet again) 'bad media' were the sole explanation of the problem (see Buckingham, 1996; Franklin and Petley, 1996). Despite increasingly authoritarian attempts to control youth crime and other forms of 'bad behaviour', there is a growing sense that children and young people are moving beyond adult control (Newburn, 1996). In this context, control of the media has a crucial *symbolic* significance for politicians and others who are seeking to demonstrate their moral authority and responsibility.

Constructing the digital generation

Nevertheless, this construction of the child 'at risk' has increasingly been offset by a very different construction of the relationship between children and digital media. Unlike those who bemoan the media's destruction of childhood innocence, advocates of the new 'digital generation' regard technology as a force of liberation for young people – a means for them to reach past the constraining influence of their elders and to create new, autonomous forms of communication and community. Far from corrupting children, technology is seen to be creating a generation that is more open, more democratic, more creative and innovative than their parents' generation. As with Seymour Papert's portrait of children's 'love affair' with computers (1996: see chapter 3), children are typically seen here to have an innate, spontaneous competence in their dealings with technology.

For example, Marc Prensky (2001a) makes a distinction between digital 'natives' (who have grown up with this technology) and digital 'immigrants' (adults who have come to it later in life) that has been widely influential in popular debate. Prensky argues that digital natives have a very different style of learning: they crave interactivity; they value graphics before words; they want random access; and they operate at the 'twitch speed' of video games and MTV. As a result, they are dissatisfied with old styles of instruction, based on exposition and step-by-step logic: they see digital immigrants as speaking in an entirely different, outdated language. Prensky (2001b) even suggests that digital natives have a very different brain structure from that of immigrants – as though technology had precipitated a form of physical evolution within a period of little more than a decade.

However, it is Don Tapscott's book *Growing up Digital: The Rise of the Net Generation* (1998) that provides the most sustained and comprehensive argument for the idea of the 'digital generation'. Tapscott's account is based on two sets of binary oppositions, between technologies (television versus the internet) and between generations (the 'baby boomers' versus the 'net generation'). He draws clear lines between the generations, based primarily on US birth-rate statistics: the 'boomers' were born between 1946 and 1964, followed by the 'bust' (1965–1976) and the 'boom echo' (1977–1997). According to Tapscott, the boomers are the 'television generation', who are defined by their relationship with that medium, just as the children of the boom echo are the 'net generation'.

Tapscott's oppositions between these technologies are stark and absolute. Television is a passive medium, while the net is active; television 'dumbs down' its users, while the net raises their intelligence; television broadcasts a singular view of the world, while the net is democratic and interactive; television isolates, while the net builds communities; and so on. Just as television is the antithesis of the net, so the 'television

opposite

generation' is the antithesis of the 'net generation'. Like the technology they now control, the values of the 'television generation' are increasingly conservative, 'hierarchical, inflexible and centralized'. By contrast, the 'N-Geners' are 'hungry for expression, discovery and their own self-development': they are savvy, self-reliant, analytical, articulate, creative, inquisitive, accepting of diversity and socially conscious. These generational differences are seen to be *produced* by technology, rather than being a result of other social, historical or cultural forces. Unlike their parents, who are portrayed as incompetent 'technophobes', children are seen to possess an intuitive, spontaneous relationship with digital technology. 'For many kids', Tapscott argues, 'using the new technology is as natural as breathing' (1998: 40). Technology is the means of their empowerment – and it will ultimately lead to a 'generational explosion'.

Growing up Digital takes the reader through a series of areas – cognition, play, learning, family, consumption and work. In each case, the argument is essentially the same: technology offers a new form of empowerment for young people; and this is producing a generation gap, as the habits and preferences of the older generation are coming to be superseded. From an academic vantage point, it is perhaps rather easy to mock these kinds of arguments: they lack scholarly caution and qualification, and the evidence on which they are based is unrepresentative and often anecdotal. Tapscott is a management consultant, entrepreneur and motivational speaker and, as such, academic virtues are likely only to dilute his appeal. Yet in fact many of his arguments come quite close to the kinds of ideas that circulate in the discourse of policy-makers – and, I would suggest, in the academy as well. For this reason, it is worth exploring his claims more closely.

Tapscott argues that technology produces a wide range of social, psychological and even political changes. Five key claims are particularly relevant to our concerns here.

1   First, technology is seen to create new styles of communication and interaction. Among the ten themes that Tapscott sees as characteristic of web-based communication, he includes independence and autonomy, emotional and intellectual openness, innovation, free expression, immediacy, and an investigative approach. The internet provides new means for constructing community: it is an active and participatory medium which is about distributed communication from 'many to many'. These new communities are inclusive and require the creation of new kinds of trust. They are about breaking down walls, and they allow the creation of new

kinds of relationships, in the form of both friendships and new family life-styles: the internet, Tapscott argues, will give rise to 'a new kind of open family' characterized by equality, dialogue and mutual trust.

2   Secondly, the internet also produces new styles of playful learning. Unlike the television generation, the net generation is inquisitive and self-directed in learning. It is more sceptical and analytical, more inclined towards critical thinking, and more likely to challenge and question estab-lished authorities than previous generations. Net-based learning is interac-tive, rather than a matter of transmission. Where old-style education was teacher-dominated and authoritarian, digitally based education is non-linear and learner-centred, based on discovery rather than the delivery of information. The net transforms the teacher into a facilitator whose input has to be customized to learners' needs. Above all, learning via the internet is 'fun': learning is play and play is learning, and so 'the net is a place where kids can be kids'. At the same time, this new style of learning is also par-ticularly appropriate to the so-called knowledge economy, and to the new kinds of employment that are emerging there. In this new world, the old knowledge hierarchies no longer apply, and the working environment is one of personal networking, innovation and openness.

3   These new conditions of education, work and social life also require new competencies – or new forms of 'literacy'. This is apparent to some degree in the innovative, informal styles of language that are emerging on the internet – emoticons and so on – and in the changing conventions of language use (or 'netiquette'). More broadly, however, internet commu-nication is seen to require and produce new intellectual powers, and even 'more complex brain structures': it results in a kind of accelerated develop-ment, and young people who do not have access to it will be 'developmen-tally disadvantaged'. The net generation not only has different skills in terms of accessing and navigating through information, it also processes and evaluates information in a radically different way from the television generation. This new orientation towards information is natural and spon-taneous rather than learned: it somehow connects with the inherent condi-tion of childhood. → BABIES.

4   At each of these levels, technology is implicitly seen to have direct psychological effects. Yet it also has consequences at a more profound and fundamental level: it provides new ways of forming identity, and hence new forms of personhood. For all the reasons identified above, the net generation is seen to be high in self-esteem: the use of digital media imparts an enhanced sense of efficacy and self-worth, not only for young people with disabilities, but for all. In the digital world, the child is the

actor. Via the medium of chat, the internet provides opportunities for experimentation and play with identity, and for the adoption or construction of multiple selves. By offering communication with different aspects of the self, it enables young people to relate to the world and to others in more powerful ways. —▷ Autism.

5   Finally, the internet is also seen to be leading to the emergence of a new kind of politics. The net itself is distributed and democratic: it is a collectively shared, non-hierarchical delivery system that serves as 'a medium for social awakening'. Its effects on offline behaviour are also inherently democratizing. According to Tapscott, the net generation is more tolerant, more globally oriented, more inclined to exercise social and civic responsibility and to respect the environment. Technology is radicalizing them, just as television has ultimately led the baby boomers to accept the status quo.

A different story

In many ways, these are familiar arguments. To a greater or lesser extent, they are shared by many popular and academic commentators on the impact of digital media, and they have also been increasingly popular within education (e.g. Oblinger and Oblinger, 2005). They place a generational spin on what has been called the 'Californian ideology' – the form of 'cyber-libertarianism' favoured not just by internet activists, but also (perhaps paradoxically) by many marketing gurus (Barbrook and Cameron, 1996). Despite the evident pleasures of such wishful thinking, it is important to restate some of the fundamental limitations of these arguments.

Tapscott's approach is clearly based on a form of technological determinism. From this perspective, technology is seen as an autonomous force that is somehow independent of human society, and which acts upon it from outside. This view connects with a familiar rhetoric about the 'information society' (or the 'knowledge economy'), which similarly appears to attribute a determining power to some disembodied force ('information'). As we have seen (chapter 2), this perspective has been widely challenged, both for its reductionism and for its tendency to reify technology, as though it existed independently of human activity.

These kinds of ideas carry a particular emotional charge when it comes to the discussion of childhood. The combination of 'childhood' and 'technology' serves as a powerful focus for much broader hopes and fears about social change, and, in this sense, Tapscott's argument can be seen as a mirror image of the Alliance for Childhood position (Cordes and Miller,

2000). In both cases, the fundamental question here is how we understand the causal relationships that are at stake. As I have argued, contemporary developments in technology may indeed present new risks and opportunities for children. But these developments can only be adequately understood in the light of other changes – for example, in the political economy of children's culture, the social and cultural policies and practices that regulate and define childhood, and the everyday social realities of children's lives. These latter changes themselves can also be overstated, and frequently are; but, in any case, it makes little sense to consider them in isolation from each other.

This technologically determinist stance means that there are many issues and phenomena that Tapscott and other such technology enthusiasts are bound to ignore. He neglects the fundamental continuities and interdependencies between new media and the 'old' media (such as television) that he so despises – continuities that exist at the level of form and content, as well as in terms of economics. As I have suggested, a longer historical view clearly shows that old and new technologies often come to co-exist: particularly in the area of media, the advent of a new technology may change the functions or uses of old technologies, but it rarely completely displaces them. On average, members of the 'net generation' in fact spend more of their time watching television than they do on the internet; and of course there are many members of the 'television generation' who spend much of their working and leisure time online.

Tapscott's relentlessly optimistic view inevitably leads him to ignore many of the downsides of the internet – the undemocratic tendencies of many online 'communities', the limited nature of much so-called digital learning, and the grinding tedium of much technologically driven work. He also romanticizes young people, offering a wholly positive view of their critical intelligence and social responsibility that is deliberately at odds with that of many social commentators.

He is also bound to ignore the continuing 'digital divide' between the technology rich and the technology poor, both within and between societies. In common with other technology enthusiasts, Tapscott believes that this is a temporary phenomenon, and that the technology poor will eventually catch up – although this is obviously to assume that the early adopters will stay where they are. It is also to assume – as Tapscott very clearly does – that the market is a neutral mechanism, and that it functions simply by giving individuals what they need. The possibility that technology might be used to exploit young people economically (Seiter, 2005), or indeed that the market might not provide equally for all, does not enter the picture. The complacency of this argument is at least compounded by the view that children growing up without access to such technology – for example, in less wealthy countries – are likely to be 'developmentally disadvantaged'.

Tapscott's approach is also bound to ignore what one can only call the *banality* of much new media use. Recent studies (e.g. Facer et al., 2003; Holloway and Valentine, 2003; Livingstone and Bober, 2004) suggest that most children's everyday uses of the internet are characterized not by spectacular forms of innovation and creativity, but by relatively mundane forms of information retrieval. What most children are doing on the internet is visiting fan websites, downloading music and movies, e-mailing or chatting with friends, and shopping (or at least window-shopping). Technology offers them different ways of communicating with each other, or pursuing specialist hobbies and interests, as compared with 'offline' methods, but the differences can easily be overstated.

The technologically empowered 'cyberkids' of the popular imagination may indeed exist; but even if they do, they are in a minority, and they are untypical of young people as a whole. In general, there is very little evidence of the internet being used by young people to develop global connections: in most cases, it appears to be used primarily as a means of reinforcing local networks among peers. Young people may be 'empowered' as consumers – at least in the sense of being able to access a much wider range of goods and services much more easily. But as yet there is little sense in which they are being empowered as citizens: very few are using the technology to engage in civic participation, to communicate their views to a wider audience, or to get involved in political activity (Livingstone, Bober and Helsper, 2005). As Warschauer (2003) points out, the potential for multimedia production – which requires the latest computers and software and high bandwidth – is actually quite *inaccessible* to all but the wealthy middle classes. Research also indicates that young people may be much less fluent or technologically 'literate' in their use of the internet than is often assumed: observational studies suggest that young people often encounter considerable difficulties in using search engines, for example – although this is not to imply that they are necessarily any *less* competent than adults in this respect (Cranmer, 2006; Livingstone and Bober, 2004; Schofield and Davidson, 2002).

Aside from those who are denied access to this technology, there are also many who positively refuse or reject it, for a variety of reasons (Facer and Furlong, 2001; Roe and Broos, 2005; Selwyn, 1998b). Only a relatively small proportion of young people are driven by a desire to purchase the latest technological gadgets or participate in the latest form of online culture; and, rather than being regarded as 'cool', they are still often dismissed by their peers as 'geeks' (Holloway and Valentine, 2003). In general, one could argue that, for most young people, technology *per se* is a relatively marginal concern. Very few are interested in technology in its own right, and most are simply concerned about what they can use it for.

Ultimately, like other forms of marketing rhetoric, the discourse of the 'digital generation' is precisely an attempt to construct the object of which it purports to speak. It represents not a description of what children or young people actually are, but a set of imperatives about what they should be or what they need to become. To some extent, it does describe a minority of young people who are actively using this technology for social, educational and creative purposes; yet it seems very likely that most of these people are the 'usual suspects', who are already privileged in other areas of their lives, and whose use of technology is supported by their access to other forms of social and cultural capital.

The new digital divide

Despite the limitations of these arguments, it remains the case that most young people's experiences with technology are now taking place outside school, in the context of what has been termed 'techno-popular culture' (Facer et al., 2003). And the contrast between what happens there and what happens in the classroom is often very striking. Of course, some new media technologies – such as computer games and mobile phones – are largely excluded from the classroom (although, as we shall see in chapter 6, there have been some problematic attempts to incorporate them for educational purposes). Yet even where the same medium is being used – as in the case of the internet – the difference is very clear. As I have suggested, young people's use of the internet outside school is largely dominated by the desire for communication and entertainment. It is embedded within the everyday culture of the peer group, and it is also inextricably connected with a wider media culture of movies, television, pop music and video games. Yet in school, most students' uses of the internet are extremely limited.

This is partly because few schools offer extended or unrestricted access. Time for access is often limited, and depends upon students being able to make the case for 'legitimate' educational uses (which are often narrowly defined). Students' use of e-mail is often tightly regulated, and most schools will not permit instant messaging or the use of social networking sites.

Access is often confined to approved websites only, and many schools employ filtering systems that turn web surfing into an obstacle course. As Lawson and Comber (2000b) suggest, the use of filters represents a response to growing 'moral panics' about the dangers of children's access to pornography and (to a lesser extent) 'hate sites'. Interestingly, concerns about the increase in commercial material online feature much less strongly in schools' rationales for filtering – and indeed the UK government's National Grid for Learning contains numerous links to commercially branded sites. Even so, filters are typically very crude and unreliable, and students frequently complain about how they block access to sites that are needed for perfectly legitimate reasons. Research also suggests that – as with other attempts at surveillance – the use of filters (as well as more direct forms of observation by teachers) is frequently resisted (Burbules and Callister, 2000; Goodson et al., 2002; Hope, 2005; Selwyn, 2006). Students will frequently claim that they can evade filters, through a range of inventive and devious strategies, and some boast of their skill in hacking into teaching staff files (a strategy Hope (2005) calls 'sousveillance'). Students recognize that complete and effective control is impossible, and many enjoy the playful 'cat-and-mouse' game that ensues.

Of course, there are some good reasons for these restrictions. Even if the dangers of the internet often appear exaggerated, it is clearly rife with potential distractions. Nevertheless, the use of filtering software is both an ineffective response and a rather self-defeating constraint on students' ability to seek out information and to communicate. As I shall argue in more detail in chapter 8, a more constructive approach would be to inform students about potential risks, and enable them to regulate their own uses of the medium – although, in my view, such an approach would need to go well beyond narrow concerns about students' moral 'safety'.

When it comes to homework, some teachers offer web-based assignments, but these are often restricted to visiting prescribed sites. Others are reluctant to set such work at all, not least because they cannot assume that students enjoy internet access at home (Valentine et al., 2005). Some argue that such concerns are overstated, and that students could well use public access points, for example in their local library, though others suggest that any such expectation is bound to be socially divisive if even one student in the class is not online (see Seiter, 2005; and Sutherland-Smith et al., 2003). However, as Valentine et al. (2005) point out, students who have good internet access at home will be advantaged in any case, even if teachers do not explicitly ask for the internet to be used – and so a digital divide will remain. Here again, there may be good reasons for such limitations, but they can end up simply reinforcing a gap between in-school and out-of-school practices.

In practice, as we have seen, most students' uses of computers in schools are confined to a comparatively narrow range of software applications. Formal ICT classes – in which much of this use occurs – focus primarily on the mastery of decontextualized skills in word processing, file management, Powerpoint presentations and the construction of databases. Such classes are typically taught by maths and technology specialists who, in secondary schools, tend to monopolize the available ICT suites, restricting access for other subject teachers (Reynolds et al., 2003). There is a strong focus here on mainstream clerical applications – in effect, on the teaching of 'Microsoft Office'. ICT skills are rarely integrated with the teaching of mainstream subjects, and many subject teachers implicitly regard this as a distraction from their main concerns. In common with other National Curriculum subjects, the ICT curriculum in the UK is defined in terms of a sequence of level descriptors and attainment targets, and assessed via standardized tests. As Bridget Somekh (2004) observes, students are typically assumed to know nothing about these media, and little account is taken of variations in their prior experience. Meanwhile, although many secondary schools now have their own websites, these are used mainly for school publicity (Ofsted 2004): students' work can only reach a wider audience if it does not conflict with the imperatives of schools' public relations.

By contrast, young people's use of technology in the home is often much less limited and restricted. Shazia Mumtaz (2001), for example, found in a UK study that there were significant differences between students' uses of computers at home and in school, in terms of the frequency and amount of use, the type of hardware and software available, and the ways in which they were able to use it. While home uses were dominated by games, the internet, e-mail and chat, school uses were dominated by word processing and the use of spreadsheets; and while home uses were often extensive, diverse and open-ended, school often posed restrictions on students' autonomous access and use. Unlike the decontextualized skills training of ICT classes, uses of technology in the home are also more directly related to young people's existing interests and motivations. These findings have been echoed by several other recent studies (e.g. Downes, 1999; Facer et al., 2003; Kent and Facer, 2004; Lewin, 2004; Livingstone and Bober, 2004; Sutherland-Smith et al., 2003).

In this situation, it is not surprising that many children are bored and frustrated by their use of new media in schools. Much classroom work with technology is bound to appear unexciting when compared with the complex and extensive multimedia experiences some students have outside school. This applies particularly to students who are intensive users of technology at home, although not only to them. In one US study, Douglas Levin and Sousan Arafeh (2002) found that such 'net-savvy' students were very positive about the benefits of the internet for their education, using it as a virtual library, tutor, study group and guidance counsellor. However, they were very disillusioned by their schools' uses of technology, criticizing the poor quality of access, the obstacles posed by filters, and the unengaging, teacher-directed ways in which the internet was used. Similar findings emerge from a British replication of this study (Selwyn, 2006). Here, however, many students were quite pragmatic, even resigned, about what their schools could offer: they begrudgingly accepted that schools were likely to remain heavily regulatory institutions, and that their use of the internet was simply one example of this.

These studies focus largely on students who already enjoy high levels of access outside school – in Levin and Arafeh's study, for example, these amounted to around 30 per cent of the whole school populations. However, there is little reason to believe that students who do not have outside access will find such practices any more engaging – let alone that they will compensate for the inequalities of access outside school. Furthermore, such studies should not be taken to imply that 'net-savvy' students are not in need of assistance in using the medium. Levin and Arafeh point out that such students' expressions of confidence may disguise the fact that they often encounter difficulties in locating useful information and in evaluating its reliability; and they also note that such students were annoyed by the 'push' elements of the medium, for example in the form of advertising pop-ups.

These studies confirm the idea that the use of technology in schools may serve to accentuate inequalities between students, rather than ameliorate them. As Attewell and Battle (1999) also found, there is a danger of a *Sesame Street* effect' here. An intervention designed to enable poorer children to 'catch up' educationally with their more affluent counterparts may end up widening existing inequalities based on social class, ethnicity and gender, since it is boys, middle-class children and whites (who enjoy greater access outside school) who are likely to benefit most from it.

However, this new 'digital divide' between in-school and out-of-school use could also be seen as symptomatic of a much broader phenomenon – a widening gap between children's everyday 'life worlds' outside school and the emphases of many education systems. While the social and cultural experiences of children have been dramatically transformed over the past fifty years, schools have signally failed to keep pace with change. As proponents of technology often point out, the classrooms of today would be easily recognizable to the pioneers of public education of the mid-nineteenth century: the ways in which teaching and learning are organized, the kinds of skills and knowledge that are valued in assessment, and even a good deal of the actual curriculum content, have changed only superficially since that time. Indeed, some have argued that schooling is now heading determinedly backwards, retreating from the uncertainty of contemporary social change towards the apparently comforting stability of a new 'educational fundamentalism', in which traditional relationships of authority between adults and children can be restored (Kenway and Bullen, 2001). The weakening of existing patterns of social hierarchy has led to an increasingly desperate attempt to reassert discipline in schools, which is manifested in what Goodson et al. (2002) call the 'micro-management' of the curriculum, of assessment and of student behaviour.

Popular culture has always been a key focus of this struggle for control. Traditionally, of course, schools have sought to exclude popular culture, or at least to 'teach against' it by seeking to expose its limitations and its inferiority to legitimate 'high' culture. The history of media education in schools has been strongly informed by this kind of 'discriminatory' approach (see Buckingham, 2003). The advent of digital technology has opened a new front in this struggle, and has led to schools adopting new technical and disciplinary strategies in their attempts to police students' popular cultural practices. As we shall see in the following chapters, it has also led to efforts to incorporate elements of popular culture with the aim of 'enchanting the disenchanted child' (Beastall, 2006). Yet whichever strategy it adopts, it remains the case that the school is no longer in control of the socialization and enculturation of children – if indeed it ever was. For better or worse, new popular cultural practices have come more and more to challenge the legitimacy of schooling, and hence its claim to sustain established forms of social power.

This is not to posit an absolute opposition between 'school culture' and 'children's culture'. The school is inevitably a site for negotiation (and indeed for struggle) between competing conceptions of knowledge and cultural value. Nevertheless, there is now an extraordinary contrast between the high levels of activity and enthusiasm that characterize children's consumer cultures and the passivity that increasingly suffuses their schooling. Of course, teachers have perennially complained about children's weakening 'attention span', although in fact the levels of intense concentration and energy that typify children's playground engagements with phenomena such as Pokémon are quite at odds with the deadening influence of mechanical testing that currently prevails in many classrooms (Buckingham and Sefton-Green, 2003). Children are now immersed in a consumer culture that appears to position them as active and autonomous; yet, in school, a great deal of their learning is passive and teacher-directed. Indeed, as Jane Kenway and Elizabeth Bullen (2001) point out, the 'knowledge politics' of children's consumer culture often explicitly oppose that of formal schooling, presenting teachers as dull and earnest, worthy not of emulation but of well-justified rejection. Like a Rabelaisian 'carnival', children's media culture has increasingly become an arena in which authoritarian values of seriousness and conformity are subverted and undermined. In this context, it is hardly surprising if children come to perceive schooling as marginal to their identities and concerns – or, at best, as a kind of functional chore.

Conclusion

So how should schools respond to this new digital divide? Clearly, they need to be aware of the range and diversity of young people's experiences of media and technology outside school. They need to improve students' access to technology, to use more engaging software, and to allow more opportunities for open-ended, creative uses of media. However, it is too simplistic to suggest that schools should simply mimic or seek to incorporate these 'informal' uses of technology into their work. As I shall argue in the next two chapters, a merely celebratory stance towards the activities of the so-called digital generation can result in a kind of fashionable superficiality. Merely playing around with the latest technological gadgets or repackaging tired educational content with the trappings of techno-culture is unlikely to achieve any lasting gain. The issues I have raised in this chapter – particularly in relation to the growing commercialization of digital culture and the diversity and inequalities in young people's experiences – pose more significant and far-reaching challenges for schools. As I shall argue, taking young people's digital culture seriously will require a more rigorous, and indeed a more critical, approach.

6

Playing to Learn?[1]

Rethinking the Educational Potential
of Computer Games

Advocates of educational technology have frequently looked to children's leisure-time experiences as a source of new approaches to learning. As we have seen, children's use of technology outside the classroom is often regarded as somehow more authentic and more natural than what happens in school. Seymour Papert (1996), for example, extols the value of what he calls 'home-style' learning, seeing it as self-directed, spontaneous and motivated in ways that 'school-style' learning is not. Marc Prensky (2006) and Don Tapscott (1998) also look outside the school for alternatives to what they regard as the old-fashioned, instructional style of 'baby boomer' teachers. Similar arguments have increasingly been made by academic researchers, who have looked to children's leisure uses of digital technology – for example in the form of computer games – as a means of challenging the narrow and inflexible uses of ICTs in schools (e.g. Lewin, 2004; Mumtaz, 2001; Somekh, 2004). Jerry Wellington (2001), for example, believes that technology inherently fosters a more flexible, open-ended, student-led style of learning, and he suggests that this 'marvellous platform for learning' is more attuned to the 'informal' learning style of the home than that of the school, which he characterizes as rigid and conformist. As we saw in chapters 1 and 2, marketeers and policy-makers have also been keen to emphasize the importance of learning in the home. Technology companies clearly regard the home as an important and desirable market, although policy-makers have been rather more interested in extending the reach of the school into the home, for example by reasserting the importance of homework. Yet, even here, there has been some recognition of the more authentic kinds of learning that are believed to occur through children's 'informal' interactions with new media and technology.

The idea that young people might be learning from popular culture – and that schools should be paying more attention to this – is by no means new, nor is it confined to digital media. For example, our research on young people's learning about sex and relationships (Buckingham and Bragg, 2004) found that the media were often regarded as much more valuable than other sources of information and advice, particularly schools. While children were bored and alienated by sex education classes, and frequently embarrassed by their parents' clumsy efforts, they were keen to learn about such issues through teenage magazines and soap operas – although that is not to suggest that they were necessarily any more trusting or uncritical of what they found there. To some extent, this was about content: the media were often seen to speak more frankly and openly about sexual matters than either parents or schools. However, it was also a matter of style: young people looked to the media because they generally did not lecture or talk down to them. Above all, the media were seen to provide young people with opportunities to find out for themselves, in their own time and in their own way. The children we interviewed clearly wanted to be in charge of their own learning, and to make up their own minds about such matters.

These arguments are, if anything, even stronger when it comes to new media. Young people's everyday uses of computer games or the internet involve a whole range of informal learning processes, in which there is often a highly democratic relationship between 'teachers' and 'learners'. Children learn to use these media largely through trial and error – through exploration, experimentation and play; collaboration with others – in both face-to-face and virtual forms – is an essential element of the process. Playing certain types of computer games, for example, can involve an extensive series of cognitive activities: remembering, hypothesis testing, predicting and strategic planning. While game players are often deeply immersed in the virtual world of the game, dialogue and exchange with others is crucial. And game playing is also a 'multi-literate' activity: it often involves interpreting complex three-dimensional visual environments, reading both on-screen and off-screen texts (such as games magazines and websites) and processing auditory information. In the world of computer games, success ultimately derives from the disciplined and committed acquisition of skills and knowledge (Carr et al., 2006).

Likewise, online chat and instant messaging require very specific skills in language and interpersonal communication (Davies, 2006; Tingstad, 2003). Young people have to learn to 'read' subtle nuances, often on the basis of minimal cues. They have to learn the rules and etiquette of online communication, and to shift quickly between genres or language registers. Provided they are sensible about divulging personal information, online chat provides young people with a safe arena for rehearsing and exploring aspects of identity and personal relationships that may not be available elsewhere. Again, much of this learning is carried out without explicit teaching: it involves active exploration, 'learning by doing', apprenticeship

rather than direct instruction. Above all, it is profoundly soci
matter of collaboration and interaction with others, and of partic
a community of users.

In learning with and through these media, children are also learning
how to learn. They are developing particular orientations towards information, particular methods of acquiring new knowledge and skills, and a
sense of their own identities as learners. They are likely to experience a
strong sense of their own autonomy, and of their right to make their own
choices and to follow their own paths – however illusory this may
ultimately be. In these domains, they are learning primarily by means of
discovery, experimentation and play, rather than by following external
instructions and directions.

Even so, there are some important limitations to this. Media content is
of course not necessarily neutral or reliable: it represents the world in particular ways and not others, and it does so in ways that tend to serve the
interests of its producers. Activities such as chat and game play are heavily
bound by systems of rules – even if the rules are not always explicitly
taught, and even if they can sometimes be broken or bent. The structure
or 'architecture' of software itself (for example, of links on the internet)
imposes very significant constraints on the ways in which it can be used.
And the social worlds that users enter into as they participate in these
activities are by no means necessarily egalitarian or harmonious. For all
these reasons, we need to be wary of simply *celebrating* children's 'informal'
experiences of media and technology; and, as we shall see in this chapter,
there are good reasons to be cautious about the idea of simply extending
those experiences into the more 'formal' context of the school.

Over the past few years, the key focus of this debate has been on computer games. Not least by virtue of their popularity with (some) young
people, games have been seen to offer more effective, engaging and even
liberating styles of learning than those currently dominating school classrooms. James Gee, for example, argues that games involve processes of
learning that are 'deeper and richer than the forms of learning to which
[children] are exposed in school' (Gee, 2005: 112). In this chapter, I intend
to challenge some of these more celebratory claims about the nature of
learning from games, and to point to some glaring absences in the analysis
– not least in terms of its implications for education.

Games and learning: making the case

The recent interest in computer games in education is more than simply
a reflection of their growing popularity and commercial significance. It also

reflects the emergence of some of the new discourses about learning and the new political imperatives that we have identified in earlier chapters. Most simply, games are seen to provide a means of 'enchanting the dis-enchanted child' (Beastall, 2006) – and particularly boys, who are being increasingly outpaced by girls in the race for educational success. Yet games also appear to permit more personalized forms of learning and to accommodate different learning styles; and they are often seen to embody the more 'informal' approach that educators are keen to co-opt. In this sense, the debate about games in education provides an interesting test case of the validity of some of these broader arguments.

Marc Prensky and James Paul Gee are without doubt two of the most influential advocates of the potential of computer games for learning. In some respects, their approaches are quite different. Prensky is a games designer and CEO of an e-learning company called 'Games2train', which works for a range of corporate clients devising training tools: he describes himself as 'an internationally acclaimed speaker, writer, consultant, futur-ist, visionary, and inventor' (Prensky, 2006: 253). Gee, by contrast, is an academic – a former theoretical linguist who has written several influential books on sociolinguistics, literacy and education, and for whom games are a relatively recent preoccupation (Gee, 2003, 2004, 2005). Prensky has been publicly critical of what he sees as the academic 'jargon' of Gee's work (Prensky, 2003), although his latest book, *'Don't Bother Me, Mom – I'm Learn-ing!'* (2006), includes a foreword and contributions from Gee.

Significantly, neither Gee nor Prensky make any significant reference to the burgeoning academic literature in 'games studies'. There is now an extensive body of research on games, encompassing textual analysis, theo-retical accounts of the characteristics of the medium, and studies of the games industry (for introductions to such work, see Atkins, 2003; Carr et al., 2006; Juul, 2005; Newman, 2004; Wolf, 2002). Even more surpris-ingly, neither author refers in any detail to the growing body of empirical research on game play (for reviews and examples, see Carr et al., 2006; Copier and Raessens, 2003; Durkin, 1995; Gunter, 1998; Taylor, 2003). Their accounts of the experience and consequences of play are typically anecdotal, or based on their own experiences as players. These are crucial absences, and they reflect the way in which the debate about games in education has tended to neglect the nature of games as a *cultural form* much more broadly.

In some respects, Prensky is making a narrower case than Gee. His over-riding aim is to advocate the value of games and to counter the arguments of their critics – and he does this primarily by emphasizing their importance for learning. Both in his books and on his website (www.gamesparent-steachers.com), he urges parents and teachers to talk to children about games, to take them seriously, and to teach with and about them. According to Prensky, 'complex' games make children better, more successful people: they teach them to co-operate with others, to develop moral sensitivity, to understand how business works, and even to stay healthy. Above all, games teach children to think: they enable them to develop skills – such as reasoning, problem-solving and decision-making – that are 'immediately generalizable' to real-life situations (Prensky, 2006: 8).

By contrast, Gee is making a much more general argument about learning and education: while he too is keen to celebrate the value of games, there is a sense in which games are merely an instance or a vehicle for the more general theory of learning – and the critique of 'traditional schooling' – that he is seeking to develop. Unlike Prensky, Gee does not directly argue that games should be used in schools – although he does not argue against this: rather, his argument is that learning in schools should become more 'playful' or 'game-like', reflecting the forms of learning that he identifies as characteristic of 'good' games (Gee, 2005: 30).

In *What Video Games Have to Teach us about Literacy and Learning* (2003), Gee uses his own and his young son's experience of games to develop a set of thirty-six 'learning principles'. These principles are too lengthy to explain in detail here, but it is worth noting some key emphases. According to Gee, meaningful learning (which includes learning in games) is necessarily active; it is multimodal, involving multiple sign systems (such as images, writing and sounds); it entails participation in 'affinity groups' or 'affinity spaces', where people with shared interests and goals come together; it involves a kind of 'moratorium', where learners feel free to make choices and take risks; it includes the provision of rewards, feedback and opportunities for repeated practice; it is ordered and scaffolded, for example by introducing progressively more challenging tasks, and by providing information 'just in time', and 'on demand'; it involves skills being acquired in the context of activity, rather than in fragmented ways, or through abstract exercises; and it provides opportunities for self-reflection, both on the content of the learning and on the way in which it is learnt.

In all these respects, Gee argues, games offer learning experiences that are more compelling and challenging than those that are provided in schools. In his subsequent book *Situated Language and Learning* (2004), he links this argument to his earlier work on literacy. Gee argues that, for less privileged children, there is typically a mismatch between their use of language in the home and the demands posed by academic varieties of language in school, and schools fail to address this by persistently focusing on the surface aspects of reading (for example by teaching synthetic phonics). Meanwhile, for these (and indeed most) children, popular culture offers equally, if not more, complex experiences of language – even if these remain largely unrecognized by schools; and gaming in particular is an area where children typically encounter quite demanding, specialized forms of written text.

According to Gee, 'good' games allow multiple solutions to problems and afford different learning styles: as learners probe the game world, develop hypotheses and strategies, probe again and rethink, they develop the ability to recognize more abstract patterns – something which Gee regards as a fundamental 'human need'. Games also teach the skills that are required for successful play, for example in the 'training levels' or early stages of a game; and they do so not through abstract instruction, but in the context of real play, and by progressively presenting players with challenges that lie at the edge of their existing competence. By contrast, he argues, learning in school emphasizes the decontextualized mastery of skills and information; it does not provide opportunities for learners to build connections with their prior experiences or their real-world identities; it fails to provide sufficient opportunities for embodied, practical activity; and it isolates learners from the social networks (or 'affinity spaces') that might support their learning. It is, essentially, unsituated learning.

Gee's theory shares some key emphases with the constructivist (or con-structionist) approach of Papert and others, discussed in chapter 3 – most notably in its criticisms of formal instruction and its emphasis on activity and 'learning by doing'. However, Gee also regards learning as something that is mediated by tools – particularly linguistic or semiotic tools – and hence as inescapably social, and in this respect he draws much more on the work of Vygotsky than Piaget (indeed, at many points, Gee appears to be recasting familiar Vygotskyan concepts such as 'scaffolding' and 'zone of proximal development' in a new terminology). From this perspective, learning involves participation in particular 'semiotic domains' – that is, social arenas in which there are shared methods and resources for con-structing and communicating meaning. Science, for example, is one such domain, and gaming is another. In both cases, participants have to acquire a form of 'literacy' that will enable them both to 'read' (or recognize) and to 'write' (or produce) the kinds of meanings that are accepted within the domain. In this respect, learning is inextricably linked to social action, and to social identity – that is, to people's sense of themselves as participants in particular social domains. In game play, as in learning, we typically project new identities that may in turn come to influence our real-life identities.

As I shall argue, there are some aspects of learning that this theory appears to marginalize or ignore; and it may not be applicable to all forms of learning. Even so, there is little that is new about it, and most of the arguments seem quite obvious and uncontroversial. My main concern here is not so much with the validity of the theory as with its derivation from, and application to, computer games. Here there are grounds for several criticisms.

Constructing digital learners

Both Gee and Prensky base their arguments on a set of very broad assertions about how technology has changed young people's consciousness and style of learning. Both clearly espouse the 'digital generation' rhetoric discussed in chapter 5. As we have seen, Prensky constructs a binary opposition between 'digital immigrants' and 'digital natives', and he presents a long list of the new ways in which digital natives communicate, create, socialize and learn (Prensky, 2006: 41–51). Gee occasionally uses the same terms (e.g. 2003: 39), but he also draws a distinction between 'Millennials' and 'Baby Boomers' – for example on the basis of a (highly contentious) account of the different television programmes that have been popular with these different generations (Gee, 2004: 100–3). In both cases, the distinctions are drawn in stark and absolute terms. Natives, it appears, all play computer games, while immigrants do not; natives know everything about technology, while immigrants are merely incompetent and ignorant; natives speak 'an entirely new language', which immigrants cannot understand; natives are always multi-tasking, while immigrants can only cope with one thing at a time; and so on. Like explorers returning from distant lands, both writers see their role as being to explain the activities of this exotic new species for the benefit of their confused and puzzled teachers and parents.

As we have seen, Prensky's argument is reinforced by what he regards as definitive evidence about the 'plasticity' of the human brain. Despite the fact that children's brains have not adapted sufficiently over thousands of years to enable all of them to read and write, it appears that, within the space of one generation, technology has brought about fundamental evolutionary changes that are making children unrecognizable even to their own parents. Children have apparently been 'reprogramming their brains' to accommodate the speed, interactivity and non-linear structures of computer games (Prensky, 2006: 35) – and this has resulted in physical differences in the organization of their brains.

Gee's argument here is a more sociological one. The changing requirements of 'new capitalism', he argues, require children to become 'shape-shifting portfolio people' (Gee, 2004: 91–115). Work in the post-Fordist economy is project-based, involving collaboration, networking and flexibility – and these, he argues, are skills that are strongly developed within the 'affinity spaces' and identity play of games. Gee claims that this new style of learning is not merely applicable to the affluent, but that all workers are now required to develop 'portfolios' of transferable skills, experiences and achievements that they can manage in flexible ways. This description might appear quite appropriate to an elite of so-called knowledge workers, although it is certainly debatable how far it can be extended to employment in general. However, Gee effectively denies the continuing significance of social class or cultural capital in this process: it is the portfolio that counts, and the building of portfolios appears to be a wholly individual responsibility (ibid.: 106). Both Prensky's physiological assertions and Gee's sociological ones are highly contentious, and neither are supported with sufficient evidence. Yet they clearly illustrate how the argument about games in education is connected with some of the broader discourses of learning I have identified in earlier chapters.

The limits of celebration

Both in education and more broadly, the debate about computer games has been conducted in extremely polarized terms. Broadly speaking, games have been framed in public debates in terms of predictable anxieties about their harmful effects – and, as with older media, much of the concern has focused on the issue of 'violence' (see Squire, 2002; Jenkins, 2006). This leaves advocates of games such as Gee and Prensky with the task of allaying such anxieties, and of having to prove that games and their users are not as stupid as they are frequently made out to be. This often results in a merely celebratory stance that ignores significant aspects of the phenomenon it is so keen to justify.

Thus, Gee's book *Why Video Games are Good for your Soul* (2005) finds him waxing lyrical about 'the beautiful symphony of images and actions' that is 'Castlevania'; and revelling in the 'exhilarating' feeling of control that is encouraged by the military simulation 'Full Spectrum Warrior'

(2005: 33, 49). While issues of learning continue to be his main preoccupation, his self-professed 'dream' is 'just to celebrate the potential of good video games, the technologies by which they are made, the intelligence by which they are designed and played, and the pleasures that are part and parcel of that intelligence' (ibid.: 118). Games are good for the soul, Gee argues, because they feed 'the soul's desire for agency, control and meaningfulness': they 'hold out the promise of imagining new worlds and setting sparks loose that may make people want to make those worlds real' (ibid.: 119). (This strangely timeless, universal conception of the human mind – or indeed the soul – fits awkwardly with Gee's sociocultural approach to cognition.) Likewise, both Gee and Prensky have a wholly benign view of the online communities – or 'affinity spaces' – that surround gaming. Prensky, for example, asserts that such online communication is 'norm-free' (2006: 42), while Gee describes such spaces as non-hierarchical, lacking in discrimination, and accepting all forms of knowledge as valid (2004: 85–7).

In this case, there are significant questions to be raised about *which* games are discussed and which are left aside. Gee, for example, confines himself largely to discussing what he calls 'good' games, although the criteria by which these are identified are not made clear. At best, the argument appears quite tautological: what he calls 'good' games are games that illustrate his 'learning principles' – which presumably 'bad' games do not. Elsewhere (Gee, 2005: 1–2) he asserts that 'good games are games that lots of gamers agree are good', which might appear to equate quality with commercial success (an issue to be addressed below) – although in fact he then goes on to undermine this by asserting that, in his view, some games are good despite the fact that only a minority of gamers appear to enjoy them. In practice, both Gee and Prensky largely confine themselves to particular game genres – notably role-playing games, strategy games and simulations (which Prensky refers to as 'complex' games). There are many genres of popular games – puzzle games, sports games, platform games, 'beat-em-ups' and 'first-person shooters', for example – that they largely ignore. This clearly raises questions about the general applicability of their arguments, and about the extent to which their preferred genres are actually representative of gaming more broadly. (Interestingly, Prensky refers to the fact that the largest market for games is middle-aged women playing puzzle games on the internet – a fact which might appear to challenge his assertions about gaming and the 'digital natives'.)

Furthermore, this celebratory stance leads to a paradoxical position on the question of media effects. Both Gee and Prensky challenge (in my view, entirely correctly) some of the more naïve and exaggerated assertions about the effects of 'violence' in games: they argue that only a minority of games are violent, and that the evidence that such games cause heightened aggression is both limited and questionable (Gee, 2005: 5–7; Prensky, 2006: 16–20). However, Prensky in particular then proceeds to make similarly naïve and poorly supported claims about the *positive* effects of games. He cites endorsements from a surgeon who believes that game playing leads to fewer mistakes in operations and a geneticist who believes it helps him recognize visual patterns in numerical data, and he repeatedly notes the use of games by the US military in its training programmes. He asserts that game players are more likely to succeed in business and to earn more money than non-players; that gamers are better at collaborating and problem-solving; and, even more broadly, that 'being successful at playing today's computer games helps you succeed in life' (2006: 116).

Prensky and Gee do not ignore 'violent' games, although here it seems that the only learning that takes place is pro-social, or entirely divorced from the overt content. For example, Prensky implies that players of such games somehow retain only positive moral lessons, accepting some messages ('fighting is tough') and rejecting others ('everybody is an enemy') (2006: 69). Games such as 'Grand Theft Auto' appear to have only cathartic effects, and to teach players that there are consequences for 'negative choices' (ibid.: 74–5). Parents are even urged to discuss the ethical implications of such games with their children (ibid.: 111) – an approach which would seem rather to miss the point.[2] Likewise, Gee argues that games such as 'Metal Gear Solid' and 'Return to Castle Wolfenstein' do not reward linear, goal-oriented strategies or mindless macho behaviour, and as such could be seen to be teaching more positive lessons (Gee, 2005).

Another strategy both authors adopt here – albeit inconsistently – is to suggest that the narrative scenarios and content of games are simply irrelevant, mere 'eye candy'. Gee suggests that experienced players quickly see through this superficial 'window dressing' to 'the underlying rules, strategy spaces, and emergent possibilities for problem solving' (2006: XX). This is an approach that effectively separates *learning* from *knowledge* – or the 'how' from the 'what' – and implies that the latter is somehow irrelevant. Prensky appears to share this view, but somehow applies it only to 'violent' games. Elsewhere, he is keen to extol the virtues of games that have some relationship with established curriculum content – so-called serious games, such as the simulations 'Roller Coaster Tycoon' and 'The Sims', the prototype science and history games produced by MIT, such as 'Supercharged' and 'Revolution', and health-related games – and, most problematically,

'America's Army', a game that was designed to function as a recruitment tool for the US military. In this case, the games *are* seen to teach 'content' that is directly applicable to real-life situations – although the ability of simulations to replicate real-life situations fully is obviously quite limited.

While contemporary games are clearly diverse, participation in many of the games these authors discuss is effectively premised on an interest in scenarios that are well-established aspects of male adolescent fantasy – sword-and-sorcery narratives, science fiction and action movies. While Gee recognizes in passing (for example, 2004: 113) that there may be grounds for a cultural critique of games content, and occasionally feels bound to apologize for some of the ideological dimensions of his favoured games (such as the military simulation 'Full Spectrum Warrior': 2005: 63), he tends to bracket this off as irrelevant to his main enquiry. Indeed, he goes on to challenge what he defines as the 'content fetish' of contemporary schooling, implying that authentic learning is somehow independent of content. Yet within specific 'semiotic domains', certain types of knowledge – as well as certain types of learning – are clearly more valid and legitimate than others: to use one of Gee's examples (2004: 118), knowing Mendel's laws is more important in most powerful domains than knowing the names of all 150 Pokémon. To remove 'content' from the account is to remove significant grounds for judgement, and somehow to ignore the relationship between knowledge and social power: what matters is not simply *how* you know but also *what* you know.

The final aspect of games that is fairly systematically ignored in these accounts is their commercial dimension. As a games designer himself, Prensky is predictably keen to promote a positive view of the industry – for example, describing games designers as 'among the most creative and intelligent people in the world' (2006: 68). Yet, for an academic, Gee also appears to have an extraordinarily uncritical sense of how the games industry works:

> If a game cannot be learned well, then it will not sell well, and the company that makes it is in danger of going broke . . . If only to sell well, good games have to incorporate good learning principles in virtue of which they get themselves well learned. Game designers build on each other's successes and, in a sort of Darwinian process, good games come to reflect yet better and better learning principles. (Gee, 2004: 57)

It would be interesting to consider how this 'Darwinian' account might be applied to other areas of the cultural industries, such as book publishing, the cinema or television. To say the least, research on the games industry suggests that the processes through which games are produced, marketed and distributed are rather more complex – and significantly less benign – than Gee implies (e.g. Kline et al., 2003).

There is a similar neglect in Gee's account of 'affinity spaces'. For example, he makes a good case for the conceptual and linguistic complexity of Pokémon – although one might not necessarily wish to go so far as describing it as 'perhaps the best literacy curriculum ever conceived' (2005: 84). He also points to the intensely sociable nature of children's interactions around such phenomena (2004: 8–10). Yet what he sweeps aside is the role of commerce: children's participation in such phenomena is highly contingent on their ability to purchase particular commodities (such as the trading cards) – and these are transactions in which children are not all equal. As we have argued elsewhere, children's participation in such phenomena is indeed active, but it is also inextricably connected with the operations of consumer capitalism (Buckingham and Sefton-Green, 2003). As a result, the 'affinity spaces' of phenomena such as Pokémon do not provide a level playing field: on the contrary, they are spaces in which relations of power and inequality are inevitably rehearsed and reproduced.

The game of learning

According to James Gee, 'for humans, real learning is always associated with pleasure and is ultimately a form of play – a principle almost always dismissed by schools' (2004: 71). The equation of learning with play, and both with pleasure, is of course a staple theme in the marketing of educational media: as we shall see in chapter 7, the industry's obsessive insistence on 'fun learning' reflects an implicit rejection of the contrary view – that learning might actually involve work, and that work might not always be pleasurable. In this respect, it reflects a suppression of aspects of learning – and indeed of play – that might be more difficult to address.

For Gee and Prensky, the pleasure of gaming derives directly from the fact that it involves learning. According to Prensky, 'the true secret of why kids spend so much time on their games is that they're learning!' (2006: 5). In this respect, both authors adopt what Brian Sutton-Smith (1998) has identified as a 'rhetoric of progress': like many contemporary educationalists, they seek to justify play on the grounds that it contributes to the development of the child's intellectual faculties, and hence to their progress towards adult maturity. As Sutton-Smith suggests, this rhetoric typically neglects other aspects of play that might be seen as somehow 'anti-social', pointless or irrational. For example, he draws attention to an alternative notion of play as 'frivolity', as something that can oppose and challenge the traditional work ethic; and he also discusses 'play as power' – as something that necessarily entails competition and conflict. By contrast, the rhetoric of 'play as progress' sees value only in the aspects of play that contribute directly to learning.

Furthermore, the notion of pleasurable learning as an innate 'human need' neglects the possibility that pleasure might not always be such a good thing. For example, Gee extols the ability of game play to provide 'projective identities'. In playing a game such as 'Full Spectrum Warrior', we take on the role of a professional soldier: the game allows us to 'feel control . . . to experience *expertise*, to feel like an expert' – feelings that, he argues, are often quite lacking in real life (2005: 49). More broadly, he asserts that, in role-playing games, 'people get to be things and live lives they could never live in reality'; they allow players 'to have experiences and travel to places that even the rich cannot buy and keep for themselves in real life'; and they enable us to feel that 'we are the heroes of our own story', rather than 'the victims of forces beyond our control', as we often feel in real life (2005: 104–5). Leaving aside for the moment the suggestion that games are somehow equivalent to real life, is it not possible that this vicarious experience might be somehow problematic? This is perhaps most obviously the case with the militaristic scenario of a game such as 'Full Spectrum Warrior', but it could be argued more broadly. Traditional critics of 'mass culture' would perceive these qualities as a further indication of the role of popular culture as a kind of compensation for people's powerlessness, and a substitute for real political change.

Conversely, the identification of learning with pleasurable play neglects the possibility that some forms of learning might necessarily involve frustration, boredom and endless repetition – and indeed, be actively unpleasurable. On one level, many of the general arguments Gee is making might equally be applied to playing football, or learning a musical instrument. Yet anyone who engages in these things knows that learning is far from always pleasurable. As a keen amateur jazz musician, I know that if I don't put in regular time on practising my scales, my playing will be good for nothing; and much of the gratification I receive here is, to say the least, deferred. Abstract, decontextualized skills practice is precisely what sportsmen and women are doing when they are training. Achieving fluency and improving performance in these areas often involves frustration, yet in the world of games it appears that the only frustration is what Gee calls 'pleasurable frustration'.

A further difficulty with this account is the implication that what is learnt through game play will necessarily transfer to other situations. In this respect, there are some striking similarities between these authors' account of computer games and Papert's arguments about the benefits of LOGO (see chapter 3). Thus, Prensky argues that the skills acquired through game play – to do with collaboration or problem-solving, for example – are 'immediately generalizable'. For instance, gamers learn to take prudent risks or to make decisions in games, and therefore become better at doing so in business situations (Prensky, 2006: 8). Prensky even extends this argument to game content, arguing that gamers will learn 'real-life' skills from simulation games, for example about how to manage theme parks, trade financial instruments, or find their way around offshore oil platforms – although, as we have seen, he seems unwilling to extend this approach to violence in games (2006: 65). Obviously, this argument fails to acknowledge that games are *representations*: for Prensky, games offer an unmediated 'experience of life' that is indistinguishable from real-world experience (ibid.: 79). 'The Sims', for example, is praised on the grounds that it 'directly and explicitly helps you learn about life' (ibid.: 73) – as though the characters and situations in the game were simply neutral reflections of reality.[3]

Theoretically, this view of the transferability of skills (and even of content) fits awkwardly with Gee's insistence on the 'situated' nature of learning – the notion that learning is 'embodied' and specific to particular social practices, rather than somehow transcending them. When extended to the classroom, this approach implicitly sanctions an instrumental approach to using media in which the *representational* character of such texts is simply ignored.

So what, finally, are the implications of these arguments for schools? As we have seen, both Gee and Prensky are exceptionally negative about schools and teachers. Both writers set up a polar opposition between the authentic, pleasurable learning afforded by games and the 'sheer drudgery', boredom and 'painful learning' of school (Prensky, 2006: 85). For Gee, school is characterized by its absolute neglect of each and every one of the 'learning principles' he outlines: it is simply defined by what it is not. However, the evidence for such claims about schools is simply not forthcoming. Gee's *Situated Language and Learning* is subtitled *A Critique of Traditional Schooling*, but it does not at any point consider what actually happens in such 'traditional' schools. Gee's only evidence about schools comes from studies of innovative science classrooms (Gee, 2003) – which are precisely not the 'traditional' classrooms he so roundly condemns.

As I have noted, both authors' proposals for a revision of schooling are exceptionally vague and generalized. Prensky makes some sketchy proposals for using games in the classroom (an issue we will consider in more detail shortly), but elsewhere all we have is a generalized assertion that learning in schools needs to become more 'playful' and game-like. Prensky argues that the 'education world' needs to become more like the 'games world', and imagines a more 'user-centered' educational system, in which bricks-and-mortar schools will be replaced by a competitive market akin to that of entrepreneurial capitalism (2006: 87–90). Gee, meanwhile, fails to offer even these kinds of utopian prescriptions: school is so far removed from the authentic learning of games that it seems almost impossible to reimagine it.

Whether or not one shares these authors' utopian view of gaming culture, it seem fairly obvious that schools are bound to be very different from gaming communities in many respects. In terms of my earlier discussion of the dimensions of 'formality' in learning (chapter 2), these two contexts are necessarily different in terms of *content*, *social relations* and *learning styles*. Learning in schools – and, indeed, a good deal of learning outside schools – involves a relationship with a specialist teacher who knows more about a particular subject area than the learners. It also involves a structured curriculum, which provides a guide to what is important to learn, and a way of judging what learners are learning. It often involves areas of knowledge or skill that are much more difficult for learners to acquire on their own, or simply through 'experience' – including what one might call theoretical or conceptual knowledge and analytical thinking. This is not to suggest that 'informal' learning, for example of the kind that occurs within game communities, is invalid; simply that there are certain kinds of learning that inevitably require a more 'formal' approach. Of course, schools are not necessarily always effective in achieving this; but this does not justify simply writing them off.[4]

Games in the classroom

The notion that computer games might be directly used in classrooms is not new; but interest in this approach has grown significantly in recent years. In the UK, key organizations such as BECTA, Futurelab and the Learning and Skills Development Agency have all commissioned reviews of research and small-scale projects on this issue, funded directly or indirectly by government (BECTA, 2001; Kirriemuir and McFarlane, 2004; Mitchell and Savill-Smith, 2004; McFarlane et al., 2002). All these reports are broadly positive about the *potential* of using games, particularly in respect of learners' motivation, but empirical evidence about actual classroom use is extremely limited. As with research on educational ICTs more broadly, research in this field has rarely managed to escape the 'Hawthorne effect': that is, researchers tend to write as 'defenders' of games (Kirriemuir and McFarlane, 2004: 7), and their uses of them in the classroom are often sustained by their own high levels of enthusiasm. Such empirical projects also tend to be extremely well resourced in terms of staff time and technical support.

Most of the research in this field is very negative about specifically 'educational' games – or what are frequently termed 'edutainment' games. Such games are generally seen to be lacking in the qualities that make 'real', commercial games so engaging for players: they are mostly single-player games, with unsophisticated graphics and limited interactivity. The development budgets of such games are typically a fraction of those of major commercial games; and 'edutainment' is generally seen within the industry as an unprofitable and 'unsexy' area. More to the point, perhaps, these games are primarily marketed to (and recommended to children by) parents and teachers as specifically relevant to particular areas of the school curriculum – or indeed to particular standardized tests. (These kinds of games will be discussed more fully in the following chapter.)

By contrast, researchers have been significantly more interested in the potential of using mainstream commercial games in the classroom. Both BECTA and the Department for Education and Skills have supported projects in this field, in which particular games have been piloted by teachers (BECTA, 2001; McFarlane et al., 2002). The kinds of games most frequently referred to in these studies are simulations and strategy games (such as 'Sim City', 'Age of Empires', 'City Traders' and 'The Sims'), as well as some 'edutainment' adventure games for younger children. Meanwhile, the most important empirical study of actual classroom use, by the Danish researcher Simon Egenfeldt-Nielsen (2005), focuses on a historical strategy game, 'Europa Universalis II'. As this implies, the games selected mostly have some relevance to existing curriculum subjects – although in fact the teachers involved in these studies frequently observed that the content of the games still did not connect sufficiently with their own curriculum, particularly at secondary level. While teachers apparently valued the generic 'thinking skills' and the need for collaboration demanded by some games, it appeared that this alone was not enough to justify their use (McFarlane et al., 2002: 12–13).

Taken together, these studies indicate several significant obstacles to the effective classroom use of games – not all of which are easy to overcome. Some of these are logistical. To a greater extent than many other ICTs, the use of games demands substantial investments of time, both on the part of teachers preparing to use them and in the classroom itself. As Gee and others amply demonstrate, games are often extremely complex to master, and they frequently require a sustained period of 'apprenticeship' before the player attains even a basic level of competence. There are significant additional obstacles here in terms of the lack of teacher training, the difficulty of locating appropriate good-quality games, and incompatibility with existing hardware systems in schools (Kirriemuir and McFarlane, 2004; Egenfeldt-Nielsen, 2005), and there is little reason to believe that these will be easily overcome.

A further difficulty is to do with students' varying levels of interest and familiarity with games to begin with. Gender is clearly a significant factor here. It is generally agreed that games are more likely to interest boys than girls – or at least that boys and girls will have different levels of investment in different types of games. As I have noted, games are often seen as a means of re-engaging disaffected boys (BECTA, 2001) – although the issue of boys' 'underachievement' is complex, and unlikely to be resolved simply by throwing technology at the problem (see Epstein et al., 1998). Egenfeldt-Nielsen's study, for example, found that girls were less enthusiastic than boys about learning through games, and tended to be marginalized by the boys in the classroom. Undoubtedly, there are some girls who *are* interested in gaming, and it is possible that the market may be becoming less male-dominated over time (Carr et al., 2006). Yet even irrespective of gender, there are significant implications in terms of equity of using a medium in which some students are likely to be experts while others are merely novices. Despite Prensky's generalizations about 'digital natives', surveys repeatedly show that young people who have a developed interest in games (to the point of playing them for more than an hour a day, for example) are a fairly small minority (e.g. Livingstone and Bovill, 1999; Roberts et al., 2003). At the very least, this again suggests that, if we intend to use games in the classroom, we will need to teach *about* the medium, and not merely to teach *through* it, as though it were a neutral tool.

The use of games is also inevitably affected by the existing attitudes of parents, teachers and – most importantly – students. All are likely to have preconceptions about the medium, and many of these may well be negative. Thus, Egenfeldt-Nielsen (2005) found that many of his (older) students – particularly those who were more academically oriented – regarded the use of games as somewhat trivial, and as a distraction from the serious business of learning; and for this reason, they tended to ignore their potential educational value. This echoes UK research, where the use of game-style simulations in science lessons was also found to result in students taking the class less seriously (Sutherland et al., 2005). While it may be possible to overcome such preconceptions, the use of games faces a significantly steeper uphill struggle in this respect than many other media.

Further difficulties follow from the qualities of engagement and 'immersion' that their advocates see as crucial to the appeal of games. This is particularly the case with simulation games. Research has consistently suggested that debriefing is absolutely crucial to the learning that simulations may promote (Edwards and Mercer, 1987; Buckingham et al., 1995: chapter 8). Yet encouraging students to step back from the immediate experience of the game and to reflect on the broader issues at stake often proves extremely difficult: students may become so involved in play that they positively resist the teachers' questions and interventions (BECTA, 2001). For example, in the case of the history simulation studied by Egenfeldt-Nielsen (2005), the students often failed to connect their experience of the game with the broader historical concepts at stake, and they were also distrustful of the ways in which the scenarios of the game conflicted with their knowledge of the historical 'facts'. As this implies, some instruction on the part of the teacher is vital here; yet this appears to conflict with the idea that learning should occur (as it were) 'by stealth', and in the context of 'embodied activity'.

Ultimately, as with much of the research on ICTs more broadly, evidence about the effectiveness of computer games as means of learning is quite limited. As Egenfeldt-Nielsen (2005) points out, there are some grounds for claiming that the use of games can increase *motivation*, at least for some students; but there is little evidence that it results in increases in *learning* – not least because researchers have not systematically compared the use of games with other teaching approaches. Yet in the absence of solid empirical evidence about the actual use of games in the classroom, sweeping claims about their value – often drawn from an uncritical reading of the work of games advocates such as Prensky and Gee – continue to be recycled, not least in government-sponsored reports.

As with the research on programming (see chapter 3), one of the most significant questions is whether the skills or understanding developed in game play *transfer* to other situations. In fact, research frequently suggests that children who spend significant amounts of time playing commercial games are likely to be those who achieve most poorly in school – as well as scoring less in measures of sociability and self-esteem (e.g. Roe and Muijs, 1998). The value of such research is decidedly questionable (like most 'effects' research, it establishes correlations rather than proof of causality); but if games were as valuable in terms of developing children's thinking and collaborative skills as their advocates claim, one would surely expect to see at least some evidence of a 'payoff' in terms of learning in school. It is more plausible that expertise in games might transfer to other areas of ICT; yet while some research suggests that game players may be more confident (or at least 'playful') in their dealings with technology, there is no convincing evidence, for example, that experienced games players are any more skilled in handling word processors or databases than non-players (Kirriemuir and McFarlane, 2004: 14–15).

Many of these reviews of research conclude with recommendations for the games industry: they note the limitations of 'edutainment' games and the difficulty of using mainstream commercial games in the classroom, and suggest that the industry needs to address the needs of education more effectively. Yet the chances of this occurring are quite limited: the games market itself is certainly very profitable for some, but it is also extremely volatile, and most major companies are likely to regard any connection with education as the kiss of death when it comes to marketing. Meanwhile, as I have noted, more explicitly educational – or 'edutainment' – games are often produced on very limited budgets, which has significant implications in terms of the quality of graphics and the level of interactivity, and hence on their ability to engage reluctant learners.

Conclusion

Computer games have increasingly been seen – not only by researchers and games enthusiasts, but also by educational policy-makers – as a means of revitalizing the use of technology in schools. By building connections between classroom uses of technology and children's out-of-school experiences, they have been regarded as a way of capitalizing on the benefits of 'informal' learning, and of validating the diverse 'learning styles' of different students. As I have suggested, the use of games appears to fulfil several of the imperatives that are now emerging from the new discourses of learning that are circulating among educational policy-makers (and among those who seek to influence them).

As we have seen, advocates of games typically make some very strong claims about their educational value. Clearly, playing games can involve a significant amount of learning, and in some cases it can be a demanding, engaging and intellectually challenging activity – as well as an intensely pleasurable one. I have no intention of denying this. Nor would I entirely reject the theories of learning on which such arguments have been based. At least in the case of some game genres, play often involves a self-directed, collaborative form of learning, in which learners are actively generating hypotheses, solving problems and taking strategic risks. I would absolutely contest the popular view of game play that sees it merely in terms of narrow preoccupations about 'violence', or as just a form of mind-numbing distraction.

However, there are many aspects of game play, and of the cultural phenomenon of computer games, that are less amenable to this kind of celebration. Advocates of computer games typically evade difficult questions about representation in games, and ignore the commercial dimensions of the games industry. They represent gaming 'communities' as wholly benign, and ignore the complex ways in which social power operates within them. They talk in selective ways, about particular types of games and about particular aspects of play; they recycle tired generalizations about young people; and they trade in quite unsubstantiated assertions about the positive effects of games.

When it comes to the use of games in education, there are numerous obstacles that teachers face. Some of these are logistical, but others are a consequence of the real difficulties of learning from games, and of their relation to the curriculum. There are also significant questions about equity and the ability of all students to gain equal access to learning, which are perhaps more acute here than in many other areas of media and technology. Ultimately, the evidence that using games results in significant increases in students' learning – and that this learning *transfers* to other areas – is far from adequate.

So am I proposing that teachers should simply ignore computer games? On the contrary, I continue to maintain that we need to bridge the 'new digital divide' between schools and children's out-of-school cultures – and, for many children, that includes the culture of computer games. In doing so, however, we will need to move well beyond a one-dimensional, defensive approach. Rather than mere celebration, we need to develop a much more rigorous and critical – but also more creative – engagement with children's out-of-school cultures. Before outlining this more fully, however, it is necessary to address the broader phenomenon of 'edutainment' in more detail.

That's Edutainment

Digital Media and Learning in the Home

'Education, education, education' – Tony Blair's declaration of his three main priorities in 1997 in the forthcoming general election serves as an index of what has become a growing preoccupation within contemporary British culture. Education, Blair asserted, 'will be the passion of my government'. 'Levering up standards and achievement' in schools and banishing 'the deadening culture of low expectations' would, he argued, be the key to reversing Britain's economic and social decline. And through a variety of policies, including the reintroduction of grouping by 'ability', the extension of national testing and the use of new technology, New Labour promised to 'open up opportunities for all children', regardless of their social background (Blair, 1997: 159–76).

This evangelistic emphasis on education now extends well beyond efforts to raise 'standards' in schools. The government has increasingly sought to harness 'parent power' – employing a consumerist rhetoric that has been taken over wholesale from the Conservatives. Appealing directly to parents has been seen as a means of wresting control from an 'education establishment' that is still considered recalcitrant and resistant to change. Thus, there has been a growing emphasis on parental choice and involvement in schooling, while national testing and school league tables have purported to provide parents with the information they need to identify the 'best' school for their children. 'Home–school agreements' have attempted to place the 'partnership' between parents and schools on a quasi-legal basis, by specifying parents' responsibility for supporting the practices of the school.

Over the past decade, there has also been a growing insistence on the importance of parental involvement in children's learning at home. As with many New Labour initiatives, there is a combination of egalitarianism and authoritarianism in this approach. It appears to be motivated by a democratic rhetoric about equalizing opportunity, and about giving parents access and power in relation to education. Yet education is also increasingly seen to be responsible for the moral regulation of children – for keeping idle hands busy, and thereby preventing the possibility of delinquency and crime. Thus, the government has repeatedly emphasized the value of homework and funded a whole range of new initiatives that seek to extend the reach of schooling into children's leisure time, such as 'summer universities' and homework clubs. There has been growing interest in what is termed 'family learning' – that is, 'planned activity in which parents and children come together, to work and learn collaboratively' (Ofsted, 2000: 5). Meanwhile, the continuing expansion of national testing has created an atmosphere of growing competition, not only between schools but also among parents and children themselves. In all these respects, the government has promoted an educational work ethic that children are expected to carry with them from the classroom into the home.

This new emphasis on education in the home could be regarded as symptomatic of a much broader 'curricularization' of family life – that is, as a way of transforming children's leisure and everyday interactions into a form of educational 'work' (Walkerdine and Lucey, 1989). Such initiatives frequently rest on normative assumptions about 'good parenting' or 'healthy family life', against which many parents and families are implicitly found lacking. They offer ideals that the majority of parents – and particularly the disadvantaged – may find impossible to achieve and, in this respect, they may result merely in feelings of guilt and inadequacy (cf. Urwin, 1985; Duxbury, 1987).

In this new climate, education has become a source of growing anxiety for many parents. Parents are increasingly concerned about their child's ability to pass the tests, and to gain entry to a 'good' school or a 'good' university. For some, this is about the aspiration to move up the social ladder, but for others it reflects an anxiety about the possibility of falling back down. Furthermore, the demand for parental involvement in education has arisen just at a time when mothers are more often working outside the home, and when the form of family life is changing (via the rise in divorce and single parenthood). For those in employment in the UK, working hours appear to be rising; and for parents, there is accordingly a premium on 'quality time'. Particularly for parents who lead pressured lives, one solution is to throw money at the problem: paying for educational goods and services offers the promise of educational advantage which they may feel unable to secure on their own behalf, or in their own time.

Commercial companies have not been slow to grasp the new opportunities that have arisen here. As I have noted (chapter 1), commercial involvement in education has been significantly extended in recent years, not least through the privatization of basic services, the growth of marketing in schools and the involvement of private companies in school management. Yet parents represent a market that could ultimately prove significantly more lucrative than schools. Through a combination of broader social imperatives and particular marketing appeals, parents are being placed under increasing pressure to 'invest' in their children's education by providing additional resources at home.

Thus, private home tutoring is booming, and is now becoming available for children at an ever younger age, and there has been a marked expansion in the commercial provision of supplementary classes, not just in 'extras' such as the arts but also in 'basics' such as maths and literacy. This is a largely unregulated market: there is no system of inspection, and no requirement that providers should be qualified (Ireson, 2004). Yet it represents what one researcher has aptly termed a 'shadow education system' that can only exacerbate inequalities in children's achievement (Bray, 1999).

Private tutoring is just one aspect of what Stephen Ball and Carol Vincent (2005) call the 'making up' of the middle-class child – the parents' attempt to fill the child's spare time with educationally 'enriching' activities. The dance lessons, swimming lessons, music lessons, horse-riding lessons, French lessons, gym classes, computing classes and so on that such parents increasingly urge their children to attend are all privately provided and purchased. This typically results in what Valerie Walkerdine (1999: 10) calls the 'full diary syndrome' of the middle-class child – the child whose every waking minute is scheduled with educationally worthwhile, stimulating activities, for fear that they might lapse into what are seen as more dangerous pastimes, like slumping in front of the TV or hanging out aimlessly in the street. This proliferation of extra-curricular activities facilitates a kind of CV-building that, for some middle-class children, appears to begin at an ever earlier age. It also leads to a view of the child as a parental project for development – since the success of the child inevitably reflects back on the parent. In this sense, one could even argue that the child has become an object to be displayed, a positional commodity or a marker of parental 'distinction' (cf. Bourdieu, 1984).

Media and publishing companies have also sought to capitalize on the emergence of this new market. On one level, this is nothing new. As Carmen Luke (1989) and others have pointed out, the modern 'invention' of childhood was accompanied by a whole range of pedagogic initiatives aimed at parents and children, including primers, advice manuals and instructional books and playthings. Authors such as Ellen Seiter (1993), Stephen Kline (1993) and Gary Cross (1997) have traced the growth of the toy market in the early twentieth century, which was partly founded on beliefs about the developmental and educational value of play. Like many adults of my generation, I can certainly recall being bought encyclopaedias, information books and educational magazines by my parents; and, of course, a sub-sector of the publishing and media industries has always subsisted on appealing to parents' educational aspirations for their children.

Yet as the sets of encyclopaedias countless children were bought in previous decades have now been largely superseded by their online versions, there has been a significant expansion in the market for broadly 'educational' toys, software, books and magazines targeted at the domestic consumer. Thus, there has been a proliferation of educational magazines, particularly aimed at pre-school children and their parents; the market for popular information books has become crowded with increasingly glossy and attractive new products; and, building on the faltering home software business, we are now seeing the emergence of a significant new market in interactive 'e-learning', led by well-established television companies (Buckingham and Scanlon, 2003a). Industry research has suggested that the overall value of the educational resources market (including print and digital media) in the UK is around £350 million per year (PWC, 2002); and while homes still represent a smaller share of this market than schools, the domestic market is clearly regarded as ripe for further expansion. As with educational technology more broadly, the UK is seen to be in a key position to dominate world markets: indeed, the New Labour peer Lord Puttnam has argued that digital technology should be used to transform Britain into the 'Hollywood of Education'.[1]

Perhaps the most extreme manifestation of this phenomenon has been the boom in materials aimed at very young children. In addition to books, magazines and educational toys, there is now a large range of DVDs, CD-ROMs and educational websites targeting the parents of pre-schoolers, and even of babies. One market leader is 'Baby Einstein', a range of 'developmental' DVDs aimed at under-twos, which has now generated a series of sub-brands in the form of 'Baby Shakespeare', 'Baby Newton', 'Baby Mozart' and (implausibly enough) 'Baby Van Gogh'. (Significantly, the company has recently been bought by Disney.) More recent entrants to this market include 'Brainy Baby', 'Brilliant Baby' and 'Smart Baby', while a practical guide to using such approaches is symptomatically entitled *Baby Power: Give your Child Real Learning Power* (Wade and Moore, 2000). Such materials typically emphasize 'curiosity' and 'discovery', and seek to distance themselves from negative associations of 'hothousing'; but, nevertheless, their pedagogic intent is quite tightly defined (Seetharaman, 2006). As Majia Nadesan (2002) has shown, such products are typically marketed on the basis of claims drawn from a popularized version of so-called brain science (infant neurological research). Such research is certainly questionable – for instance in the case of the so-called Mozart effect, where playing Mozart to infants was deemed to stimulate their spatial-temporal cognition. Yet these materials undoubtedly appeal to middle-class parents anxious that their children should not merely reach developmental norms, but significantly exceed them.

As this implies, the marketing of such goods and services often seeks to appeal to parents' 'better nature' – their sense of what they *should* be doing in order to qualify as Good Parents. This is perhaps most transparently the case with the marketing of home computers, which frequently involves claims about how they can 'help your child to get ahead' in the educational race (Nixon, 1998). Information technology, it is typically argued, will give children an 'educational edge' on the competition and help them 'move to the front of the class'. Indeed, the home computer could be seen as one of the indispensable 'symbolic goods' of contemporary parenting (Cawson et al., 1995).

Likewise, the marketing of educational software to parents emphasizes its ability to 'make homework fun', and thereby enable the child to achieve better results at school (Buckingham et al., 2001). A great deal of the educational software targeted at the domestic market is packaged with explicit claims about its relevance to particular National Curriculum attainment targets or standardized tests. Such packages frequently contain 'assessment technology' that will enable parents to measure their child's progress in acquiring 'essential skills' and 'mastering fundamentals' – although this often sits awkwardly alongside claims about the 'magic' and 'enchantment' that such software affords.

Nevertheless, as this implies, companies are having to target a dual market here. Such material has to satisfy parents' expectations about what counts as valid education, and hence as a worthwhile way for their children to spend their time; and yet, if children are to be persuaded to use it in their leisure, it also has to qualify as pleasurable and entertaining. To some extent, this accounts for the emergence of 'edutainment', a hybrid mix of education and entertainment that relies heavily on visual material, on narrative or game-like formats, and on more informal, less didactic styles of address. At least on the face of it, this material embodies a form of 'popular' pedagogy that is much less authoritarian – and much more 'interactive' – than that of formal schooling. These new forms of 'edutainment' are offered both as an acceptable leisure-time pursuit and as a glamorous alternative to the apparent tedium of much school work. Children, it is typically argued, will gain a competitive edge on their peers – and yet they will not even know that they are learning.

My aim in this chapter is to outline some of the characteristics of this emerging market, focusing particularly on 'edutainment' software such as CD-ROMs, games and websites. The chapter concentrates in turn on the production of such media and the changing strategies of the educational software industry; the design, form and pedagogy of these digital texts; and the ways in which they are used by consumers, both parents and children. The material here is drawn primarily from two substantial empirical projects, which involved interviews with industry personnel, analysis of selected products and surveys and interviews with parents and children.[2]

Selling learning: educational software

The market in educational software needs to be understood in relation to broader tendencies in the media industries. As I have noted (chapter 5), the contemporary media are characterized by substantial commercial competition. There has been a concentration of ownership, in both production and distribution, and a degree of technological convergence, largely as a result of digitization. Companies increasingly have to think on a global scale, and to develop properties that can be marketed across a range of media platforms. While successful companies are generating greater profits, the pace of change has also created a considerable degree of instability and uncertainty. In many ways, the key imperative is one of *risk management*: strong branding, series publishing and cross-media promotion are key means of regulating demand and ensuring a degree of predictability in the marketplace. In the field of education, however, provision is also directly affected by government policy. The National Curriculum and national testing provide a very clear indication of what 'counts' as valid learning, and hence a powerful means of regulating and predicting consumer demand. This is the case in well-established areas such as book publishing (see Buckingham and Scanlon, 2003a), as well as in new media.

In fact, the market for educational CD-ROMs, which expanded rapidly during the late 1990s, has now effectively stagnated. Part of the reason for this is obviously to do with competition from the internet (which I will consider in more detail below); but there are other reasons too. As in print

publishing, the overriding tendency within the educational software industry is towards monopoly, or at least oligopoly. The UK's four leading
educational software companies are all owned by global multinationals:
TLC (formerly The Learning Company) and Europress are owned by the
US-based toy companies Mattel and Hasbro respectively; Havas is owned
by the French-based media corporation Vivendi; and the fourth is Disney.
Dorling Kindersley, formerly one of the UK's market leaders, was taken
over in 2000 by the media conglomerate Pearson, and is now no longer
producing software. Before these takeovers, Europress had been a family-
owned company for thirty years, and Dorling Kindersley was owned by
its founder, Peter Kindersley.

The scope for innovation in the field of software publishing is less than
in the case of books, since the costs of entry into the market, and the costs
of production, are much higher. Here, smaller companies are significantly
more vulnerable. Because of the high production costs, software must be
even more clearly designed for a global market than is the case with books.
Changing the language on a CD-ROM is relatively straightforward,
although accents may also have to be changed (most US CDs are 'revoiced'
for the UK market); but the cost of changing the visual design of an interactive product is generally prohibitive.

The general uncertainty within this sector has of course been accentuated by the rapid pace of technological change. During the 1990s, the
market in reference books was severely hit by the advent of CD-ROMs,
and particularly by the practice of 'bundling' *Encarta* and other reference
works with the purchase of home computers. However, the market in
CD-ROMs is now in turn being undermined by the popular dissemination
of the internet, which is arguably much more effective both in terms of
the quantity of information and in terms of searchability.

This development has specific implications for particular areas of
content. Software publishers are keen to avoid replicating the kind of
material that they believe is more effectively provided on the internet (for
example, in an area such as geography); although the high level of parental
anxiety surrounding 'adult' content on the internet, together with the
degree of specialism and linguistic difficulty of much web-based material,
may still work in favour of age-targeted CD-ROMs. However, several
software publishers are taking advantage of technological convergence and
attempting a 'multi-platform' approach, for example by linking books or
CD-ROMs with specially selected sites, or using a CD-ROM purchase as
the basis for a limited-time subscription to dedicated sites from which
additional material can be downloaded.

In future, it seems likely that educational content will be produced for a range of media formats, in line with the general tendency towards 'multimedia synergy' or 'integrated marketing'. For instance, the use of licensed characters may be more likely to occur in the educational software market in future, as a result of the concentration of ownership described above. However, publishers are also wary about upsetting brand identities. Some argue that associating entertainment characters with educational products may undermine both aspects. Furthermore, hitting the right time is crucial when it comes to media tie-ins – Dorling Kindersley effectively went bankrupt following an ill-advised attempt to cash in on a new *Star Wars* film – and may be less appropriate for educational products, which are intended to have a longer shelf-life.

As in book publishing, the logic here is to capitalize on existing successes rather than to take the risk of new or one-off products. CD-ROM series such as 'Reader Rabbit', 'Adi', 'Learning Ladder' and (formerly) Dorling Kindersley's 'Explorer' have a defined brand identity that – among other things – can provide a substantial visual presence in shop displays. Publishers also seek to build long-term brand loyalty through offering a range of titles that progress up the age range, and this also offers economies of scale in terms of production costs. Although brand identities can become stale, the inevitable result is a form of conservatism: texts are produced according to a formula which can be repeated across different subject matter. Here again, the companies that are best placed to benefit from this situation are those that already have well-established brand identities; and, as a result, the scope for innovation on the part of smaller companies or new entrants to the market is bound to be reduced.

These tendencies have been accentuated by the retailing of educational software – which, at least in Britain, has proven to be particularly problematic. Very few high-street stores specialize in software, and most of their business is in games. Large computer stores tend to focus primarily on hardware, and are notoriously alienating for female customers (who may be more likely than fathers to be looking for educational packages for their children). There are multi-purpose high-street outlets, which tend to have very limited display space and can only stock a small range of titles; and in Britain – unlike, for example, in France – specialist bookstores have generally been reluctant to stock software. In comparison with books, software packages are also quite highly priced, and are unlikely to be seen as an 'impulse buy'. In general, it is impossible to try out such programs before you buy, which means that the packaging is vital, but the fact that the boxes are therefore relatively large inevitably reduces the range of titles that can be stocked or displayed. Finally, there are few sources of independent advice about available titles – or even advertising – available to potential consumers.

To some degree, government policy would appear to offer software publishers and retailers a degree of predictability and security. As I have noted, the market is heavily dominated by the imperatives of national testing. In some large computer stores, what used to be called the 'education' or 'learning' section is now called simply 'National Curriculum'. The packaging of educational software frequently includes prominently displayed claims about its relevance to national tests; and some packages make great play of their 'state-of-the-art assessment technology', which enables parents to test their children's progress against SAT targets. This is likely to be even more the case with software than with books, given the instability of the industry, the high production costs and the high price to the consumer. To a much greater extent than with books, the (parent) consumer needs to be provided with significant grounds to *justify* their purchase.

As a result, the range of educational material available on CD-ROM is currently dominated by reference works and drill-and-practise packages; and it is likely to become even narrower in the future. There is limited scope for innovation within the industry, as smaller producers are being marginalized and larger companies are concentrating on 'safer' material. Meanwhile, few consumers know what is available or where to go in order to buy it. For this and other reasons (to be discussed below), the use of educational software in the home is often failing to live up to the promises that have been made on its behalf.

Learning online

If the prognosis for educational software is not good, it remains to be seen whether the internet will provide a more profitable alternative. Here again, economic uncertainties exercise a considerable constraint on the kinds of material that are made available to the consumer.

Online learning is an industry that is only just beginning to take shape, with many different players jostling for position in what is becoming a very competitive market. In the UK, a few of the companies involved have a public remit to offer educational content, such as the BBC and Channel 4. Others are commercial companies with a stake in other media, for example Granada, Pearson, the *Times Educational Supplement* and *The Guardian*. Software companies such as Europress and TLC are particularly interested in the possibilities of the internet because of the decline in the CD-ROM market, and some companies (such as RM) which originally supplied ICT hardware are diversifying into new markets, including educational websites. Meanwhile, other companies (from McDonalds to Cadbury's) are using broadly 'educational' sites as a means of promoting their own products or services; and of course there is a wide range of non-profit organizations, schools and individuals creating educational sites.

One of the main issues facing commercial companies is how to make a return on their investment. Subscription and advertising are two of the leading possibilities. Spark Learning, for example, is a medium-sized e-learning company that has developed an elaborate system for generating income based on advertising, subscription fees from parents and schools, and sponsorship from London Electricity. In addition, its site has links to the high-street store W. H. Smith and other retailers. Spark Learning has also partnered with the BBC to produce a range of books, magazines and CD-ROMs. Other such companies have developed sites which can only be used in conjunction with other media, either print or digital: so, for example, Pearson has a study guides package, comprising online testing and resources which can be accessed only by students who have purchased the books.

One of the problems with charging a subscription fee is that consumers have become so accustomed to free content on the internet that it may now be difficult to persuade them to pay. While subscription is an established method for pornography (Di Filippo, 2000), it seems less likely to be effective in relation to education – even for parents who identify education as one of the reasons for buying a computer in the first place. Some companies have attempted to operate on a 'loss-leader' principle, and several sites that started out as free services are now subject to a subscription or pay-per-view charge – although this approach is only feasible for companies who can sustain losses in the short term. Getting parents to subscribe to another product (such as a magazine) which is linked to the website may be another way of overcoming this barrier. Meanwhile, the government's funding to schools for online resources via its e-learning credits initiative may provide a boost for this sector – although this may be offset by the BBC's new service 'BBC Jam', which is free to both homes and schools. Even with additional funding, schools may be more likely to recommend free sites, on the basis that these will be accessible to a greater number of children at home (see Scanlon and Buckingham, 2003).

Advertising and sponsorship raise different problems. As I have noted, the internet is increasingly being used as a means of advertising to children

(Fabos, 2004; Seiter, 2005), though it is generally considered far less acceptable to advertise on *educational* websites. For example, the eligibility rules for the DfES's Curriculum Online portal state that advertising should be kept to a minimum. Despite this, marketeers have found ways of introducing advertising, product placements and company branding into educational sites. Indeed, there appear to be some contradictions in the DfES's policy here, since there are several commercial sites linked to the National Grid for Learning and to Gridclub, its official site for seven- to eleven-year-olds.

In some instances, of course, the website is not intended to generate direct revenue in its own right, and so immediate profit is not the issue. This is most obviously the case for 'amateur' providers, and for promotional sites such as Cadbury's (whose main business is selling chocolate). In other cases, publishers are putting samples of material on the internet as a form of advertising for their books, while some companies have tried to target the home market by combining online content with small-group and online tuition (albeit with little success to date). Given the difficulties in generating revenue from the internet, companies with interests in other areas are currently at a significant advantage – as are publishers in other media, who have libraries of available content that can be transferred to the new medium, often with minimal interactivity (generating what is sometimes described as 'shovelware').

Established media companies also have a huge advantage in terms of reaching their target audience. For example, broadcasters will advertise their own websites, or provide programmes which are linked to websites, and the sites can also serve as a means of selling merchandise related to programmes. For smaller companies, reaching the target audience is far more difficult, and the home market is significantly more elusive than schools. There is relatively little market research, and little or no advertising of websites in publications which target the home market, for example parenting or computer magazines. At the same time, company branding is likely to prove particularly important in this market. Given the amount and diversity of content available on the web, and the lack of 'quality control', both schools and parents may be inclined to choose well-known brands such as the BBC or Channel 4, thereby making the task of the smaller, lesser-known companies even more difficult.

In practice, producers argue that the way to reach the home is through the school, particularly if schools give a direct endorsement of a particular site – thereby indicating yet another way in which private companies are using public institutions as a means of commercial marketing. The advent of 'learning platforms', which allow children to have access at home to material they use in school (see chapter 2), may also enable some companies to target both the home and the school market. Here again, smaller companies are bound to find it harder to survive, and may have little option but to work with larger conglomerates.

BBC Jam – the BBC's 'digital curriculum' – clearly exemplifies this tendency. As a well-established, publicly funded multimedia corporation, the BBC is ideally placed to play a leading role in the e-learning market. It has a strong brand and a reputation for producing educational materials for homes and schools. It has access to content and expertise, and its websites can be linked to other media products, for which customers have to pay. It has effectively been given permission by the government to use licence fee income to fund its e-learning provision – despite the fact that this will not be accessible to all licence fee payers. It is perhaps not surprising that its activities in this area have attracted such widespread opposition, not just from its commercial rivals, but also from defenders of public service broadcasting (see Scanlon and Buckingham, 2003).

Here again, there is a significant gap between the emerging reality of e-learning and the rhetoric that has often accompanied it. The notion that the web would result in a decentralized communication environment and the rise of an artisanal 'cottage industry' of producers – envisaged by, among others, Nicholas Negroponte (1995) – has not been borne out. Ultimately, as is also the case with book publishing, the tendency may be for the home market to be led by developments in the schools market. As I have suggested, the schools market is more predictable and more easily reached and, at least in the short term, it is also more immediately lucrative. One consequence of this is that the available content necessarily comes to be dominated by the National Curriculum. There are few commercial incentives for companies to provide diverse and innovative content, or to cater for areas outside the core National Curriculum subjects, particularly as the market becomes more competitive. In these respects, the combination of market forces and the influence of government policy is bound to result in a narrowing both of the available content and in terms of what *counts* as meaningful learning.

The limits of interactivity

As I have noted, educational software is frequently sold on the basis of strong claims about its relevance to the National Curriculum and to standardized testing. According to one manufacturer we interviewed, simply changing the packaging in order to emphasize such traditionally educational claims – 'covers the whole Key Stage 1 maths curriculum' – resulted in significant increases in sales. Indeed, software that is imported from other countries is often repackaged specifically in order to emphasize such claims (Buckingham and Scanlon, 2003a). However, such marketing is also characterized by arguments about the value of 'interactivity'. It is in this respect that CD-ROMs are seen to have the advantage over older media – and it is this quality of interactivity that is often seen to guarantee 'fun' and to ensure children's motivation to learn. Yet to what extent are such claims justified?

Advocates of digital technology in education are often dismissive of the majority of commercially produced CD-ROMs, and of the 'marketing hype' that surrounds them. For example, Aldrich et al. (1998: 321) claim that such packages are 'poorly constructed, consisting simply of a mishmash of images, sounds and video that offer little more than light entertainment'. Lydia Plowman (1996a: 263) argues that educational packages are often no more than 'electronic books . . . betraying the material's origin in a different format and failing to maximise the potential of a new medium'. John Robertson (1998) argues that the multimedia encyclopaedias and edutainment packages that now dominate the market have a degree of superficial sophistication, but are much less 'interactive' and 'empowering' than the software tools that were available in the 'golden age' of educational computing in the 1980s. Seymour Papert (1996) likewise condemns the more popular 'instructional', back-to-basics software packages, particularly those which attempt to 'deceive' children into believing that they are simply playing a game.

To some degree, this is a matter of economics. As I have noted, the production budgets of most educational software packages are minuscule compared with those of the majority of commercial games. Such packages are often poorly designed, which creates difficulties even for quite 'computer literate' users. In our research on educational software (Buckingham and Scanlon, 2003a) we encountered problems that will be familiar to many users, and which were echoed by some of the parents whom we asked to evaluate them: programs would refuse to install (or uninstall); they would quit unexpectedly because an error of type 67 occurred; or they would plague the user with seemingly arbitrary menus or instructions. In several instances, so-called intuitive interfaces appeared to leave too much to the imagination: we were occasionally left facing a frozen screen, not knowing where to click in order to proceed, or alternatively were carried along on a particular sequence, not knowing how to escape from it. Even when one has mastered the interface, there is a sense in which much of the content of a CD-ROM is discovered quite accidentally: there are often 'secrets' in multimedia whose existence may not be known, and which may therefore be impossible to discover (Plowman, 1996b).

The gap between such packages and commercial games will be glaringly apparent to most children, however much their parents may encourage them to play educational games on the computer. To move from 'Tomb Raider' to Dorling Kindersley's 'Become a World Explorer', or from 'The Adventures of Zelda' to 'Adi's Attic' (Knowledge Adventure), is to move from a world that is challenging and compulsive to one that must quickly seem impoverished and constraining. While the graphics and sound environments of educational packages are much more limited, it is the lack of profound interactivity that is particularly striking.

Researchers have outlined several dimensions or levels of interactivity in educational packages (e.g. Laurillard, 1987; Sims, 1997), but the fundamental variables are to do with the degree of control offered to the learner and the nature and extent of the feedback that is provided. These dimensions vary between different 'genres' of CD-ROM packages. For example, in the case of so-called living books, much of the interactivity is relatively superficial. Here, each screen (or page) contains a wealth of animated objects that can be activated by the user. Yet, as Aldrich et al. (1998) suggest, the interactivity here is largely a matter of 'physical activities at the interface': the user 'acts' (for example, by clicking on an object or an icon) and the computer responds. This kind of 'reactive interactivity' can often be quite gratuitous: the user clicks aimlessly, more or less at random, and is rewarded with 'humorous' noises and pieces of animation – albeit at the expense of becoming distracted from the ongoing narrative.

Likewise, the 'drill-and-skill' packages that tend to dominate the market tend to employ very limited forms of interactivity. Most of these packages focus on providing practice in decontextualized 'skills' (for example in literacy and numeracy), or on fact-based subject content (such as science or history). The learner can adjust the level or pace of questioning, but their input is generally confined to selecting from a range of multiple-choice options. In fact, such packages rarely attempt to *teach*: they are more likely to confine themselves to *testing* skills or knowledge that learners are assumed to have already acquired. Feedback is generally provided only in the form of test scores, and success is reinforced by rewards that are often extrinsic to the activity itself (such as the opportunity to play a game, as in the case of the 'Maths Blaster' series). The interactivity here is essentially linear and hierarchical, and it reflects a narrowly behaviourist conception of learning (Seiter, 2005: 4–6).

By contrast, what we have termed 'exploration' packages do tend to provide a greater degree of control for the user. These packages typically invite the user to find their way through a particular landscape or location, in which a range of different types of information or activities may be embedded. They generally offer a variety of ways of searching and navigating one's way through the available material. Most educational packages of this kind (such as Dorling Kindersley's 'Explorer' series) contain written text alongside games, quizzes and competitions, as well as short animations and various 'bells and whistles' that attempt to make information retrieval 'fun'. Even so, the feedback to the user is often minimal, and is mostly confined to support in the form of help messages. Here again, the material is largely in the form of decontextualized 'facts' and, in a sense, the key activity is more like *browsing* than purposeful information retrieval. In this sense, the learning that occurs here is akin to a game of 'Trivial Pursuit', and there are clearly significant questions about how far the mere accumulation of information might be seen to lead to genuine knowledge.

Interactivity is more at a premium in educational simulation games. 'Sim Town', for example, a 'junior' version of 'Sim City', is a town planning simulation that allows users to create their own town using a 'tool box' consisting of roads, buildings, utilities and so on; animated people then appear to occupy the town, multiplying seemingly uncontrollably. In this sense, the game provides both a high degree of control, or at least a great many choices, and a developed form of feedback – in that the user sees the consequences of those choices, for example in the form of overcrowding, pollution, floods or fires. Such packages provide a simulated context in which performance (skills, recall of knowledge) is made to *matter* at a level that goes beyond simply getting a score on a test; and, in this respect, they avoid the largely decontextualized approach of the other genres discussed above. As such, they are likely to prove much more engaging, particularly over the longer term. Even so, the direct relationship between choices and consequences is not made explicit: one can watch the development of one's town, or simply click away hoping to succeed through trial and error, but the lack of explanation means that the user may miss some of the broader conceptual principles that are at stake.

As this implies, 'interactivity' takes many different forms and serves many different purposes. Yet in many cases, it seems to amount to little more than a marketing promise, or a superficial ornament. Compared with the experience of many computer games, the interactivity afforded by most educational software must ultimately be seen as quite impoverished.

Learning (and playing) online

To what extent do these criticisms apply to online resources, in the form of educational websites specifically targeted at the home market? Our analysis of two such sites (Buckingham and Scanlon, 2004) points to some significant limitations in the kinds of material currently on offer. We looked at two UK sites aimed at primary school children: Gridclub, the official DfES site provided by Channel 4 (in partnership with Intuitive Media and Oracle); and Spark Island, a smaller subscription site produced by Spark Learning and sponsored by London Electricity. Both sites feature a range of educational activities, including quizzes, games and compilations of 'surprising facts', while Gridclub also offers production software (for example for generating music or drawings) and message boards.

Both sites seek to adopt a more 'informal' and 'interactive' approach to learning. This is partly manifested in their reliance on visual material and their comparative avoidance of written text. Both also provide a range of ways of navigating, and much of the guidance that is provided is also in a visual form. Even so, there are significant limitations here. Particularly in the case of Spark Island, the restricted bandwidth means that different areas of the site often take a long time to load and there is limited use of sound, while even in Gridclub, which is significantly more extensive, the site is quite hierarchically structured, and it is difficult to move quickly from one area to another. As with the CD-ROMs discussed above, much of the educational content is provided by means of multiple-choice quizzes, 'drill-and-skill' activities and basic information retrieval. Even where production tools are on offer – for example, in Gridclub's 'Art Factory' – the functionality is significantly less than in most commercially available packages.

Predictably, much of the content on both sites is strongly flagged in terms of its relevance to the National Curriculum. In the case of Spark Island, the subscription funding model means that the site has to appeal more directly to parents; and while Gridclub is free to access, it remains an official government-funded site. Even so, the two sites address the learner in rather different ways. Spark Island addresses the family as a whole, implicitly presuming that the site will be accessed by parents and children together (at least for some of the time). It uses a form of 'automated personalization' that will be very familiar to recipients of junk mail, appearing to address the user in person while nonetheless slotting them into a limited range of predetermined categories (or, in this case, National Curriculum 'levels'). By contrast, Gridclub addresses the child more directly, seeking to adopt what one of its producers called a 'cool and edgy' tone. Thus, Gridclub incorporates some elements of 'tween' culture, such as news about pop groups and fashion, and references to parents or family are much less apparent. Even so, there are distinct limits to this 'youth-oriented' approach: news of the latest *Pop Idol* competition or 'what's hot in the shops' sits awkwardly alongside 'SATs Magic' and the 'OWL Literacy Hour Site'. Ivor Goodson et al. (2002) are not alone in criticizing Gridclub's focus on skills practice, or in finding it quite conventionally 'school like'.

Both sites incorporate simple games, mostly in a simple drill-and-practise format or using elements of the action-adventure genre. This is particularly the case in the area of mathematics. Gridclub, for example, includes maths games that involve travelling across a volcanic island, tracking down burglars, or joining 'Battlestar Mathematica's elite fighting force', while, in keeping with its parental appeal, Spark Island is a little more sedate, featuring scenarios based on space travel, racing and card games. However, rather than integrating the mathematical content with the game play, the two are often detached from each other: progress in the game is typically based on answering decontextualized arithmetic questions that have no relevance to the scenario or the narrative of the game. As with the 'drill-and-skill' packages described above, the user is given no credit for knowing how to approach the problem, even if they get the answer wrong, and no support or feedback beyond being told whether or not they are correct. In this respect, the sites appear to reinforce a dominant view of mathematics as a matter of mastering disembodied skills, and as a subject of absolutes in which the learner is either right or wrong.

Furthermore, the 'entertainment' elements of these games are typically contained in the visual mode, whereas the 'educational' elements are contained in written text – which further reinforces the detachment between them. In terms of game theory (see Scanlon et al., 2005), the 'ludic' elements of such games (that is, their challenges and rewards) are largely extraneous to the learning: they provide only *extrinsic* motivation, rather than motivation that is intrinsic to the main activity at hand (cf. Covington and Mueller, 2001). As a result, the incentives to play are quite limited. When we discussed these games with children, they were predictably scathing about their limitations when compared with 'real' computer games; and if they played them at all, they would set them to the easiest setting, enabling them to bypass most of the educational content and go directly to the game. As this implies, such attempts to 'make maths fun' by means of computer games are at best superficial and at worst self-defeating: games are by no means automatically motivating.

There are various reasons for the limitations of these sites. To some extent, they are technical and economic – to do with constraints on bandwidth, and the lack of investment that is needed to create highly interactive sites. They might also be attributed to a failure of imagination – an inability to recognize the unique 'affordances' of the new medium (Livingstone, 2002: 245), or indeed to take the pleasures of popular culture sufficiently seriously. However, they are also symptomatic of the broader difficulties in seeking to combine 'education' and 'entertainment' (see Buckingham and Scanlon, 2003a). Indeed, in some respects it is the very formulation of the problem in this way that causes the difficulty. It seems to rest on an assumption that we need to sugar the pill – that learning is somehow inherently unpalatable, and that it has to be disguised with a coating of pleasure. Yet it could be argued that all entertainment is educational, in the sense that somebody is bound to learn something from it, and that all education has to be entertaining, in the literal sense of having to engage the learner. As Marshall McLuhan once said, 'anyone who tries to make a distinction between education and entertainment doesn't know the first thing about either of them.' If we are seeking to re-engage disaffected learners, we need to do more than adorn teaching materials with computerized bells and whistles – to 'jazz up' the curriculum with a superficial gloss of kid-friendly digital culture. Dressing up SATs tests or multiplication tables with a veneer of 'fun' is a strategy that most children quickly see through.

Learning coming home

To what extent, and in what ways, are these kinds of 'edutainment' materials actually used in the home? Research suggests that, while many parents buy computers in order to support their children's education, they are used predominantly for 'non-educational' purposes; and likewise, while some parents invest considerable amounts of money in educational software, it is often left unused. While some parents are keen to monitor their children's activities on the computer – particularly on the grounds of 'safety' – few spend significant amounts of time collaborating with their children in using software or the internet. All the research would suggest that children's uses of computers in the home are dominated by playing games, by information-seeking related to hobbies or other media enthusiasms, and (increasingly) by instant messaging and participation in social networking sites. While children do use computers for specific homework assignments, the spontaneous use of educational software remains very limited (Facer et al., 2003; Livingstone and Bovill, 1999; Papadakis, 2001; Roberts et al., 2003).

In an early study, conducted well before the widespread dissemination of the internet, Joseph Giacquinta et al. (1993) found that uses of educational software in the home were extremely rare, even in families with relatively high levels of enthusiasm and technical knowledge. Few parents had the time or the expertise to support their children's use of such material, and mothers in particular were less enthusiastic about computers in general – although they typically played a more important role than fathers in supporting their children's education. The parents seemed to regard the *provision* of the computer as the limit of their educational role. They were reluctant to buy expensive software that they were unable to test before purchase, and they often had a low opinion of the packages they had seen. Meanwhile, schools were generally failing to integrate computers into subject learning, and were not interested or able to support their use in the home. As Giacquinta et al. suggest, the extent to which computers actually deliver on their educational 'promise' depends on the social context and the social relationships that surround them – or what they call the 'social envelope'. As with teachers (see chapter 4), the extent to which parents engage with the technology depends on whether they see it as having real benefits, and on whether it coincides with their own priorities as parents.

These general findings are supported by several other studies. Our research on children's uses of 'creative' multimedia software, conducted in the mid-1990s, found that, while children were certainly aware of the potential of the technology, they were rarely in a position to exploit it (Sefton-Green and Buckingham, 1996). They understood in principle what their *computers* could do – for example in digital animation, design, sound and video editing, and 'multimedia authoring' – but they rarely engaged in such activities themselves. Some of the reasons for this were essentially 'technical', and in this respect the machines (or the advertisements for them) seemed to promise more than they were capable of delivering. However, there were also some important social reasons why the technology was not living up to its creative potential. Very few parents knew how to support their children in using the computer in this way, although children in middle-class families, whose parents or relatives were often more familiar with technology, were in a better position. This lack of social connectedness was also reflected in the absence of an *audience* for this material. Children described how they would show their productions to their mum or stick their designs on their bedroom wall, but otherwise nobody ever saw or knew about them – a striking contrast with the intensely sociable culture of computer gaming.

More recently, Lucinda Kerawalla and Charles Crook (2002, 2005) have again pointed to the underuse of educational software in the home. Logging children's use of computers, they found that almost two-thirds of their time was spent on playing commercial games, and that the 'educational' games that were widely available in most of the homes in their study were used for less than 10 per cent of the time. Even where several edutainment titles were freely provided to the families, the novelty quickly wore off, and in several cases the packages were left unopened (Kerawalla and Crook, 2005). These authors suggest that many parents do not get involved because their children are resistant to them adopting a 'teacherly' role, and parents themselves may also be uneasy about 'orchestrating' educational activities for their children on the computer (Kerawalla and Crook, 2002: 768–9). This is not to say that the children did not need support in using the software – several of them ran into difficulties, or failed to discover potentially useful features. Even so, several parents found the glossy publicity images of family togetherness around the computer quite unreal, and even laughable. As these authors conclude, the 'ecology' of family life may well prove quite resistant to this kind of educational use: as one parent memorably put it, 'it's a bit like exercise machines, you have great intentions but the reality's a bit different' (ibid.: 765).

This gap between the educational aspirations that surround home computers and the realities of everyday use was also apparent in our own research (Buckingham and Scanlon, 2003a, 2003b). Here too, education was cited as one of the reasons for buying the computer in the first place, yet there were mixed feelings about whether it was being used in the manner originally intended. Some parents found that their children were only willing to use the computer for games, and complained that educational software was 'boring', while others were concerned because their children seemed to be abandoning books. Ultimately, however, most parents seemed unwilling to force the issue: they accepted that their children were unlikely to enjoy a didactic approach to education in the home, and that they would often leave materials unused for this reason.

Our research suggests that there is a clear 'educational divide' between parents who are able to invest in such resources and those who are not. In line with other large-scale surveys, we found that personal computers and internet access were more likely to be available in middle-class families, and significantly less available in single-parent families and in families where parents were unemployed. The latter were also less likely to buy educational software, to use educational websites, or to buy information books. Middle-class parents were also more likely to say that they helped their children with their homework.

However, class was not the only factor in play here. In our in-depth interviews with parents across a range of social class backgrounds, we found quite different orientations to education which were only partly to do with parents' own class 'trajectories' (cf. Reay, 1988). While some parents were quite assiduous in supporting their children's homework, others resisted the idea that they should be seen as surrogate teachers. Even so, the majority of parents experienced a degree of pressure to support their children's school work at home, and to invest in home tutoring, additional private lessons, home computers and educational materials. Obviously, for those who have fewer economic resources, this option is less available, and to pursue it may require some difficult choices; and as such, the commercialization of out-of-school learning seems almost bound to exacerbate educational inequalities.

In our analysis, we identified three distinct types of computer buyers: the 'enthusiasts', the 'resisters' and the 'followers'. The enthusiasts believed strongly in the educational potential of computers, even though some of them appeared to know little about computers themselves: they seemed to feel that, although it was too late for them to learn, they did not want their children to 'miss out'. The 'resisters', some of whom were relatively affluent, seemed to have reluctantly given in to the need for a home computer. Some expressed resentment that marketeers were 'blackmailing' parents into buying computers by appealing to anxieties about their children's education, while others argued that books were more reliable sources of information, and that the internet provided too many opportunities for 'cheating'. Ultimately, however, they were resigned to the necessity of what one called 'joining the rest of the planet'. The majority of the parents we interviewed were somewhere between these two positions, and could be described as 'followers': although they had some reservations about computers, they seemed to feel that computers were something that everyone had, and therefore they had to get one too.

In some families, there was an ongoing struggle between 'new' and 'old' media, which partly reflected generational and gender differences. The older children (aged eleven to thirteen), particularly the boys, expressed considerable enthusiasm for the internet in preference to books as a source of information. However, several mothers expressed a personal preference for books, and regret or discomfort regarding computers. Fathers tended to be seen as experts on computers, although mothers were still primarily responsible for their children's learning in the home. As Giacquinta et al. (1993) also found, there may be a danger of a new 'education gap' emerging here, along the lines of gender as well as social class.

Having bought a computer, however, several of the parents in our sample found that it was not being used in the way they had hoped. They reported that their children were unwilling to use educational software packages more than once because they found them repetitive and simplistic. Few families were making extensive use of educational software. Parents did not necessarily know about the software that was available, or where to obtain it; and the fact that it cannot generally be previewed prior to purchase was a significant disincentive, as compared with books. Several of the parents and children whom we interviewed had invested in software that turned out to be of poor quality, or did not live up to the promises of its packaging. Most had bought little beyond the packages that came 'bundled' with the computer itself.

We found similar responses when it came to educational uses of the internet (Buckingham and Scanlon, 2003b). Here again, parents reported that their children tended to use the internet for entertainment rather than education. Some argued that this was because their children were too young to be using it on a regular basis for education: when computers were used in this way, it was usually for school assignments in subjects such as history or geography. Broadly speaking, children appeared to be accessing sites which were little more than books in digital form – thereby providing support for parental complaints that the internet does not provide anything which children could not get from books. Nonetheless, children generally preferred using the computer to reading books for information: although they did not always seem to know where to go on the internet to find the information they needed, they still preferred this method to using catalogues and book indexes in the library. Their schools did not often recommend sites, and children generally found sites by using search engines. Alternatively, they would return to a site they had found useful in the past or go to well-known sites such as the BBC, reflecting the importance of branding (as noted above). None of the parents was especially proactive in terms of helping their child locate educational sites, and none said they would be inclined to pay to subscribe to such a site.

Although all the families in our study had good internet access (in some cases for several years), we found little evidence of intensive use of educational sites. There were several reasons for this: parents' lack of knowledge of the sites available; the limited nature of homework assignments; the greater appeal for children of other (entertainment) uses of the computer; technical difficulties in accessing sites; and the lack of engagement offered by the sites that were known to be available. Here again, many years after Giacquinta et al.'s early study (1993), it would seem that the educational promise of home computing is still a long way from realization.

Conclusion

The domestic market in 'edutainment' media has significantly expanded in recent years, partly due to initiatives from government, but also as a result of the industry's continuing drive to generate new sources of profit. Government policy on education has placed a growing competitive pressure on parents and children; and one response to this is to spend money on goods and services that appear to guarantee educational advantage – although of course this is an option that is not equally available to all. Yet despite their aspirations and good intentions, there is little evidence that parents are actually supporting their children's educational uses of computers in the home. One key reason for this is simply that much of the educational material available is limited and of poor quality – and children find it significantly less engaging than most of the other things they can do with computers. As I have suggested, these limitations can be seen at least partly as a consequence of the constraints imposed by the commercial market.

However, the most significant reason for this failure may be to do with the inherent differences between the social context of the home and the context of the school. The idea – promoted by some enthusiasts for educational computing – that new technology will automatically result in new, more liberating styles of 'informal learning' in the home seems somewhat questionable. To say the least, such expectations may be out of step with the everyday realities of family life. The 'ecology' or 'social envelope' of the home is very different from that of the school – and, many would argue, necessarily so. By and large, children do not wish to spend their free time engaging in anything that closely resembles school work, and many parents also resist the idea that they should be regarded as surrogate teachers. Indeed, as the kinds of learning that are promoted within formal education become ever narrower and more reductive, it may be that children will be more and more inclined to resist the pressure to learn outside school. Anxious parents may represent a 'soft touch' for marketeers, but children may not be so easily persuaded.

8

Digital Media Literacies[1]

An Alternative Approach to Technology in Education

I have argued that there is a widening gulf between many young people's experiences of media technology outside school and the ways in which it is currently being employed in the classroom. For more experienced users, these increasingly appear to be two quite separate worlds. So how can we bridge this 'new digital divide'? In the two preceding chapters, I have considered two potential answers to this question that I believe are fundamentally misguided.

Advocates of computer games in education have made a strong case for the kinds of learning that some games undoubtedly entail. Yet they have tended to provide a narrowly celebratory account which fails to address many of the broader social, economic and cultural dimensions of games. The implications of these arguments for schools are also far from clear: all we have are generalized prescriptions for more 'playful' forms of learning, or suggestions for educational uses of games that are (to say the least) undeveloped. Past experiences of using computer games in the classroom point to some very significant problems and difficulties that have yet to be adequately addressed.

The use of games for learning is typically part of a broader strategy of combining education and entertainment. As we saw in chapter 7, this notion of 'edutainment' – or 'fun learning' – is a key sales pitch for companies targeting the home market, for example with educational software packages and websites. Yet the material that is produced here is often lacking in precisely the qualities that make 'non-educational' media so engaging for children: it is often little more than a repackaging of the traditional curriculum with a superficial gloss of 'techno-popular' culture. Here again, there is little evidence that such materials are being effectively used in the home, or even that children are particularly interested in them.

Both strategies seem to imply that the 'new digital divide' between home and school can be overcome if we simply import elements of the home (or of children's leisure culture) into the school – or indeed vice versa. From this perspective, the use of technology and of aspects of popular culture is seen to be somehow inherently motivating, particularly for 'disenchanted' learners. The so-called digital generation will, it seems, be magically re-engaged in education through the transformative influence of new technology. In my view, such arguments fundamentally misconceive most young people's relationships with technology, and they also dramatically overestimate its power. Furthermore, they seem to misunderstand the nature of the school as a social institution. As we have seen, one reason why such strategies are doomed to fail – or at least are condemned to superficiality – is because the school is inevitably and necessarily a different type of context from the home.

Of course, there are several critics – such as Seymour Papert and James Gee – who appear to regard contemporary schooling as a kind of educational wasteland. Some persistently proclaim that digital technology will result in the imminent demise of the school, although they are typically rather vague as to what will replace it. I will revisit some of these arguments in my final chapter. Personally, I do not share this generalized rejection of the school, nor do I believe that we can afford simply to write it off. On the contrary, my proposals in this chapter are based on a strong sense of what schools should be doing – and, in some instances, already are.

Why media education?

So if these strategies are essentially mistaken, what is the alternative? In this chapter, I argue that schools need to place a central emphasis on developing children's critical and creative abilities with regard to new media – and that we need a form of 'digital media literacy' as a basic educational entitlement. My account draws on a fairly well-established body of educational practice, which (at least in the UK) has a long history – although it has remained largely on the fringes of the mainstream compulsory curriculum (Buckingham, 2003). I intend to provide an overall rationale for this approach, as well as some concrete indications of what it involves in practice and the difficulties that it entails. While there is much that might be said about the potential of informal, out-of-school settings in this respect (see Buckingham et al., 2005), my focus here is primarily on schools.

In line with my broader argument in this book, the emphasis here is not on *technology*, or indeed on *information*, but on *media*. Digital media cannot be adequately understood if we persist in regarding them simply as a matter of machines and techniques, or as 'hardware' and 'software'. The

internet, computer games, digital video, mobile phones and other contemporary technologies provide new ways of mediating and representing the
world, and of communicating. Outside school, children are engaging with
these media not as technologies, but as *cultural forms*. The problem with
most educational uses of such media is that they continue to be regarded
as merely instrumental means of delivering information – in effect, as
neutral tools or 'teaching aids'.

Media education provides a developed alternative to this approach,
which I believe is both more rigorous and more engaging for students. I
define media *education* as the process of teaching and learning about media,
and media *literacy* as the outcome – the knowledge and skills learners
acquire. To some extent, media literacy is something that people gain in
any case through their everyday encounters with the media, and it can
obviously be developed in a range of situations, not just schools. But
schools do have a central role to play here. Media education, as it is now
defined, is both a critical and a creative enterprise. It provides young people
with the critical resources they need to interpret, to understand and (if
necessary) to challenge the media that permeate their lives; and yet it also
offers them the ability to produce their own media, to become active participants in media culture rather than mere consumers. It therefore involves
the rigorous analysis of media texts, in terms of the visual and verbal 'languages' they employ and the representations of the world they make available; the study of the companies and institutions that produce media, and
how they seek to reach their target audiences; and the creative production
of media in a range of genres and formats. (For recent accounts of media
education, see Buckingham, 2003; Burn and Durran, 2007; McDougall,
2006; and for a review of research in the field, Buckingham et al., 2005.)

This contemporary form of media education has evolved over a
comparatively long period: the first proposals for teaching about popular
media in UK schools date back to the early 1930s (Leavis and Thompson,
1933). Historically, schools have often perceived themselves to be caught
up in what Neil Postman (1992) calls a 'media war' (see chapter 3). Teachers have repeatedly been urged to protect children from what are seen as
the harmful influences of the media, and to win them over to what are
believed to be more wholesome pursuits. This approach is often driven by
the kind of superficial 'moral panics' about children and media that routinely make the headlines. We need to teach children about media in order
that they can be saved from violence or premature sexualization or eating
disorders – or indeed from any of the other social ills for which the media
are regularly deemed to be responsible. This approach is still dominant in

some parts of the world – including the United States; but in Britain and in many other countries we have developed a much broader and less protectionist approach that has been informing practice in many schools for several decades.

Contemporary media education does not begin from the view that the media are necessarily and inevitably harmful, or that young people are simply passive victims of media influence. On the contrary, it begins from students' existing knowledge and experience of media, rather than from the instructional imperatives of the teacher. It does not aim to shield young people from the influence of the media, and thereby to lead them on to 'better things', but to enable them to make informed decisions on their own behalf. Rather than seeking to protect children from the media, it aims to develop their *understanding* of, and *participation* in, the media culture that surrounds them (Bazalgette, 1989). Advocates of this approach emphasize the importance of media education as part of a more general form of 'democratic citizenship', although they also recognize the importance of students' enjoyment and pleasure in the media.

Media education has faced an uphill struggle in gaining recognition within the education system, both in the UK and internationally (see Buckingham and Domaille, 2004). Nevertheless, in recent years it has begun to be acknowledged by policy-makers, at least in the field of media. As we move towards a more market-led, technologically rich media environment, governmental regulation of media is focusing increasingly on the need to produce 'informed consumers'. The UK government minister for culture, media and sport, Tessa Jowell, is on record as saying that media literacy is as important for children today as more established subjects such as English, maths and science,[2] and our new media regulator, Ofcom, has a responsibility under the 2003 Communications Act to 'promote media literacy' through its publications and research initiatives. Obviously, media education is more than simply an alternative to media regulation, although (as I shall indicate below) the definition adopted by Ofcom is in fact rather broader than this would imply.

To date, there has been relatively little dialogue between media educators and advocates of technology in education – although such a dialogue is now beginning to develop. As we shall see in this chapter, media educators are increasingly engaging with information and communication technologies, both as objects of study and as means of enabling students to engage in media production. Meanwhile, ICT as a curriculum subject often uses and refers to students' out-of-school experiences of popular culture, not least in attempting to make the work more relevant to their lives.

Growing numbers of ICT teachers are making use of the potential of the technology for creative production – for example, with students producing their own websites. In practice, however, few ICT teachers are concerned with the critical questions that are central to media education, and, as I have argued, a great deal of ICT teaching is based on the decontextualized practice of technological 'skills' (see Somekh, 2004; Watson, 2001). In this respect, media education could be seen to provide the kind of critical and conceptual framework that ICT as a specialist subject currently lacks.

However, these arguments also apply to the use of technology in the curriculum as a whole. As the Italian author Umberto Eco (1979) once wrote about the potential of using television in education: 'if you want to use television to teach somebody, you must first teach them how to use television.' Education *about* the media, he argued, was an indispensable prerequisite for education *with* or *through* the media. The same is true of digital media. If we want to use the internet or games or other digital media to teach, we need to equip students to understand and to critique these media: we cannot regard them simply as neutral means of delivering 'information', and we should not use them in a merely functional or instrumental way.

The literacy metaphor

Over the past twenty years, there have been many attempts to extend the notion of literacy beyond its original application to the medium of writing. As long ago as 1986, one of the leading British researchers in the field, Margaret Meek Spencer, introduced the notion of 'emergent literacies' in describing young children's media-related play (Spencer, 1986), and the call for attention to 'new' or 'multiple' literacies has been made by many authors over subsequent years (Bazalgette, 1988; Buckingham, 1993a; Tyner, 1998; and many others). We have seen extended discussions of visual literacy (e.g. Moore and Dwyer, 1994), television literacy (Buckingham, 1993b), cine-literacy (British Film Institute, 2000), and information literacy (Bruce, 1997). Exponents of the so-called New Literacy Studies have developed the notion of 'multiliteracies', referring both to the social diversity of contemporary forms of literacy and to the fact that new communications media require new forms of cultural and communicative competence (Cope and Kalantzis, 2000).

This proliferation of literacies may be fashionable, but it raises some significant questions. Popular discussions of 'economic literacy', 'emotional literacy' and even 'spiritual literacy' seem to extend the application of the term to the point where any analogy to its original meaning (that is, in relation to written language) has been lost. 'Literacy' comes to be used merely as a vague synonym for 'competence', or even 'skill'. (And it is worth noting in this respect that such analogies are much more difficult to make in other languages, where the equivalent term is more overtly tied to the notion of writing – as in the French word '*alphabétisation*'.)

The term 'literacy' clearly carries a degree of social status, and to use it in connection with other, lower status, forms such as television is thus to make an implicit claim for the latter's validity as an object of study. Yet, as uses of the term multiply, the polemical value of such a claim – and its power to convince – is bound to decline. Thus, while recognizing the significance of visual and audio-visual media, some scholars challenge this extension of the term, arguing that 'literacy' should continue to be confined to the realm of writing (Barton, 1994; Kress, 1997); others dispute the idea that visual media require a process of learning analogous to the learning of written language (Messaris, 1994). The analogy between writing and visual or audio-visual media such as television or film may be useful at a general level, but it often falls down when we look more closely: it is possible to analyse broad categories such as narrative and representation across all these media, but it is much harder to sustain more specific analogies, for example between the film shot and the word, or the film sequence and the sentence (Buckingham, 1989).

So what are the possibilities and limitations of the notion of 'digital literacy'? Is it just a fancy way of talking about how people learn to use digital technologies, or is it something broader than that? Indeed, do we really need *another* literacy?

Defining literacy: the limits of competence

Many educational conceptions of literacy tend to define it in terms of a set of skills or competencies. The definition of media literacy adopted by the UK media regulator Ofcom (2004) – itself an adapted version of an earlier US definition (Aufderheide, 1997) – provides a fairly clear and succinct example of this approach: 'media literacy is the ability to access, understand and create communications in a variety of contexts'. *Access* thus includes the skills and competencies needed to locate media content, using the available technologies and associated software. At least in Ofcom's usage, it also includes the ability to regulate (or self-regulate) access, for example by being aware of potential risks and using regulatory mechanisms and systems of guidance. *Understand* includes the ability to decode or interpret media, for example through an awareness of formal and generic conventions, design features and rhetorical devices. It also involves a knowledge of production processes and of patterns of ownership and institutional control, and an ability to critique media, for example in terms of the accuracy or reliability of their representations of the real world. Finally, *create* involves the ability to use the media to produce and communicate one's own messages, whether for purposes of self-expression or in order to influence or interact with others.

Of these, 'access' is perhaps the easiest to identify and measure – and it may be partly for this reason that much of Ofcom's subsequent research on media literacy has focused on this aspect (e.g. Ofcom, 2006). In terms of official definitions of print literacy (cf. Levene, 1986), access could be seen as a form of *functional* literacy: it is essentially a matter of whether people know enough about media and technology to be able to function in society at a fairly basic level. As we shall see, most definitions of 'digital literacy' (or 'internet literacy' or 'computer literacy') tend to focus more or less exclusively on this dimension of access. By contrast, 'understanding' and 'creativity' are much harder to assess. What *counts* as a valid or legitimate or desirable form of understanding or creativity is not something that can easily be agreed upon.

Indeed, sociological and anthropological studies of print literacy (e.g. Heath, 1983; Street, 1984) have clearly shown that literacy cannot be regarded as merely a set of competencies that live in people's heads. On the contrary, literacy is a phenomenon that is only realized in and through social practices of various kinds. In studying literacy, we cannot confine our attention to the isolated encounter between the reader and the text. We need to take account of the interpersonal context in which that encounter takes place (where the text is read, with whom, and why) as well as the broader social and economic processes that determine how texts are produced and circulated. This implies that literacy is inevitably a contested field. Some manifestations of competence or understanding are bound to be perceived as more socially legitimate than others. As such, literacy is inevitably related to the question of who owns and controls information and the means by which it is generated and distributed. Definitions of literacy are thus necessarily ideological, in that they imply particular norms of social behaviour and particular relationships of power. For this reason, the meaning of literacy is open to negotiation and debate: it is not something that can easily be reduced to a set of skills which can be taught in abstract terms, and then be applied and tested.

Equally controversially, one can argue that literacy also contains a *critical* dimension. When we describe somebody as a 'literate' person, we do not simply mean that he or she is able to read and write. Particularly in an educational context, the notion of literacy generally implies a more reflexive approach. Literacy in this broader sense involves analysis, evaluation and critical reflection. It entails the acquisition of a 'meta-language' – that is, a means of describing the forms and structures of a particular mode of communication – and it involves a broader understanding of the social, economic and institutional contexts of communication, and how these affect people's experiences and practices (Luke, 2000). According to advocates of the 'multiliteracies' approach (Cope and Kalantzis, 2000), literacy education cannot be confined simply to the acquisition of skills or the mastery of particular practices; it must also entail a form of 'critical framing' that enables the learner to take a theoretical distance from what they have learned, to account for its social and cultural location, and to critique and extend it.

Internet literacy: from access to critical understanding

There is undoubtedly a tension here between a broadly social or critical model of media literacy and what we might call a competency-based approach – and this is a tension that needs to be more fully explored. However, most conceptions of 'digital literacy' are a long way from addressing these more complex issues. The notion of digital literacy is not new. Indeed, arguments for 'computer literacy' date back at least to the 1980s. Yet, as Goodson and Mangan (1996) have pointed out, the term is often poorly defined and delineated, both in terms of its overall aims and in terms of what it actually entails. As they suggest, rationales for computer literacy are often based on dubious assertions about the vocational relevance of computer skills, or about the inherent value of learning with computers, of the kind we have considered in earlier chapters. In contemporary usage, digital (or computer) literacy often appears to amount to a minimal set of skills that will enable the user to operate effectively with software tools or to perform basic information-retrieval tasks. This is essentially a *functional* definition: it specifies the basic skills that are required to perform particular operations, but it does not go very far beyond this.

For example, the British government has attempted to define and measure the ICT skills of the population alongside traditional literacy and numeracy as part of its *Skills for Life* survey (Williams et al., 2003). This survey defines these skills at two levels. Level 1 includes an understanding of common ICT terminology; the ability to use basic features of software tools such as word processors and spreadsheets; and the ability to save data, copy and paste, manage files, and standardize formats within documents. Level 2 includes the use of search engines and databases and the ability to make more advanced use of software tools. In the 2003 survey, over half of the sample of adults was found to be at 'entry level or below' (that is, not yet at Level 1) in terms of practical skills. Other research also suggests that adults' ability to use search engines for basic information retrieval, for example, is distinctly limited (Livingstone, van Couvering and Thumim, 2005: 23–4).

Another context in which the notion of digital literacy has arisen in recent years is in relation to online safety. For example, the European Commission's 'Safer Internet Action Plan' has emphasized the importance of internet literacy as a means for children to protect themselves against harmful content. Alongside the range of hotlines, filters and 'awareness nodes', it has funded several educational projects designed to alert children to the dangers of online paedophiles and pornography – although in fact it is notable that many of these projects have adopted a significantly broader conception of internet literacy that goes well beyond the narrow concern with safety. The 'Educaunet' materials, for example, provide guidance on evaluating online sources and assessing one's own information needs, as well as recognizing the necessity and the pleasure of risk for young people (see www.educaunet.org).

Even so, most discussions of internet literacy tend to place the primary emphasis on *information*. The key concern is with locating and using information – and, to a lesser extent, with evaluating and producing it. Yet, as I have argued (chapter 5), it is no longer particularly useful to think merely in terms of 'information technology': with the growing convergence of media (which is driven by economics as much as by technology), the boundaries between 'information' and other media have become increasingly blurred. In most children's leisure-time experiences, computers are much more than devices for information retrieval: they convey images and fantasies, provide opportunities for imaginative self-expression and play, and serve as a medium through which intimate personal relationships are conducted. Recognizing this certainly means broadening our conception of technology – not least in education. 'ICTs' are clearly no longer just a matter of desktop computers, or indeed necessarily of 'computers' at all. However, it also means acknowledging the fact that digital media are *cultural forms* that are inextricably connected with other visual and audio-visual media.

In practice, most approaches to digital literacy are concerned primarily with promoting more efficient uses of the medium – for example, via the development of advanced search skills (or so-called power searching) that will make it easier to locate relevant resources amid the proliferation of online material. This ability to *access* or locate information is undoubtedly important, yet the skills children need in relation to digital media go well beyond this. As with print, they also need to be able to evaluate and use information critically if they are to transform it into knowledge. This means asking questions about the sources of that information, the interests of its producers, and the ways in which it represents the world, and understanding how technological developments and possibilities are related to broader social and economic forces.

Popular guides to the internet have begun to address the need to evaluate online content. For example, Paul Gilster's *Digital Literacy* (1997) is concerned primarily with what he calls the 'survival skills' that users need to locate internet sources. He provides guidance on web searching, engaging in dialogues with web authors, and issues such as copyright online, although he also suggests some approaches to verifying the provenance of online information. Likewise, David Warlick's (2005) *Raw Materials for the Mind: A Teacher's Guide to Digital Literacy* is principally a how-to guide, including step-by-step instructions on setting up internet mailing lists or retrieving information from web pages, as well as suggestions for classroom projects; he too offers brief guidance on evaluating the credibility and reliability of online resources, for example by researching the author or 'backtracking' the URL. As Livingstone, van Couvering and Thumim (2005) point out, there are overlaps here between this notion of digital (or specifically internet) literacy and the older concept of 'information literacy', which derives primarily from library and information sciences.

Ultimately, however, these formulations tend to operate with a fairly functional conception of literacy. They focus on technical 'know-how' and procedures that are relatively easy to acquire, and on skills that are likely to become obsolete fairly rapidly. Much of the discussion appears to assume that information can simply be assessed in terms of its factual accuracy. From this perspective, a digitally literate individual is one who can search efficiently, who compares a range of sources, and who sorts authoritative from non-authoritative and relevant from irrelevant documents (Livingstone, van Couvering and Thumim, 2005: 31). There is little recognition here of the symbolic or persuasive aspects of digital media, of the emotional dimensions of our uses and interpretations of these media, or indeed of aspects of digital media that exceed mere 'information'.

Nicholas Burbules and Thomas Callister (2000) go somewhat further, arguing that web users need to become 'hyperreaders', who are able to read selectively and to evaluate and question the information they encounter online. 'Hyperreaders' will compare different information sources; assess how the authority of sites is claimed and established; analyse who produced the site, and why they did so; and consider what might be absent, and why. These authors draw particular attention to the role of web links, arguing that links in themselves serve rhetorical functions, not least in supporting claims to credibility; as well as guiding and controlling users' access to information, they also express meanings, suggest inferences and ultimately betray particular biases. However, Burbules and Callister challenge the idea that these procedures will necessarily enable the user to arrive at objective truth: rather, the aim is to enable users to become more critically aware of how the medium works – and they argue that this can be effectively achieved not only through analysis, but also by students learning to produce their own hypertexts.

Bettina Fabos (2004) and Ellen Seiter (2005) are more specifically concerned with the commercial dimensions of online information. They draw attention to the increasing role of sponsorship, online marketing, product placement, data mining and other means of gathering commercial information about users; and, as they point out, most young people (and indeed most teachers) are less likely to be aware of these aspects than they are, for example, of the role of commercials on television. As Seiter argues, for most users 'the Internet is more like a [shopping] mall than a library: it resembles a gigantic public relations collection more than it does an archive of scholarship' (2005: 37–8).

Fabos (2004) is particularly concerned about the unthinking use of commercial search engines in schools, and she provides a useful review of schools' attempts to promote more critical evaluation of online content. These typically include addressing issues such as the authorship and sponsorship of sites; the accuracy and objectivity of information; and the currency, scope and depth of sites. However, Fabos argues that such evaluation 'checklists' are often less than effective, and that students may feel inadequate assessing sites when they are unfamiliar with the topics they cover. Her classroom research suggests that, in practice, students largely failed to apply these criteria, instead emphasizing speedy access to information and appealing visual design.

More to the point, however, such 'web-evaluation' approaches appear to presume that objective truth will eventually be achieved through a process of diligent evaluation and comparison of sources. They seem to imply that sites can simply be divided into those that are reliable, trustworthy and factual, and those that are biased and should be avoided. In practice, such approaches often discriminate against low-budget sites produced by individuals and in favour of those whose high-end design features and institutional origins lend them an air of credibility. The alternative, as Fabos suggests, is to recognize that 'bias' is unavoidable, and that information is inevitably 'couched in ideology'. Rather than seeking to determine the 'true facts', students need to understand 'how political, economic, and social context shapes all texts, how all texts can be adapted for different social purposes, and how no text is neutral or necessarily of "higher quality" than another' (Fabos, 2004: 95).

Laura Gurak (2001) makes a similar argument for what she terms 'cyberliteracy'. 'To be truly literate online,' she maintains, 'users must understand the economic and political forces that are shaping information technologies' (2001: 12). As she argues, 'technological literacy' is typically confined to learning how to use a computer and a keyboard, or how to do online searches. By contrast, a *critical* literacy would involve the ability to understand and make informed judgements about the place of technology within society and culture. The internet, she claims, is by no means a neutral technology: it has been socially shaped in particular ways, not least by the powerful commercial, governmental and military interests that have determined its basic architecture. In this sense, as I have argued, the question of literacy is inevitably connected with broader questions of social power.

This position, which Fabos (2004) defines as characteristic of 'critical literacy' research (e.g. Luke, 2000), is also the one adopted by media educators – and, indeed, I would argue that media education has a more concrete and coherent framework for addressing such issues. In the following sections of this chapter, I outline a media educator's approach to digital literacy, focusing firstly on the world wide web, and secondly on computer games.

Media literacy goes online

There are four broad conceptual aspects that are generally regarded as essential components of media literacy. These have been most coherently elaborated over the past twenty years by media educators in the UK and increasingly around the world: a fuller discussion may be found in my book *Media Education* (Buckingham, 2003). While digital media clearly raise new questions and require new methods of investigation, this basic conceptual framework continues to provide a useful means of mapping the field. It may be summarized as follows.

Representation   Like all media, digital media represent the world, rather than simply reflecting it. They offer particular interpretations and selections of reality which inevitably embody implicit values and ideologies. Informed users of media need to be able to evaluate the material they encounter, for example by assessing the motivations of those who created it and by comparing it with other sources, including their own direct experience. In the case of information texts, this means addressing questions about authority, reliability and bias, and it also necessarily invokes broader questions about whose voices are heard and whose viewpoints are represented, and whose are not.

Language   A truly literate individual is able not only to use language, but also to understand how it works. This is partly a matter of understanding the 'grammar' of particular forms of communication, but it also involves an awareness of the broader codes and conventions of particular genres. This means acquiring analytical skills and a meta-language for describing how language functions. Digital literacy must therefore involve a systematic awareness of how digital media are constructed and of the unique 'rhetorics' of interactive communication: in the case of the web, for example, this would include understanding how sites are designed and structured, and the rhetorical functions of links between sites (cf. Burbules and Callister, 2000: 85–90).

Production   Literacy also involves understanding who is communicating to whom, and why. In the context of digital media, young people need to be aware of the growing importance of commercial influences – particularly as these are often invisible to the user. There is a 'safety' aspect to this: children need to know when they are being targeted by commercial appeals, and how the information they provide can be used by commercial corporations. But digital literacy also involves a broader awareness of the global role of advertising, promotion and sponsorship, and how they influence the nature of the information that is available in the first place. Of course, this awareness should also extend to non-commercial sources and interest groups, who are increasingly using the web as a means of persuasion and influence.

Audience   Finally, literacy also involves an awareness of one's own position as an audience (reader or user). This means understanding how media are targeted at audiences, and how different audiences use and respond to them. In the case of the internet, this entails an awareness of the ways in which users gain access to sites, how they are addressed and guided (or encouraged to navigate), and how information is gathered about them. It also means recognizing the very diverse ways in which the medium is utilized, for example by different social groups, and reflecting on how it is used in everyday life – and indeed how it might be used differently. (In some respects, of course, the term 'audience' (which is easily applied to 'older' media) fails to do justice to the interactivity of the internet – although substitute terms are no more satisfactory (Livingstone, 2004)).

Box 8.1 indicates some of the issues that might be addressed in applying this framework specifically to the world wide web, and is developed from Buckingham (2003). It incorporates several of the key concerns of the 'web-evaluation' approaches discussed above, but sets these within a broader context. (Different issues would undoubtedly need to be explored in relation to other uses of the internet, such as e-mail, instant messaging or blogging.)

Box 8.1   The world wide web: issues for study

Representation

- How websites claim to 'tell the truth', and establish their authenticity and authority
- The presence or absence of particular viewpoints or aspects of experience
- The reliability, veracity and bias of online sources
- The implicit values or ideologies of web content, and the discourses it employs

Language

- The use of visual and verbal 'rhetorics' in the design of websites (for example, graphic design principles, the combination of visuals and text, the use of sound)
- How the hypertextual (linked) structure of websites encourages users to navigate in particular ways

- How users are addressed: for example, in terms of formality and 'user-friendliness'
- The kinds of 'interactivity' that are on offer, and the degrees of control and feedback they afford to the user

Production

- The nature of web authorship, and the use of the internet by companies, individuals or interest groups as a means of persuasion and influence
- The technologies and software that are used to generate and disseminate material on the web, and the professional practices of web 'authors'
- The significance of commercial influences, and the role of advertising, promotion and sponsorship
- The commercial relationships between the web and other media such as television and computer games

Audience

- The ways in which users can be targeted by commercial appeals, both visibly and invisibly
- The nature of online 'participation', from web polls to message boards to 'user-generated content' and blogs
- How the web is used to gather information about consumers
- How different groups of people use the internet in their daily lives, and for what purposes
- How individuals or groups use and interpret particular sites, and the pleasures they gain from using them
- Public debates about the 'effects' of the internet, for example in relation to online safety and 'addiction'.

Towards game literacy

The approach outlined here is not only applicable to 'information' media (if indeed the web can any longer be seen as merely a source of 'information'). In principle, it can also be applied to other aspects of digital media, including 'fictional' media such as computer and video games. As we saw in chapter 6, there is a growing interest in using computer games in education – but, here again, most proposals implicitly conceive of games as a neutral 'teaching aid'. In line with Eco's argument about television (quoted above), I would argue that we also need to be teaching young people about games as a *cultural form* – and that this is a necessary prerequisite for using games in order to teach other curriculum areas.

To date, most proposals for teaching about games in schools have been developed by teachers of English or language arts (e.g. Beavis, 1998, 2000). As such, these proposals tend to emphasize the aspects of games that fit most easily with English teachers' traditional literary concerns, for example with narrative or the construction of character. In terms of our four-part framework, the emphasis is on language and to some extent on representation; but there is little engagement with the more sociological issues to do with production and audience that are important concerns for media teachers.

Equally significantly, this quasi-literary approach can lead to a rather partial account of the textual dimensions of games – which itself raises significant issues about the definition of 'game literacy'. Clearly, there are many elements that games share with other representational or signifying systems. On one level, this is a manifestation of the convergence that increasingly characterizes contemporary media: games draw upon books and movies, and vice versa, to the point where the identity of the 'original' text is often obscure. Users (players, readers, viewers) must transfer some of their understandings across and between these media, and to this extent it makes sense to talk about 'literacies' that operate – and are developed – across media (Mackey, 2002). More fundamentally, computer games are almost invariably 'multimodal' texts (Kress and van Leeuwen, 2001) – which is to say that they often combine different communicative modes, such as still and moving images, sounds and music, speech and writing, and so on. Different games (or genres of games) will use and combine these modes to different degrees and in different ways, and this will vary according to the functions the different modes perform. Games also employ broader elements that are similar to, or analogous with, other media. Thus, many games have characters, and it is possible to analyse these characters, for example, in terms of fairly conventional literary criteria (such as the distinction between 'flat' and 'rounded' characters that derives from E. M. Forster, 1927) or in terms of structuralist paradigms (such as the functions of hero, donor, helper and so on identified by Vladimir Propp, 1970). Many games also have, or use, narratives, and it is possible to analyse these narratives, for example, in terms of semiotics (e.g. Hodge and Tripp, 1986) or narrative theory (e.g. Genette, 1980). These are among the approaches applied in our analysis of role-playing and action-adventure games (Carr et al., 2006).

However, analysing games simply in terms of these representational dimensions produces at best a partial account. For example, characters in games function both in the traditional way as representations of human (or indeed non-human) 'types' and as points of access to the action; but the crucial difference is that they can be manipulated, and in some instances positively changed, by the player (Burn and Schott, 2004). Likewise, many games contain and depend upon narratives to provide motivation and engagement, and yet narratives can also be developed by players, albeit in different ways in different circumstances. This points to the necessary interpenetration of the *representational* and the *ludic* dimensions of games – that is, the aspects that make games *playable* (Carr et al., 2006).

So is there also a 'literacy' that applies to the ludic dimension of games? There is a growing literature, both in the field of game design and in academic research, that seeks to identify basic generative and classificatory principles in this respect (e.g. Jarvinen, 2003; Salen and Zimmerman, 2003; Wolf and Perron, 2003). This kind of analysis focuses on issues such as how games manage time and space, the 'economies', goals and obstacles of games, and issues such as rules and conditionality. It is these ludic aspects that distinguish games from movies or books, for example. However, these elements are not separate from, or opposed to, the representational elements; any account of 'game literacy' needs to address *both* the elements that games have in common with other media *and* the elements that are specific to games (whether or not they are played on a computer).

As this implies, the analysis of games requires new and distinctive methods that cannot simply be transferred from other media – although this is equally the case when we compare television and books, for example. While some elements are shared across these media, others are distinctive to a specific medium, and hence we need to talk in terms both of a more general 'media literacy' *and* of specific 'media literacies', in the plural. Furthermore, developing 'game literacy' also needs to address the aspects of production and audience – although, here again, the term 'audience' seems an inadequate means of describing the interactive nature of play. Box 8.2 summarizes some of the key issues to be addressed in applying the media literacy framework to computer games, and draws on some other recent work in this field (Burn, 2004; Oram and Newman, 2006).

Box 8.2   Computer games: issues for study

Representation

- How games lay claim to 'realism', for example in their use of graphics, sounds and verbal language
- The construction and manipulation of game 'characters'
- The representations of specific social groups, for instance in terms of gender and ethnicity
- The nature of game 'worlds' and their relationship to real worlds (for example, in terms of history, geography and physics)

Language

- The functions of verbal language (audio and written text), still and moving images, sounds and music
- The distinctive codes and conventions of different game genres, including the kinds of interactivity – or 'playability' – that they offer
- How different game genres manage space and time (that is, narrative), and how they position the player
- The ludic dimensions of games – rules, economies, objectives, obstacles, and so on

Production

- The 'authorship' of games, and the distinctive styles of graphic artists and game designers
- The technologies and software that are used to create games, and the professional practices of game companies
- The commercial structure of the games industry (developers, publishers, marketeers), and the role of globalization
- The relationships between games and other media such as television, books and movies, and the role of franchising and licensing

Audience

- The experience and pleasure of play, and how it relates to the rules and structures of games
- The social and interpersonal nature of play, and its functions in everyday life, particularly for different social groups (for example, different genders or age groups)

- The role of advertising, games magazines and online commentary in generating expectations and critical discourse around games
- Fan culture, including the role of fan websites, fan art, 'modding', machinima and so on
- Public debates about the 'effects' of games, for example in relation to violence.

The limits of critique

The digital literacy 'recipes' I have outlined are intended only as a brief indication of the possibilities here. More detailed proposals for classroom practice can be found elsewhere (e.g. Frechette (2002) on the internet; Oram and Newman (2006) and Burn and Durran (2007) on games; and McDougall (2006)). Obviously, these approaches will vary according to the needs and interests of the students, although it should be possible to address the general conceptual issues at any level. Even so, it should be apparent that approaching digital media through media education is about much more than simply *accessing* these media or using them as tools for learning: on the contrary, it means developing a much broader *critical understanding* which addresses the textual characteristics of media alongside their social, economic and cultural implications.

Nevertheless, it is important to recognize the potential limitations of this 'critical' emphasis. There seems to be little place in some conceptions of media literacy for aspects of pleasure, sensuality and irrationality, which are arguably central to most people's experience of media, and of culture more broadly. For example, the emphasis on critical 'distance' fits awkwardly with the experience of 'immersion' and spontaneous 'flow' that is frequently seen as fundamental to computer gaming (Carr et al., 2006), or indeed with the emotional intensity and intimacy of some forms of online communication. As such, the notion of literacy might be seen to sanction a narrow, rationalistic view of how a well-regulated individual should behave in relation to the media – a view that is arguably quite at odds with how the majority of users behave, or might *wish* to behave.

Research on the teaching of 'critical' perspectives in media education has pointed to some of the dangers of an unduly rationalistic, 'counter-propagandist' approach. For example, our early classroom-based study (Buckingham et al., 1990) found that most students were quite prepared to play along with teachers' critical approaches to analysing television advertising, but that much of this was little more than a superficial exercise in 'guessing what's in teacher's mind': analysis became a mechanical classroom routine, and much of the pleasure afforded by advertising tended to disappear from view.

Many researchers have argued that such 'critical' approaches tend to be based on an oversimplified view of young people's engagements with media. Thus, Turnbull (1998) found that teachers' feminist criticisms of romantic fiction and soap operas failed to address the complex ways in which these genres were actually used by their female students; Sefton-Green (1990) found that classroom discussions of ethnic representations in the media tended to be reduced to a kind of 'language game' which failed to do justice to the subtlety of the students' own responses; and Jeong (2001) found that teaching about 'images of women' in the media seemed to be based on a simplistic view of audiences as victims of media misrepresentations, and that, as a result, the discussion of students' (and indeed teachers') personal investments in the media was marginalized.

To some extent, the difficulty here arises from the gap between teachers' critical perspectives and the changing experiences of students. Thus, Funge (1998) found that there was a considerable gap between her students' perceptions of gender in the media and the feminist theories on which much media education is based. She contends that '1970s feminism', with its emphasis on ideological deconstruction, simply fails to connect with contemporary gender politics – as embodied, for example, in the notion of 'girl power'. Likewise, Cohen (1998) found that simplistic notions of 'positive' and 'negative' images were highly problematic when teaching about the representation of 'race' in the media. He argues that that such ideas are based on a rationalistic approach, which regards racism as merely a result of irrationality or misinformation, and that they fail to address the complex ways in which such representations are interpreted and used.

On the other hand, research does point to the considerable benefits of students acquiring a critical 'meta-language' with which to analyse their own responses to media. For example, Buckingham and Sefton-Green (1994) undertook a close analysis of one student's critical writing, tracing how he gradually developed the ability to generalize about the texts he was discussing, to support his assertions with evidence, and to sustain more abstract arguments. In this case, he was able not merely to apply or illustrate theories or concepts, but also to make reflexive judgements about them (for example, by questioning the notion of 'stereotyping'). This gradual mastery of the 'correct' terminology and linguistic structures of critical writing could be seen as a form of socialization into the subject discipline, but it also reflects a developing control over one's own thought processes, and a growing conceptual sophistication. Nevertheless, research clearly shows that it is most productive to relate critical analysis to students' own concerns, tastes and identities rather than engaging in the more abstract analyses of ideology that have traditionally been prevalent in media teaching (Bragg, 2002).

Creating digital media

The understandings I have identified here are not only gained through analysis: they can also be developed – in some instances, more effectively and enjoyably – through the experience of creative production. Media literacy involves 'writing' the media as well as 'reading' them; and, here again, digital technology presents some important new challenges and possibilities. The growing accessibility of this technology means that quite young children can easily produce multimedia texts, and even interactive hypermedia – and, as I have noted, more children have access to such technology in their homes.

As with older media (Lorac and Weiss, 1981), teachers are increasingly using multimedia authoring packages as a means of assisting subject learning in a range of curriculum areas. Here, students produce their own multimedia texts in the form of websites or CD-ROMs, often combining written text, visual images, simple animation, and audio and video material (Sefton-Green, 1999a). Vivi Lachs (2000), for example, describes a range of production activities undertaken with primary school students in learning about science, geography or history. These projects generally involve children 're-presenting' their learning for an audience of younger children in the form of multimedia teaching materials or websites. One of the most challenging aspects of this work is precisely the interactivity: the students have to think hard about how different users might interpret and use what they produce, and how they will navigate their way around. Yet although the children's productions frequently draw on elements of popular culture (such as computer games), the content of the productions is primarily factual and informational – and, in this sense, the preferred genre is that of 'edutainment'.

Other potential uses of digital media have emerged from arts education. These projects often involve the participation of 'digital artists' external to the school, and their primary emphasis is on the use of the media for self-expression and creative exploration. Thus, students may experiment with the possibilities of different art forms, and the ways in which they can be combined and manipulated using the computer, in exploring themes such as 'identity' and 'memory'. The implicit model here is that of the avant-garde multimedia art work, although (here again) students tend to 'import' elements of popular culture. This work can also involve an element of critical reflection, particularly where it involves communication with a wider audience.

Rebecca Sinker (1999), for example, describes an online multimedia project which set out to develop links between an infant school and its community. The project was intended to mark the school's centenary, and to offer the children opportunities 'to investigate their own families, community, histories and experiences, exploring changes and celebrating diversity'. Using multimedia authoring software, the project brought together photography, video, drawing, storytelling, digital imaging, sound and text. Although outside experts were involved, the style of learning here was quite collaborative, and the control afforded by the technology encouraged a degree of critical reflection that might have been harder to achieve in other art forms. Perhaps most significantly, the results of the project (in the form of a website) were available to a much wider audience than would normally have been the case with children's work. As Sinker argues elsewhere, this form of multimedia production represents a form of 'learning-through-making' that is necessarily cross-disciplinary, even though it may derive initially from visual arts practice (Sinker, 2000). There is certainly a good deal of common ground here with media education, not only because of the use of digital technology, but also because such work often explicitly addresses conceptual themes and issues.

Nevertheless, there are two factors that distinguish the use of digital production in the context of media education from these other approaches. Media education is generally characterized by an explicit focus on popular culture – or at least on engaging with students' everyday experiences of digital media, rather than attempting to impose an alien 'artistic' or 'educational' practice. In the case of the internet, this means recognizing that most young people's uses of the medium are not primarily 'educational', at least in the narrow sense: as I have argued, most young people's uses of the internet are intimately connected with their other media enthusiasms – for soap operas, computer games, reality TV shows and pop celebrities – and this is bound to be reflected in the texts they produce.

Secondly, there is the element of theoretical reflection – the dynamic relationship between making and critical understanding that is crucial to the development of 'critical literacy'. In the context of media education, the aim is not primarily to develop technical skills or to promote 'self-expression', but to encourage a more systematic understanding of how the media operate, and hence to promote more reflective ways of using them.

There is a growing body of research studies suggesting that young people experience a sense of 'empowerment' that comes from the experience of being in control of the production process, and of being able to represent their own experiences, concerns and aspirations (for a systematic review of research relating specifically to digital video, see Burn, 2007). The experience of production can enable students to reflect upon their emotional investments in the media, and issues of identity formation more broadly, in ways that are harder to achieve through critical analysis alone (Bragg, 2000; De Block et al., 2005). Media production is seen by some to provide a 'safe space', in which students can explore media-related fantasies and address some of the complexities of their investments in media images (Buckingham and Sefton-Green, 1994). Several studies point to the importance of students using familiar media genres, which often serve as the basis for parodic inversions or 'deconstructions' of media codes and conventions (Buckingham et al., 1995; Grace and Tobin, 1998).

Other research indicates the specific value of digital editing technology. Reid et al. (2002) point out that editing software provides constant feedback for learners; that it allows the integration of different expressive forms and their related media (speech, music, graphic design, moving image, text); and that it allows a wider variety of publication and distribution formats and contexts, and therefore a potentially wider range of audiences. Research undertaken by a group of UK teachers (Burn et al., 2001) found that the use of digital video-editing equipment has considerable benefits for students, including an improved understanding of the language of the moving image, more purposeful collaborative group creation of video work, and a specific kind of pleasure in the manipulation of video material.

However, this is not to imply that production work is unproblematic. Research has pointed to some of the difficulties of organizing group production activities, particularly where students have different levels of prior expertise (Jeong, 2001). Male students may tend to dominate the equipment, leaving female students to perform in front of the camera (Buckingham et al., 1995). In many instances, a lack of equipment – particularly for editing – clearly inhibits work. Teachers trying to give classes an experience of video editing with one computer suffer considerable difficulty, compensating for inadequate equipment only through ingenious classroom management strategies (Reid et al., 2002).

A key issue for debate here concerns the balance between instruction and discovery, particularly in the context of production work. Some researchers advocate a looser, more exploratory approach, while others find in favour of a more structured introduction to new concepts and skills. De Block et al. (2005) argue, for instance, that too great an emphasis on structured, cognitively based work in media production can be disempowering for children. On the other hand, Reid et al. (2002) found that an approach that was too open-ended led to poorer quality video productions, whereas developing a more explicit and systematic understanding of the language of the moving image produced better work. However, this difference of emphasis should not be overstated. There is broad agreement that production work should build on children's existing media knowledge, that it should develop a more critical awareness of media texts, and that it should provide structured opportunities for children to learn how to use media technologies.

Processes and products

In these respects, the specific 'affordances' or potentialities of digital technology do make a significant difference when compared with the analogue technology that preceded it, although this also raises some new questions. Digital image manipulation and video editing are not just more efficient ways of doing the things that used to be done with analogue technology. They are certainly simpler and more flexible to use, and they enable students to achieve a 'professional' result much more easily. Yet there are some significant differences in the *process* of production that have much broader implications for students' learning.

Digital technology can make overt and visible some key aspects of the production process that often remain 'locked away' when using analogue technologies. This happens, firstly, at the point of generating images. For example, being able to take a whole series of shots on a digital camera, view them in the monitor and choose the ones you need, can make apparent a whole series of points about the selection and construction of images that might otherwise have been mere theoretical exhortations on the part of the teacher. It is possible to learn through trial and error, without worrying about the possibility of losing or erasing images, and this can allow the student to look back at earlier versions of their work and reflect upon how and why their ideas have changed. In effect, the technology allows students to engage in a process of drafting and redrafting – and, in the process, of critical self-evaluation – that is similar to contemporary

approaches to the teaching of writing. In principle, of course, these processes were possible with analogue technology, although they were always
significantly more expensive (for example in the case of Polaroid cameras)
and more extended in time.

This argument also applies to 'post-production'. Here again, complex
issues about the selection, manipulation and combination of images (and,
in the case of video, of sounds) can be addressed in a much more accessible
way than was possible using analogue technology. This is not simply a
matter of the ease of operating the software or of the range of choices
available – for example, the number of effects or shot transitions. (Indeed,
the proliferation of such choices can become a distraction, particularly for
relative beginners.) Software packages for image manipulation such as
'Photoshop' make the process of constructing imagery (for example for
film posters or adverts) much quicker and simpler than with the montage
tools of the past (glue and scissors), and, in the process, they can also
quickly demonstrate the problematic status of photographs as evidence.
Likewise, the benefit of digital editing programs such as 'iMovie' or
'MovieMaker' is that they make the process of constructing meaning –
and the choices that it entails – clearly visible. As a result, they may enable
students to *conceptualize* the process in much more powerful ways. In this
respect, much of what used to be tackled in very abstract and laborious
ways through analysis and storyboarding can now be approached in a
much more direct and flexible (not to mention pleasurable) way through
production. In the process, the boundaries between critical analysis and
practical production – or between 'theory' and 'practice' – are likely to
become increasingly blurred (see Burn and Durran, 2006).

These issues have been addressed in a series of empirical studies in this
field. Julian Sefton-Green's early case study of digital production in the
context of English teaching (Buckingham et al., 1995: chapter 3) suggests
that the technology permits a more systematic experimentation with possibilities, and hence a more conscious selection and construction of a final
version, when compared with earlier methods. In one project, students
produced film posters and edited trailers on the computer as part of a unit
of work on the book and film of *The Outsiders*. By offering the students a
high degree of control over the composition and editing of the images, and
enabling them to engage with the work in very close detail, it encouraged
them to explore a number of themes at stake in the original text, and to
consider how it might be marketed for different audiences. Nevertheless,
as Sefton-Green indicates, it is important for this knowledge to be made
explicit, and this is not something the technology itself will automatically
bring about.

Andrew Burn has conducted a series of studies looking at the impact of digital technology on students' engagement with the moving image. For example, he shows how using a digital package to 'grab' and then manipulate frames from films enables students to achieve greater analytical understanding of elements that might otherwise be noticed only in a much more condensed or subliminal way (Burn, 1999). In another study, students' digital editing of a film trailer is seen to offer a degree of flexibility and control – through reordering the shots, experimenting with shot transitions, stretching and condensing sequences, speeding up and slowing down – which is comparable to that afforded by writing (Burn and Reed, 1999). Editing and manipulating media images in this way, Burn argues, somehow mimics the infinite flexibility of the process of mental image-making or 'visual thinking'; and, as the software develops, this process is likely to become increasingly intuitive. (See also Archer, 2007; Burn et al., 2001; Potter, 2005; Reid et al., 2002.)

Burn's ultimate objective here is to develop a comprehensive analysis of the 'grammar' of moving images, and, in this respect, it takes us back to the question of 'media literacy' and to some of the problems that surround the analogy between print and other media. Importantly, Burn uses functional linguistics rather than a more traditional form of grammar, which means that he is seeking to identify functional equivalents between media rather than parallels in terms of form or structure – so, for example, he seeks to identify the specific ways in which images are transformed, combined or 'fixed', rather than looking for visual equivalents of sentences, tenses or negatives (Burn and Parker, 2001). Whether or not this might add up to a 'grammar' remains to be seen; even if it does, there are bound to be further questions about how that grammar might be taught (see Burn and Durran, 2006). The interesting question here is whether the level of control afforded by digital technology somehow automatically encourages a more systematic approach. Burn's research certainly suggests that students quickly perceive the need for a technical meta-language, which in turn helps their collaborative decision-making (Burn et al., 2001), although whether this necessarily encourages them to reflect on the broader cultural and social investments that are at stake in their productions is a more open question.

The meanings of 'access'

Despite the considerable potential of this technology, it is possible that it may be differentially realized by those on different sides of the 'old' digital divide. Outside school, children have very different levels of access to technology, and to the skills that are required to use it. As I have argued, it would be quite romantic to assume that they all have some kind of automatic expertise with technology, or that they will necessarily be able to learn to use it easily and quickly. Indeed, the majority of software programs students might use for media production are designed for professionals and are very time-consuming to learn. Nevertheless, research suggests that middle-class children have significant advantages, as a result of their parents' greater experience of computers at work and their involvement in other social networks (Facer et al., 2003).

Julian Sefton-Green (1999b) describes the consequences of this in developing courses on web design and computer games production in the context of a youth arts project in London. Young people, mainly from impoverished backgrounds, were recruited onto courses in both of these areas; but the differences between the students' prior experiences of the two forms had a significant effect on how both courses developed. In the case of the web design course, the primary problem was the fact that virtually none of the students who attended these courses (in 1998) had ever used the web before. By contrast, all the students came to the computer games courses with extensive 'consumer' knowledge about games. The students also had a sense of how the games industry worked, and how the course might relate to media production in the real world – although some rather romantically hoped that the course might further their career aspirations. Nevertheless, they generally had a clear understanding of why and how games *as products* were designed and manufactured. By contrast, in the case of the web courses, the students had no clear idea of what professional (or indeed amateur) web producers might do, and only a very general sense that being competent to work in an online medium might have vocational relevance.

This prior knowledge led to very clear differences when it came to encouraging critical discussion, but it also had an influence on what students were able to produce. Neither group of students possessed basic skills in working with production software; but in the case of the web course, they needed to develop skills in using browsers before moving on to devising their own pages and sites. Students tend to imagine only what they know they can actually make; as they become more proficient in technical skills, this in turn changes their capacity to imagine new possibilities. This was certainly apparent in the web courses. Given that most students began with limited ideas about the web itself, it was not surprising that the work they produced was limited in many respects. A further issue here is that – despite claims about the democratic potential of the web – in reality much of what young people encounter online could be seen as a form of advertising. Non-commercial online culture – particularly that produced by young people themselves – is much harder to find. As a result, the expressive models available to students are few and far between. There was a striking contrast here with the students' work on computer games. Because they knew more about games, the students were quick to come up with ideas, sketches and scenarios for their work. They brought in a great deal of material from home and were clearly very motivated. The work they produced here showed a far greater sense of ownership. Although their technical control over the software was limited, this did not seem to inhibit their imagination.

This study took place several years ago, but it would be false to assume that these differences are necessarily disappearing. Indeed, similar issues are apparent in Ellen Seiter's more recent account of an after-school computer club she ran with disadvantaged Hispanic children in Los Angeles (Seiter, 2005) and in our own research on the uses of digital media by migrant children across Europe (De Block et al., 2005). As this implies, getting 'hands-on' experience with digital technology is only the beginning. *Access* needs to be seen not merely in terms of access to technology or to technical skills, but also to *cultural forms of expression and communication*; and it needs to be acknowledged that students' access to (and familiarity with) those cultural forms is itself likely to be quite variable. This in turn has challenging implications in terms of how we teach, particularly in settings that are culturally and socially diverse.

Technology and pedagogy: the role of school

At least in principle, one could argue that digital production is part of a more general 'empowerment' of media users. By offering greater democratic access to complex forms of media production, digital technology can enable students to become writers as well as readers of visual and audio-visual media – and, indeed, begins to blur these settled distinctions. Yet even where young people do have access to digital production technology in their homes, research suggests that relatively few of them are using it in this way (Facer et al., 2003; Livingstone and Bober, 2004). The reasons for this may be partly to do with the difficulty of acquiring the relevant skills, although they are also, crucially, to do with the social context. Our early research in this area suggested that, in most cases, the home context did not provide children with sufficient social motivation to want to engage in such activities in the first place, even where they had the necessary access (Sefton-Green and Buckingham, 1996; see chapter 7).

Ultimately, whether or not the potential of digital production is realized is not simply a matter of the technology: it is primarily a question of pedagogy. For example, it remains to be seen whether the advent of digital cameras in the home will in itself make a significant difference to the conventional practice of popular photography – a practice which is predominantly a matter of selectively recording certain types of atypical family events (weddings, birthdays, holidays) as a means of constructing evidence of 'happy' social relationships. Digital technology in itself does not necessarily challenge or make apparent these choices and selections, or encourage a dialogue about them. Indeed, it may simply facilitate indiscriminate use.

Likewise, it could be argued that the new range of choices made available by digital technology does not *necessarily* make the act of constructing an image any more conscious or deliberate. In the case of digital still cameras, for example, the ease with which filters and manipulations can be applied encourages the production of stylized images, but these may well continue to be seen as distinct from pictures presented as 'evidence' of reality. Unless these basic questions about selection and manipulation are built into the process, and made the focus of conscious reflection, these new choices may well become merely an excuse for arbitrary experimentation. Likewise, the high quality of digital video can encourage pride and a sense of ownership in the product which is very motivating for students. Pop videos, for example, lend themselves to digital production because of the ease of editing. Yet the fact that it is fairly straightforward to produce something that 'looks good' does not necessarily make the work any more coherent or effective in terms of communication. Indeed, 'good effects' can mask a lack of content – and indeed of *thought* about what the product is intending to communicate – particularly if they are accompanied by a powerful music track.

The key point here is that the potential benefits of digital technology will not be realized without informed intervention on the part of teachers – and, in a different way, of peers. There remains a need for reflection, deliberation and dialogue, and opportunities and requirements for these things need to be systematically built into the process, even if they seem like a distraction from it.

In this respect, it seems particularly important to insist on the need for collaboration in digital production. In the context of media education, group work has been an established approach, not just for pragmatic reasons (to do with the shortage of technology), but also for educational ones. These arguments do not easily apply to production work with digital media. Indeed, the use of digital technology often tends to *individualize* the process of production. A computer room, even one set up for creative art work, tends to involve students working individually at screens; the teacher often has a more one-to-one relationship with individuals – although students may also work together as peer-tutors, especially to solve software problems. Attempts to build in group work often appear somewhat artificial, and students will sometimes seek to avoid dialogue and debate by dividing their labour into specialized functions that can be taken on by individuals. Particularly where there is a high level of access to the technology, the benefits of working together need to be made explicit and actively promoted. Set against the tendency towards individualization, group work needs to be perceived as a matter of mutual self-interest: students need to recognize that only by pooling resources, expertise and ideas can the job get done.

Finally, there is the question of audience. Most of the creative work that students undertake in school is designed for an audience of one: the teacher-as-examiner. The existence, or even the potential existence, of a real audience can qualitatively change how students conceptualize production work and what they learn from it (see Buckingham et al., 1995). Digital technology seems to offer some important possibilities here. The internet provides – or may in future provide – significant opportunities for young people's work to find a wider audience. There is now a growing number of sites that feature images, video and audio material produced by young people. Nevertheless, it would be wrong to overstate this. The task of bringing students' work to the point of 'publication' is often quite time-consuming, and the work often looks and feels very different from 'professional' products. In reality, few schools have published their students' multimedia work or made it more generally available via the internet, although this partly reflects schools' growing concerns about their 'public image'. Of course, finding an audience – even a relatively small and local one – is just a stage in the process rather than an end point; but, if seen in this way, it can have significant benefits in terms of students' motivation and their willingness to reflect upon their work.

In all these respects, therefore, digital technology appears to have important implications in terms of students' learning about media. Yet these changes will not occur automatically. Whether or not they are realized will obviously depend to some degree on the technology itself – on the design of the hardware and the software, and on whether they can actually deliver what they promise. However, it will also depend upon the social contexts and relationships into which it enters. The value of digital technology in this situation depends to a large extent on the *pedagogic* relationships that are established around it – for example, on how students are given access to the skills and competencies they need, how far they can control the process, and how far they can enter into a dialogue with their peers and teachers. It also depends, more broadly, on the *social* contexts that surround it – on the motivations of the students, on the ways in which cultural production relates to other aspects of their lives, on the audience for their productions, and so on. In all these respects, I would argue that the school has an absolutely vital role to play.

A cautious conclusion

This chapter has presented what I regard as a productive alternative to most current practice in using digital technology in education. It is an approach that I believe should substantially replace the compulsory specialist subject of ICT in schools and also be much more centrally integrated within the core subject of English (or language arts). Unlike many such proposals in this field, this is not merely another utopian fantasy based on a technology that has yet to be fully implemented. The kind of work I have been discussing here is already well developed in many schools and in some informal, out-of-school settings; in some countries, such as the UK, there is also a fairly well-documented history of classroom practice.

Nevertheless, media education has remained fairly marginal to the mainstream curriculum. It is increasingly widely available as a specialist option for older students, but it is rarely taught in a systematic or sustained way to younger age groups. As I have noted, media regulators and policy-makers in the UK are now becoming aware of the need for media literacy, and similar bodies in other countries are looking to the UK experience with considerable interest. Nevertheless, it has been very difficult to persuade *educational* policy-makers of the importance of this area: the UK government's Literacy Strategy for schools, for example, barely addresses media literacy, and the National Curriculum for ICT remains confined largely to functional skills training. Without official recognition of this kind, backed up with a serious programme of professional development, it is unlikely that the kind of work I have described here will become more widely disseminated.

There is a small but growing body of research on media education, some of which I have referred to in this chapter. This research points to some important limitations in current practice, particularly in the kinds of 'critical thinking' that are frequently promoted in this field, although it also provides some quite powerful evidence of its effectiveness, particularly in the case of more creative approaches. Most of this work has been conducted by, or in collaboration with, teachers themselves, and much of it has necessarily been small-scale, and even anecdotal. 'Action research' of this kind is often much more effectively attuned to teachers' needs than larger-scale academic evaluations. Nevertheless, there is now an urgent need for more sustained, longer-term studies. We need to know much more about how children at different ages might learn about media, and how their understanding might develop over time. We need to recognize the social diversity of media literacies and the social functions they serve. We need to explore more fully the relationship between the 'critical' and 'creative' aspects of media literacy, and how they might feed into each other.

Perhaps above all, we need to understand a great deal more about what makes for good practice in media education – and ultimately about whether it actually makes any difference. Some studies claim that using media-based approaches can lead to significant advances in print literacy, although they are far from conclusive (e.g. Beavis, 2001; Burn, 2003a, 2003b; McClay, 2002; Parker, 1999). The more pertinent question, however, is whether media education actually results in increasing levels of *media* literacy. Is media education effective, not so much in enabling students to pass exams, but in the sense that it influences what happens *outside* the classroom, in their everyday engagements with media? Teachers in the field have well-founded practical knowledge of what 'works' in terms of helping students to pass examinations; and there are research studies that appear to prove that, if you teach students about the media and then test them on what you have taught, they will show evidence of having learnt it (e.g. Austin and Johnson, 1997; Gadow et al., 1987; Kelley et al., 1987). However, this kind of 'input–output' measure really tells us very little about the long-term impact of media education, or its effectiveness in raising the media literacy 'level' of students. This is a difficult question, and it would be difficult whichever area of the curriculum we were looking at, but it is certainly one that needs to be answered.

To this extent, a commitment to media education might be seen to involve an 'act of faith' – although, in my view, it is a rather more well-founded one than the kind of wishful thinking that typically informs the promotion of technology in education. Ultimately, however, I would want to go further than simply calling for media education as a new specialist field. The metaphor of literacy – while not without its problems – provides one means of imagining a more coherent, and more ambitious, approach. The growing convergence of contemporary media means that we need to be addressing the skills and competencies – the multiple literacies – that are required by the whole range of contemporary forms of communication. Rather than simply adding media or digital literacy to the curriculum menu, or hiving off information and communication technology into a separate subject, we need a much broader reconceptualization of what we mean by literacy in a world that is increasingly dominated by electronic media. This is not by any means to suggest that verbal literacy is no longer relevant, or that books should be discarded. However, it is to imply that the curriculum can no longer be confined to a narrow conception of literacy that is defined solely in terms of the medium of print.

This approach to digital literacy also provides a more compelling rationale for the use of technology in education. As I have argued, most uses of computers in schools signally fail to engage with the complex technological and media-saturated environment in which children are now growing up. For the most part, they are narrowly defined, mechanical and unimaginative. The answer to this problem is not to import ever more fashionable or 'child-friendly' devices, or to sugar the pill of learning with a superficial dose of digital entertainment. Digital media literacy of the kind I have described in this chapter represents a more rigorous – but also a more enjoyable and motivating – way of addressing the educational challenges of the digital age.

9

School's Out?

The Future of Schooling in the Age of Digital Media

The use of digital technology in education has been surrounded by an enormous amount of inflated rhetoric. Marketeers seeking to sell new products and services, policy-makers claiming to address social and economic needs, educators and academics promoting broader agendas about the transformation of learning, and critics bemoaning the demise of childhood and of authentic education – all have made very far-reaching claims about the power of technology. Not all of these claims are necessarily completely false or dishonest, although there is undoubtedly a great deal of exaggerated nonsense on all sides. The technology supplements of the educational press, the latest policy documents and computer marketing literature seem to offer little more than familiar excitable hype about the most recent technological 'solutions'.

In this book, I have questioned many of the ideas that typically circulate here – notions of the 'information society', of 'personalization', of 'learning styles', that are often ill-defined and superficial. Above all, I have sought to challenge the technological determinism that persistently characterizes the debate – the notion that technology in and of itself will inevitably produce particular types of learning (whether we see them as liberating, or alternatively as mechanical and reductive). As I have argued, this approach is often aligned with a particular representation of childhood, and here, too, technology is typically seen to be either liberating or destroying some imagined essence of childhood. Technology is believed to have created a 'digital generation' that is entirely and utterly different from those that preceded it, not least in terms of how it is seen to learn.

These criticisms apply just as much to the critics of educational technology as they do to its advocates. In picking my way through these arguments, it has not been my intention merely to lend support to those who would return education to a pre-technological era. Education inevitably uses technologies of many kinds, and it has always done so: the book, the pencil and the chalkboard are technologies just as much as the computer, the video camera or the latest mobile communication device. The question is not *whether* to use technology, or even *which* technologies to use, but *why* and *how* we should use them. The polarization that characterizes this debate – the endless stand-off between the 'boosters' and the 'resisters' – has ultimately made it very difficult to address these fundamental issues.

At the same time, I would not accept that technology is merely neutral, or that its consequences are merely a result of how individual people choose to use it. Technologies come to us with inherent potentialities or 'affordances': it is much easier to use them for some purposes than for others. However, relatively few of these affordances are inevitable: the history of technology is full of examples of unanticipated consequences and even subversive uses. Technology is socially and historically shaped; the forms that it takes reflect the interests of the social actors and social institutions that play a leading role in producing it, and in determining where, when and how it will be used, and by whom.

Ultimately, however, my focus here has been on *media* rather than on *technology*. Media obviously depend upon technologies, both at the point of production and in their circulation, consumption and use. Yet to see these processes simply in terms of the application of technology is quite reductive. To regard phenomena such as the internet, computer software and games merely as 'technologies' – and particularly as *information* technologies – can lead us to ignore their status as forms of representation, culture and communication. It effectively removes them from the domain of human interaction and from broader social and cultural processes. Yet it is only in the social contexts of use that technologies have any meaning.

The new digital divide

The idea that technology in itself would radically transform education – and even result in the demise of the school – has been shown to be an illusion. Despite massive expenditure on the part of government and intensive promotion by industry, few teachers have made much use of technology in their teaching – and they have often resisted using it for quite good reasons. There has been little definitive evidence that the widespread use of technology has contributed to raising achievement – let alone to generating more creative or adventurous forms of learning for the majority of young people. Today's technology is undoubtedly more pervasive than the educational technologies of the past; but here, too, there is a significant gap between the rhetoric of marketeers and policy-makers and the realities of classroom practice.

In the meanwhile, however, digital media have come to occupy a central role in most young people's lives outside school. Children are no longer encountering these technologies for the first time in school, as was the case in the 1980s and much of the 1990s. On the contrary, digital media are now a central aspect of their popular culture. To some extent, they are engaging with these media in different ways from adults, and developing new skills and competencies in the process. New media appear to offer them the possibility of becoming communicators and cultural producers in their own right: they are being led to demand choice, autonomy and control.

Nevertheless, we cannot afford to be sentimental about this. The 'old' digital divide is still a significant factor: major inequalities persist, not merely in young people's access to technology but also in the 'cultural capital' they need to use it. The contemporary fantasy of the 'digital generation' is a stereotype that belies the considerable difficulties and frustrations that children (like adults) often experience in their dealings with new media. Furthermore, children are now being aggressively targeted as consumers: their experiences of new media are framed and defined by broader social and economic forces that they do not control, or even necessarily understand.

One result of these developments is that we are witnessing a widening gap between the culture of the school and the culture of children's lives outside school. In their leisure time, children are encouraged to see themselves as active participants, navigating their way independently through complex multimodal media environments. Yet in school, they are expected to submit to a pedagogic regime that is fundamentally premised on the testing of decontextualized skills and knowledge. By and large, the use of information and communication technology in school signally fails to engage with the ways in which young people are now relating to information, and with the ways they choose to communicate.

The danger here is that the school will become more and more irrelevant to young people's real interests and concerns. Yet, as I have argued, bridging this gap will require more than superficial attempts to combine education and entertainment or importing the latest technological gadgets. The promotion of computer games in education, for example, has been based on an uncritical celebration of the pleasures of gaming and a fundamental neglect of the nature of games as a commercial and cultural form. Analysing the market in 'edutainment' media shows how in reality the combination of commercial forces and government imperatives often results in products that are impoverished and educationally trivial. By and large, children display a considerable lack of interest in these recurrent attempts to 'make learning fun'.

It is unrealistic to suggest that this problem will be solved if schools could only become more 'informal' and more like children's out-of-school environments. Certainly, schools could do much more to improve children's access to technology, and to provide more open-ended, creative ways of using it. But the social functions of the school as an institution, and the organizational imperatives that it must follow (not least in terms of the numbers of children it must contain), mean that it is bound to be different from what happens in the world outside. Indeed, many would argue that there are very good reasons why it *should* be: schools have a role in providing a structured, systematic approach to learning, in making experiences and forms of knowledge available to children that they would not otherwise encounter, and in providing social contexts and social motivations for learning that children are unlikely to experience elsewhere.

Towards digital literacies

So how should schools respond to the increasing role of digital media in children's lives? I believe the school could play a part in equalizing access to technology, compensating for the inequalities that currently persist in the wider society – although, in doing so, we will need to acknowledge that access is a matter not simply of technology, but also of the competencies that are required to use it. Yet the fundamental question here is not *how much* access to technology young people require, but what they need to *know* about technology.

In this respect, the school could and should be playing a much more positive role in providing both critical perspectives on technology and creative opportunities to use it. Media education provides a well-developed conceptual framework and a wide range of effective classroom strategies that can make this possible. By contrast, the teaching of ICT as a school subject remains dominated by the practice of decontextualized 'skills' of a kind that most students find merely redundant. Furthermore, media education directly challenges the instrumental use of media as a transparent 'teaching aid' – an approach that now typifies the classroom uses of computers, as of textbooks and television before them.

To be sure, children are likely to acquire forms of digital media literacy outside school, simply by using these media. Yet the role of the school is to offer them experiences, perspectives and knowledge that they might not otherwise encounter. Media education provides students with crucial knowledge about the operations of the media industries, about how audiences for media are targeted and addressed, and about how media are produced and used. It offers them critical perspectives that will enable them to reach informed judgements about how media create meanings and pleasures, how they represent the world, and how they embody particular ideologies and values. And it provides them with opportunities – and, importantly, social motivations – for creative work with media that might not be available elsewhere.

Ultimately, media education implies a rethinking of the notion of literacy, which remains central to the social purpose and mission of the school. Verbal literacy will obviously remain an indispensable 'skill for life' – even if much of the written language we read will now be encountered on screens of various kinds rather than through the medium of print. At present, the British government's 'Literacy Strategy', and the 'Literacy Hour' that is now a compulsory daily requirement in primary schools, makes very little acknowledgement of the diverse forms of visual, audio-visual and digital literacy that are absolutely central to contemporary life. It seems extraordinary that the school system should continue to ignore the dominant forms of culture and communication of the last century, let alone those that are now emerging. A change is long overdue: media literacy – including digital media literacy – should be seen as a core curriculum entitlement for all children.

The end of school?

Numerous commentators have seen the advent of digital technology as a means of bringing about the end of the school as an institution. Of course, compulsory mass schooling is itself a relatively recent development, and it is not implausible that it might eventually give way to a different set of institutional or social arrangements. In fact, this seems unlikely, not least because the school serves social (and even economic) functions that are not confined to its role in respect of learning: historically, schooling has always operated partly as an agency of child-minding.

Nevertheless, this does not appear to have prevented some quite utopian thinking on these matters. As we have seen, some advocates of computer technology have argued that it will eventually replace – or even 'blow up' – the school. Such ideas have been around for many years. Seymour Papert (1980), for example, argues that the presence of computers will lead to a situation in which 'schools as we know them today will have no place'. He looks forward to a time when 'much if not all the knowledge schools presently try to teach with such pain and expense and such limited success will be learned, as the child learns to talk, painlessly, successfully, and without organized instruction' (1980: 9). Likewise, Ivan Illich's (1971) imagination of a 'deschooled' society depends upon the ability of technology to create new, decentralized networks in which the distinctions between teachers and learners, and the old institutional form of the school, will disappear. L. J. Perelman (1992) argues that the 'technological revolution' will create the 'constant, universal learning' on which the modern 'knowledge-based economy' is seen to depend. He describes a science-fiction scenario of 'hyperlearning', in which a fusion of artificial intelligence, broadband telecommunications and biotechnology will make knowledge universally accessible. In the process, he asserts, teachers will become as redundant as blacksmiths.

Other, slightly less absolutist, commentators appear to regard the school as a fundamentally conservative institution, and technology – or at least certain uses of technology – as a means of revolutionizing it. As we have seen, James Gee (2003) and Marc Prensky (2006) contrast the authentic learning that occurs as children play computer games with the apparently mindless, mechanical approach of the school. Likewise, Bridget Somekh (2004) regards schooling as inherently bureaucratic, hierarchical and even 'despotic', while the internet is inherently radicalizing – 'individualistic, anarchic, exploratory and disruptive' (2004: 168–9). ICTs, she argues, have the power 'to radically change schools', although they are likely to encounter 'institutionalized resistance' in doing so. Meanwhile, Joshua Meyrowitz (1996) argues that the traditional structure of the school – with the teacher as an authority figure and instruction proceeding in a step-by-step, graded fashion – is characteristic of a print-based culture. According to Meyrowitz, print makes it possible to control the flow of information to children and the skills they need to decode it, whereas new media disrupt this 'monopolistic structure', allowing children direct access to information in any sequence. As a result of these changes in media, children are less in awe of adult authority: they know the 'backstage' secrets of adulthood, and in some respects know more than their teachers. Following Marshall McLuhan's 'medium theory', Meyrowitz argues that the use of new media will thus inevitably result in the demise of teacher-led instruction and the emergence of more playful, co-operative, student-centred learning.

These arguments are clearly characterized by a form of technological determinism. For Perelman (1992), technology is 'the driving force of society'; Somekh (2004) argues that ICTs 'fundamentally change human ontology'; while Meyrowitz (1996) appears to believe (in line with

McLuhan) that different media inevitably result in different forms of consciousness and different arrangements of social power. These arguments also depend upon a polarized opposition between school learning and technologically based learning outside school. The school is portrayed as a kind of wasteland in which no learning of any value could possibly occur, whereas technology is seen automatically to generate new and more authentic forms of learning.

Even if technology were to supersede the school, it is interesting to speculate about how this new world of 'universal learning' might be socially organized. Ivan Illich (1971), for example, imagines a wholly decentralized system, in which individual learners would simply make contact with others with similar interests via some form of database. He rejects all types of institutionalized provision as merely forms of state surveillance and control. Yet in a capitalist society, access to educational resources is bound to involve the exchange of labour time for money, and hence the generation of profit – and indeed, as I have described, private companies are already increasingly involved at all levels in the state-funded provision of education. Far from the deschooled utopia of the network society, these developments would be more likely to result in a privatized educational dystopia – a form of educational consumerism that would be governed by market forces and characterized by expanding levels of competitiveness and inequality.

Rethinking the school

Short of the complete abolition of the education system (not to mention the immediate overthrow of capitalism), how might we reimagine the role of the school in the age of digital culture? My proposals here are almost traditional, although many might see them as equally utopian. I believe that we need to return to a 'modernist' vision of public education, and of the school as a key public-sphere institution – rather like the eighteenth-century public sphere described (or perhaps imagined) by the social theorist Jürgen Habermas ([1962] 1989). This has several dimensions.

As a public-sphere institution, the school should provide a forum for open public communication and critical debate that is equally accessible to all. It should stand between the citizen (in this case, the student) and the operations of both the market and the state. And, like the university, it should be staffed by professionals, who have the power to make their own decisions about how the business of education should be carried out. If this seems bland and uncontroversial, it is worth reminding ourselves of the inequalities of access and provision that increasingly charact education, of the growing importance of commercial compa management of schools, and of the government's view of tea matter of 'delivering' an externally defined curriculum.

While reasserting the public functions of the school, we also need to develop its connections with other public-sphere institutions – and perhaps to imagine new ones. Bridging the divide between the school and students' lives outside school can be facilitated by what might be called 'intermediate' social institutions such as libraries, adult education centres, community arts projects and even museums. School buildings constitute a valuable community resource that could be open for a wider range of activities well beyond the school day.

In this respect, schools can certainly learn from the more informal, accessible institutions that have developed around new technologies. Cybercafes, for example, have been seen as important 'liminal spaces' located at the junctions between home, school and street, online and offline spaces, and work and play (Beavis et al., 2005). Likewise, Chris Bigum (2002) provides an interesting case study of the ways in which schools can use technology (and specifically creative media technology) as a means of developing a stronger engagement with community needs and interests. In the process, the community also becomes an audience for students' creative productions. Of course, the internet itself can be seen as a public space of this kind, although it is one that is being overtaken more and more by the imperatives of business – and, in the case of schools, is largely used as a form of public relations. The need to sustain participatory, non-commercial spaces on the internet – by which I do not mean officially sanctioned and controlled spaces – is now a significant issue for public policy.

Obviously, the school is not about to disappear. Yet in an environment that is increasingly dominated by the proliferation of electronic media and the demands of consumer culture, it urgently needs to assume a much more proactive role. Technology can perhaps contribute to this, although it will not bring it about of its own accord. Ultimately, we need to stop thinking about such issues merely in terms of technology, and start thinking afresh about learning, communication and culture.

Notes

Preface

1   This package, originally designed by Bob Moy, is still available via www.devtray.co.uk.

Chapter 1   Selling Technology Solutions

1   My account of the BETT Show draws on material gathered in January 2006, and on an earlier account based on a visit in January 2000: see Buckingham, Scanlon and Sefton-Green (2001).
2   Information from EMAP website, www.emap.com, accessed January 2006.
3   Figures on attendance are drawn from ABC audit reports on the BESA website, www.besanet.org.uk. At a rough estimate, it costs the taxpayer around £1 million in teacher cover each day for staff to attend the show.
4   This figure was quoted in the opening speech by the education minister Charles Clarke at BETT in 2004.
5   Information from Prue's website, www.andertontiger.com, accessed January 2006.
6   Figures in this paragraph come from the BESA report 'Information and Communication Technology in UK State Schools' (November 2005) and the BESA website and the DfES 'TeacherNet' (www.teachernet.gov.uk) site (both accessed January 2006).
7   This is still one of BESA's organizational aims, as outlined in a 2005 press release on its website.
8   Press release, 18 November 1998: BESA web page.

Chapter 2   Making Technology Policy

1   Texts of these presentations have been available from the DfES website.
2   At the time of this publication, Futurelab was funded by the National Endowment for Science, Technology and the Arts, which is itself funded by the UK National Lottery; and its initiative in this area was also supported by Demos, BECTA (the government's British Educational Communications and Technology Agency) and the technology company Toshiba. Its primary funding now comes from the government, via the DfES.
3   *Learning Platforms: Secondary: Making IT Personal* (DfES, 2005).

Chapter 3   Techno-Topias

1   Although, as Kevin Robins and Frank Webster (1999) suggest, the Luddites have been somewhat misrepresented in this respect.

Chapter 4   Waiting for the Revolution

1   Quoted in Oppenheimer (2003: 3).
2   Of the two leading publications, *The Guardian* is owned by Guardian Media Group, which has significant commercial interests here, for example through its ownership of the website learnthings.com, while the *Times Educational Supplement* was until recently owned by Rupert Murdoch's News International.

Chapter 5   Digital Childhoods?

1   Parts of this chapter draw on material previously published in Buckingham (2000, 2006).

Chapter 6   Playing to Learn?

1   This chapter draws on discussions held as part of the 'Making games' project, funded by the UK Economic and Social Research Council (ref: RES-328-25-001).
2   On his website (www.gamesparentsteachers.com) Prensky helpfully suggests that teachers might use 'Grand Theft Auto' for 'a discussion about subcultures in society', and that 'it would also be relevant to a unit or discussion on sociology and violence in society'. Likewise, James Bond games are recommended resources for 'a discussion on gender roles in society'. No suggestions are supplied as to the nature of such 'discussions'. Much of the information about particular games on the site appears to have been taken from packaging or publishers' catalogues.
3   There are very clear ideological implications in how the world of 'The Sims' is constructed and the kinds of relationships that are possible within it. Much derives from the focus on acquiring material possessions, and on the fact that relationships have to be quantifiable. For example, Sims are liable to be unfaithful if plied with gifts – but they are also programmed to become jealous, so romantic relationships involving more than two at a time are difficult to maintain. (Thanks to Diane Carr for this point; and see also the review by Frasca, 2001.)
4   I am grateful to my colleague Michael Young for his emphasis on these points.

Chapter 7   That's Edutainment

1   Puttnam refers to his earlier remarks (which unfortunately I cannot trace) in a speech, 'Transforming the way we teach: IT and education', delivered at the Bertelsmann Foundation in Gutersloh, Germany, on 5 November 2002. See: www.netzwerk-medienschulen.de/dyn/bin/4316-4319-1-dinner_speech_lord_puttnam.pdf.
2   Both projects were conducted with Margaret Scanlon, and were funded by the Economic and Social Research Council: 'Changing sites of education: educational media and the domestic market', December 1999–November 2001 (ref: R000238218), and 'Learning online: e-learning and the domestic market', March 2002–January 2003 (ref: R000223819).

Chapter 8   Digital Media Literacies

1   Parts of this chapter draw on Buckingham (2003), particularly chapter 11, and on Buckingham et al. (2005).
2   Speech to British Film Institute/UK Film Council/Channel 4 Media Literacy Seminar, London, 27 January 2004.

References

Abbott, C. (ed.) (2002) *Special Educational Needs and the Internet: Issues for the Inclusive Classroom*. London: Routledge.

Agalianos, A., Noss, R., and Whitty, G. (2001) 'Logo in mainstream schools: the struggle over the soul of an educational innovation', *British Journal of Sociology of Education* 22 (4): 480–500.

Aldrich, F., Rogers, Y., and Scaife, M. (1998) 'Getting to grips with "interactivity": helping teachers assess the educational value of CD-Roms', *British Journal of Educational Technology* 29 (4): 321–32.

Angrist, J., and Lavy, V. (2002) 'New evidence on computers and classroom learning', *Economic Journal* 112 (October): 735–65.

Angus, L., Snyder, I., and Sutherland-Smith, W. (2004) 'ICT and educational (dis)advantage: families, computers and contemporary social and educational inequalities', *British Journal of Sociology of Education* 25 (1): 3–18.

Archer, S. (2007) 'Thought beats: new technology, music video and media education', *Media International Australia* 120: 142–55.

Armstrong, A., and Casement, C. (2000) *The Child and the Machine: How Computers Put our Children's Education at Risk*. Beltsville, MD: Robins Lane Press.

Atkins, B. (2003) *More Than a Game: The Computer Game as Fictional Form*. Manchester: Manchester University Press.

Attewell, P., and Battle, J. (1999) 'Home computers and school performance', *Information Society* 15 (1): 1–10.

Aufderheide, P. (ed.) (1997) 'Media literacy: from a report of the national leadership conference on media literacy', pp. 79–86 in R. Kubey (ed.), *Media Literacy in the Information Age*. New Brunswick, NJ: Transaction.

Austin, E., and Johnson, K. (1997) 'Effects of general and alcohol-specific media literacy training on children's decision-making about alcohol', *Journal of Health Communication* 2 (1): 17–42.

Bailey, K. V. (1957) *The Listening Schools*. London: BBC.

Ball, S. (2003) 'The teacher's soul and the terrors of performativity', *Journal of Education Policy* 18 (2): 215–28.

Ball, S. (2005) *Education Policy and Social Class: Selected Writings*. London: Routledge.

Ball, S., and Vincent, C. (2005) ' "Making up" the middle-class child: families, activities and class dispositions', paper for the British Educational Research Association conference, Glamorgan, September.

Barbrook, R., and Cameron, A. (1996) 'The Californian ideology', www.hrc. wmin.ac.uk/theory-californianideology.html.

Barton, D. (1994) *Literacy: An Introduction to the Ecology of Written Language.* Oxford: Blackwell.

Bates, A. (1984) *Broadcasting in Education: An Evaluation.* London: Constable.

Bazalgette, C. (1988) ' "They changed the picture in the middle of the fight": new kinds of literacy', pp. 211–23 in M. Meek and C. Mills (eds), *Language and Literacy in the Primary School.* London: Falmer.

Bazalgette, C. (ed.) (1989) *Primary Media Education: A Curriculum Statement.* London: British Film Institute.

Beastall, L. (2006) 'Enchanting a disenchanted child: revolutionising the means of education using Information and Communication Technology and e-learning', *British Journal of Sociology of Education* 27 (1): 97–110.

Beavis, C (1998) 'Computer games, culture and curriculum', pp. 234–54 in I. Snyder (ed.), *Page to Screen: Taking Literacy into the Electronic Era.* London: Routledge.

Beavis, C. (2000) 'Computer games as class readers: developing literacy skills for the twenty-first century', *English and Media Magazine* 41: 31–5.

Beavis, C. (2001) 'Digital culture, digital literacies: expanding notions of text', pp. 145–61 in C. Beavis and C. Durrant (eds), *P(ict)ures of English: Teachers, Learners and Technology.* Kent Town, South Australia: AATE and Wakefield Press.

Beavis, C., Nixon, H., and Atkinson, S. (2005) 'LAN cafés: cafés, places of gathering or sites of informal teaching and learning?', *Education, Communication and Information* 5 (1): 41–60.

BECTA (British Educational Communications and Technology Agency) (2001) *Computer Games in Education Project Report.* Coventry: BECTA; www.becta. org.uk/technology/software/curriculum/computergames.

BECTA (2003) *ImpaCT2: The Impact of Communication and Information Technologies on Pupil Learning and Attainment.* Coventry: BECTA.

BECTA (2004) *Content Advisory Board Report to the Secretary of State.* Coventry: BECTA.

BECTA (2005) *The Becta Review 2005: Evidence on the Progress of ICT in Education.* Coventry: BECTA.

Bigum, C. (2002) 'Design sensibilities, schools, and the new computing and communication technologies', pp. 130–40 in I. Snyder (ed.), *Silicon Literacies: Communication, Innovation and Education in the Electronic Age.* London: Routledge.

Blair, T. (1997) *New Britain: My Vision of a Young Country.* Boulder, CO: Westview Press.

Blunkett, D. (1997) 'On the starting grid', *Educational Computing and Technology* December: 11.

Bourdieu, P. (1984) *Distinction: A Social Critique of the Judgement of Taste*. London: Routledge & Kegan Paul.

Bowers, C. A. (1988) *The Cultural Dimensions of Educational Computing*. New York: Teachers College Press.

Bowers, C. A. (2000) *Let Them Eat Data: How Computers Affect Education, Cultural Diversity and the Prospects of Ecological Sustainability*. Atlanta: University of Georgia Press.

Bragg, S. (2000) 'Media Violence and Education: A Study of Youth Audiences and the Horror Genre', PhD thesis, Institute of Education, University of London.

Bragg, S. (2002) 'Wrestling in woolly gloves: not just being "critically" media literate', *Journal of Popular Film and Television* 30 (1): 42–52.

Bray, M. (1999) *The Shadow Education System: Private Tutoring and its Implications for Planners*. Paris: UNESCO International Institute for Educational Planning.

Bridges, D., and McLaughlin, T. (eds) (1994) *Education and the Market Place*. London: Falmer.

British Film Institute (2000) *Moving Images in the Classroom: A Secondary Teacher's Guide to Using Film and Television*. London: British Film Institute.

Bruce, C. (1997) *The Seven Faces of Information Literacy*. Adelaide: Auslib Press.

Buckingham, D. (1989) 'Television literacy: a critique', *Radical Philosophy* 51: 12–25.

Buckingham, D. (1993a) *Changing Literacies: Media Education and Modern Culture*. London: Tufnell Press.

Buckingham, D. (1993b) *Children Talking Television: The Making of Television Literacy*. London: Falmer.

Buckingham, D. (1996) *Moving Images: Understanding Children's Emotional Responses to Television*. Manchester: Manchester University Press.

Buckingham, D. (2000) *After the Death of Childhood: Growing Up in the Age of Electronic Media*. Cambridge: Polity.

Buckingham, D. (ed.) (2002) *Small Screens: Television for Children*. London: Leicester University Press.

Buckingham, D. (2003) *Media Education: Literacy, Learning and Contemporary Culture*. Cambridge: Polity.

Buckingham, D. (2006) 'Is there a digital generation?', pp. 1–13 in D. Buckingham and R. Willett (eds), *Digital Generations: Children, Young People and New Media*. Mahwah, NJ: Lawrence Erlbaum.

Buckingham, D. and Bragg, S. (2004) *Young People, Sex and the Media: The Facts of Life?* Basingstoke: Palgrave Macmillan.

Buckingham, D., and Domaille, K. (2004) 'Where are we going and how can we get there? General findings from the UNESCO Youth Media Education

Survey', pp. 41–54 in C. von Feilitzen and U. Carlsson (eds), *Promote or Protect? Perspectives on Media Literacy and Media Regulations*. Goteborg: Nordicom.

Buckingham, D., and Scanlon, M. (2003a) *Education, Entertainment and Learning in the Home*. Buckingham: Open University Press.

Buckingham, D., and Scanlon, M. (2003b) *Learning Online: E-Learning and the Domestic Market*. Swindon: Economic and Social Research Council.

Buckingham, D., and Scanlon, M. (2004) 'Connecting the family? "Edutainment" websites and learning in the home', *Education, Communication and Information* 4 (2/3): 271–91.

Buckingham, D., and Sefton-Green, J. (1994) *Cultural Studies Goes to School: Reading and Teaching Popular Culture*. London: Taylor & Francis.

Buckingham, D., and Sefton-Green, J. (2003) 'Gotta catch 'em all: structure, agency and pedagogy in children's media culture', *Media, Culture and Society* 25 (3): 379–99.

Buckingham, D., Fraser, P., and Mayman, N. (1990) 'Stepping into the void: beginning classroom research in media education', pp. 19–59 in D. Buckingham (ed.), *Watching Media Learning: Making Sense of Media Education*. London: Falmer.

Buckingham, D., Grahame, J., and Sefton-Green, J. (1995) *Making Media: Practical Production in Media Education*. London: English and Media Centre.

Buckingham, D., Scanlon, M., and Sefton-Green, J. (2001) 'Selling the digital dream: marketing educational technologies to teachers and parents', pp. 20–40 in A. Loveless and V. Ellis (eds), *Subject to Change: Literacy and New Technologies*. London: Routledge.

Buckingham, D., with Banaji, S., Burn, A., Carr, D., Cranmer, S., and Willett, R. (2005) *The Media Literacy of Children and Young People: A Review of the Academic Research*. London: Ofcom.

Burbules, N. C., and Callister, T. A. (2000) *Watch IT: The Risks and Promises of Information Technologies for Education*. Boulder, CO: Westview Press.

Burn, A. (1999) 'Grabbing the werewolf: digital freezeframes, the cinematic still and technologies of the social', *Convergence* 5 (4): 80–101.

Burn, A. (2003a) 'Poets, skaters and avatars: performance, identity and new media', *English Teaching: Practice and Critique* 2 (2), http://education.waikato. ac.nz/journal/english_journal/uploads/files/html/2003v2n2art1.html.

Burn, A. (2003b) 'Two tongues occupy my mouth – poetry, performance and the moving image', *English in Education* 37 (3): 41–50.

Burn, A. (2004) 'From *The Tempest* to *Tomb Raider*: computer games in English, media and drama', *English, Drama, Media* 1 (2).

Burn, A. (2007) 'Making the moving image: literacies, communities, digital technologies', in R. Andrews and C. Haythornthwaite (eds), *Handbook of E-learning Research*. London: Sage.

Burn, A., and Durran, J. (2006) 'Digital anatomies: analysis as production in media education', pp. 273–93 in D. Buckingham and R. Willett (eds), *Digital*

Generations: Children, Young People and New Media. Mahwah, NJ: Lawrence Erlbaum.

Burn, A., and Durran, J. (2007) *Media Literacy in Schools.* London: Paul Chapman.

Burn, A., and Parker, D. (2001) 'Making your mark: digital inscription, animation, and a new visual semiotic', *Education, Communication and Information* 1 (2): 155–79.

Burn, A., and Reed, K. (1999) 'Digiteens: media literacies and digital technologies in the secondary classroom', *English in Education* 33 (2): 5–20.

Burn, A., and Schott, G. (2004) 'Heavy hero or digital dummy? Multimodal player–avatar relations in *Final Fantasy 7*', *Visual Communication* 3 (2): 213–33.

Burn, A., Brindley, S., Durran, J., Kelsall, C., Sweetlove, J., and Tuohy, C. (2001) ' "The rush of images": a research report into digital editing and the moving image', *English in Education* 35: 34–47.

Carr, D., Buckingham, D., Burn, A., and Schott, G. (2006) *Computer Games: Text, Narrative and Play.* Cambridge: Polity.

Cawson, A., Haddon, L., and Miles, I. (1995) *The Shape of Things to Consume: Delivering Information Technology into the Home.* Aldershot: Avebury.

Chen, M., and Armstrong, S. (eds) (2002) *Edutopia: Success Stories for Learning in the Digital Age.* San Francisco: Jossey-Bass.

Clegg, S. (2001) 'Theorising the machine: gender, education and computing', *Gender and Education* 13 (3): 307–24.

Coffield, F. (2000) *The Necessity of Informal Learning.* Bristol: Policy Press.

Cohen, P. (1998) 'Tricks of the trade: on teaching arts and "race" in the classroom', pp. 153–76 in D. Buckingham (ed.), *Teaching Popular Culture: Beyond Radical Pedagogy.* London: UCL Press.

Cohn, E. (ed.) (1997) *Market Approaches to Education: Vouchers and School Choice.* Oxford: Pergamon.

Condie, R., Simpson, M., Payne, F., and Gray, D. (2002) *The Impact of ICT Initiatives in Scottish Schools.* Edinburgh: Scottish Executive.

Conlon, T. (2004) 'A failure of delivery: the United Kingdom's New Opportunities Fund programme of teacher training in information and communications technology', *Journal of In-Service Education* 30 (1): 115–39.

Conlon, T., and Simpson, M. (2003) 'Silicon Valley versus Silicon Glen: the impact of computers upon teaching and learning: a comparative study', *British Journal of Educational Technology* 34 (2): 137–50.

Cooper, J., and Weaver, K. (2003) *Gender and Computers: Understanding the Digital Divide.* Mahwah, NJ: Lawrence Erlbaum.

Cope, B., and Kalantzis, M. (eds) (2000) *Multiliteracies: Literacy Learning and the Design of Social Futures.* London: Routledge.

Copier, M., and Raessens, J. (eds) (2003) *Level Up: Digital Games Research Conference.* Utrecht: University of Utrecht Press.

Cordes, C., and Miller, E. (2000) *Fool's Gold: A Critical Look at Computers in Childhood*, www.allianceforchildhood.net.

Covington, M., and Mueller, K. (2001) 'Intrinsic versus extrinsic motivation: an approach/avoidance reformulation', *Educational Psychology Review* 13 (2): 157–76.

Cox, M., Abbott, C., Webb, M., Blakeley, B., Beauchamp, T., and Rhodes, V. (2004) *ICT and Attainment: A Review of the Research Literature*. Coventry: BECTA.

Cranmer, S. (2006) 'Families' Uses of the Internet', PhD thesis, Institute of Education, University of London.

Cross, G. (1997) *Kids' Stuff: Toys and the Changing World of American Childhood*. Cambridge, MA: Harvard University Press.

Cuban, L. (1986) *Teachers and Machines: The Classroom Use of Technology Since 1920*. New York: Teachers College Press.

Cuban, L. (2001) *Oversold and Underused: Computers in the Classroom*. New York: Teachers College Press.

Curran, C. (1972) *The BBC and its Educational Commitment*. London: BBC.

Dale, R., Robertson, S., and Shortis, T. (2004) ' "You can't not go with the technological flow, can you?" Constructing ' "ICT" and "teaching and learning"', *Journal of Computer Assisted Learning* 20: 456–70.

Davies, J. (2006) ' "Hello newbie! ☺**big welcome hugs** hope u like it here as much as i do! ⊞" An exploration of teenagers' informal on-line learning', pp. 211–28 in D. Buckingham and R. Willett (eds) *Digital Generations: Children, Young People and New Media*. Mahwah, NJ: Lawrence Erlbaum.

De Block, L., Buckingham, D., and Banaji, S. (2005) *Children in Communication about Migration*, final report of EC-funded project, at www.chicam.net.

De Vaney, A. (ed.) (1994) *Watching Channel One: The Convergence of Students, Technology and Private Business*. Albany: SUNY Press.

DEE (Department for Education and Employment) (1997) *Connecting the Learning Society*. London: DEE.

DfES (Department for Education and Skills) (2005) *Harnessing Technology: Transforming Children's and Learning Services*. London: DfES.

Di Filippo, J. (2000) 'Pornography on the web', pp. 122–9 in D. Gauntlett (ed.), *Web Studies*. London: Edward Arnold.

Douglas, G. (2001) 'ICT, education and visual impairment', *British Journal of Educational Technology* 32 (3): 353–64.

Downes, T. (1999) 'Playing with computing technologies in the home', *Education and Information Technologies* 4 (1): 65–79.

Durkin, K. (1995) *Computer Games: Their Effects on Young People: A Review*. Sydney: Office of Film and Literature Classification.

Duxbury, S. (1987) 'Childcare ideologies and resistance: the manipulative strategies of pre-school children', pp. 12–25 in A. Pollard (ed.) *Children and their Primary Schools*. Basingstoke: Falmer.

Eco, U. (1979) 'Can television teach?', *Screen Education* 31: 15–24.

Edwards, D., and Mercer, N. (1987) *Common Knowledge: The Development of Understanding in the Classroom*. London: Routledge.

Egenfeldt-Nielsen, S. (2005) 'Beyond Edutainment: Exploring the Educational Potential of Computer Games', PhD thesis, IT University of Copenhagen.

Elkind, D. (1981) *The Hurried Child: Growing Up Too Fast Too Soon*. Reading, MA, Addison Wesley.

Ellul, J. (1964) *The Technological Society*. New York: Vintage.

Engelhardt, T. (1986) 'Children's television: the shortcake strategy', in T. Gitlin (ed.), *Watching Television*. New York: Pantheon.

EPPI Centre (2004) *A Systematic Review and Meta-Analysis of the Effectiveness of ICT on Literacy Learning in English, 5 and 16*. London: Institute of Education, EPPI Centre.

Epstein, D., Ellwood, J., Hey, V., and Maw, J. (eds) (1998) *Failing Boys? Issues in Gender and Achievement*. Buckingham: Open University Press.

Fabos, B. (2004) *Wrong Turn on the Information Superhighway: Education and the Commercialization of the Internet*. New York: Teachers College Press.

Facer, K., and Furlong, R. (2001) 'Beyond the myth of the "cyberkid": young people at the margins of the information revolution', *Journal of Youth Studies* 4 (4): 451–69.

Facer, K., Furlong, J., Furlong, R., and Sutherland, R. (2001) 'Constructing the child computer user: from public policy to private practices', *British Journal of Sociology of Education* 22 (1): 91–108.

Facer, K., Furlong, J., Furlong, R., and Sutherland, R. (2003) *Screenplay: Children and Computing in the Home*. London: Routledge.

Fawdry, K. (1974) *Everything But Alf Garnett: A Personal View of BBC School Broadcasting*. London: BBC.

Forster, E. M. (1927) *Aspects of the Novel*. London: Edward Arnold.

Franklin, B., and Petley, J. (1996) 'Killing the age of innocence: newspaper reporting of the death of James Bulger', pp. 134–54 in J. Pilcher and S. Wagg (eds), *Thatcher's Children: Politics, Childhood and Society in the 1980s and 1990s*. London: Taylor & Francis.

Frasca, G. (2001) 'The Sims: Grandmothers are cooler than trolls', *Game Studies* 1 (1), www.gamestudies.org.

Frechette, J. (2002) *Developing Media Literacy in Cyberspace: Pedagogy and Critical Learning for the Twenty-First Century*. Westport, CT: Greenwood Press.

Frechette, J. (2006) 'Cyber-censorship or cyber-literacy? Envisioning cyber-learning through media education', pp. 149–71 in D. Buckingham and R. Willett (eds), *Digital Generations: Children, Young People and New Media*. Mahwah, NJ: Lawrence Erlbaum.

Freund, R. (2004) 'Mass customization and multiple intelligence', keynote speech at International Conference on Mass Customization and Personalization, Rzeszow, Poland: www.mass-customization.pl [accessed 8 May 2006].

Funge, E. (1998) 'Rethinking representation: media studies and the postmodern teenager', *English and Media Magazine* 39: 33–6.

Gadow, K., Sprafkin, J., and Watkins, T. (1987) 'Effects of a critical viewing skills curriculum on elementary school children's knowledge and attitudes about television', *Journal of Educational Research* 81: 165–70.

Galanouli, D., Murphy, C., and Gardner, J. (2004) 'Teachers' perceptions of the effectiveness of ICT-competence training', *Computers and Education* 43 (1–2): 63–79.

Gardner, H. (1993) *Frames of Mind: The Theory of Multiple Intelligences*. 2nd edn, London: Heinemann.

Gardner, H. (1999) *Intelligence Reframed: Multiple Intelligences for the 21st Century*. New York: Basic Books.

Garnham, N. (2000) 'Information society as theory or ideology', *Information, Communication and Society* 3 (2): 139–52.

Gates, B. (1995) *The Road Ahead*. London: Viking.

Gee, J. P. (2003) *What Video Games Have to Teach us about Learning and Literacy*. Basingstoke: Palgrave Macmillan.

Gee, J. P. (2004) *Situated Language and Learning: A Critique of Traditional Schooling*. London: Routledge.

Gee, J. P. (2005) *Why Video Games are Good for your Soul*. Sydney: Common Ground.

Gee, J. P. (2006) 'Foreword' to M. Prensky, *'Don't Bother Me, Mom – I'm Learning!'*. St Paul, MN: Paragon House.

Genette, G. (1980) *Narrative Discourse*, trans. J. E. Lewin. Oxford: Blackwell.

Gewirtz, S., Ball, S., and Bowe, R. (1995) *Markets, Choice and Equity in Education*. Buckingham: Open University Press.

Giacquinta, J. B., Bauer, J., and Levin, J. E. (1993) *Beyond Technology's Promise: An Examination of Children's Educational Computing at Home*. Cambridge: Cambridge University Press.

Gilster, P. (1997) *Digital Literacy*. New York: Wiley.

Goodson, I., and Mangan, J. M. (1996) 'Computer literacy as ideology', *British Journal of Sociology of Education* 17 (1): 65–79.

Goodson, I., Knobel, M., Lankshear, C., and Mangan, J. M. (2002) *Cyber Spaces/ Social Spaces: Culture Clash in Computerized Classrooms*. Basingstoke: Palgrave Macmillan.

Goolsbee, A., and Guryan, J. (2002) *The Impact of Internet Subsidies in Public Schools*. National Bureau of Economic Research, Working Paper 9090.

Gorard, S., Taylor, C., and Fitz, J. (2003) *Schools, Markets and Choice Policies*. London: Routledge Falmer.

Grace, D., and Tobin, J. (1998) 'Butt jokes and mean-teacher parodies: video production in the elementary classroom', pp. 42–62 in D. Buckingham (ed.), *Teaching Popular Culture: Beyond Radical Pedagogy*. London: UCL Press.

Green, H., Facer, K., and Rudd, T., with Dillon, P., and Humphreys, P. (2005) *Personalisation and Digital Technologies*. Bristol: NESTA Futurelab.

Gunter, B. (1998) *The Effects of Video Games on Children: The Myth Unmasked*. Sheffield: Sheffield Academic Press.

Gurak, L. J. (2001) *Cyberliteracy: Navigating the Internet with Awareness*. New Haven, CT: Yale University Press.

Habermas, J. ([1962] 1989) *The Structural Transformation of the Public Sphere*. Cambridge: Polity.

Hativa, N., and Lesgold, A. (1996) 'Situational effects in classroom technology implementations: unfulfilled expectations and unexpected outcomes', pp. 131–71 in S. T. Kerr (ed.), *Technology and the Future of Schooling*. Chicago: National Society for the Study of Education.

Healy, J. (1998) *Failure to Connect: How Computers Affect our Children's Minds – For Better and Worse*. New York: Simon & Schuster.

Heath, S. B. (1983) *Ways with Words*. Cambridge: Cambridge University Press.

Hennessy, S., Ruthven, K., and Brindley, S. (2005) 'Teacher perspectives on integrating ICT into subject teaching: commitment, constraints, caution, and change', *Journal of Curriculum Studies* 37 (2): 155–92.

Higgins, S. (2003) *Does ICT Improve Learning and Teaching in Schools?* London: British Educational Research Association.

Hockey, J., and Wellington, J. (1994) 'Information technology in the workplace: messages for employment and training', *British Journal of Education and Work* 6 (1): 57–74.

Hodge, B., and Tripp, D. (1986) *Children and Television: A Semiotic Approach*. Cambridge: Polity.

Holland, P. (1996) ' "I've just seen a hole in the reality barrier!" Children, childishness and the media in the ruins of the twentieth century', pp. 155–71 in J. Pilcher and S. Wagg (eds), *Thatcher's Children: Politics, Childhood and Society in the 1980s and 1990s*. London: Falmer.

Holloway, S., and Valentine, G. (2003) *Cyberkids: Children in the Information Age*. London: Routledge.

Home Office (1977) *Report of the Committee on the Future of Broadcasting*. London: HMSO [Annan Report].

Hope, A. (2005) 'Panopticism, play and the resistance of surveillance: case studies of the observation of students' internet use in UK schools', *British Journal of Sociology of Education* 26 (3): 359–73.

Illich, I. (1971) *Deschooling Society*. Harmondsworth: Penguin.

Ireson, J. (2004) 'Private tutoring: how prevalent and effective is it?', *London Review of Education* 2 (2): 109–22.

Ito, M. (2004) 'Personal, portable, pedestrian: lessons from Japanese mobile phone use', paper presented at Mobile Communication and Social Change conference, Seoul, Korea.

Jarvinen, A. (2003) 'Making and breaking games: a typology of rules', paper presented at Level Up: Digital Games Research Conference, Utrecht.

Jenkins, H. (2006) 'The war between "effects" and meanings: rethinking the video game violence debate', pp. 19–32 in D. Buckingham and R. Willett (eds), *Digital Generations: Children, Young People and New Media*. Mahwah, NJ: Lawrence Erlbaum.

Jeong, H.-S. (2001) 'Theory, Practice and "Empowerment" in Media Education: A Case Study of Critical Pedagogy', PhD thesis, Institute of Education, University of London.

Jones, K. (2002) *Education in Britain: 1944 to the Present*. Cambridge: Polity.

Juul, J. (2005) *Half-Real: Video Games between Real Rules and Fictional Play*. Cambridge, MA: MIT Press.

Kasesniemi, E.-L. (2003) *Mobile Messages: Young People and a New Communication Culture*. Tampere: Tampere University Press.

Kelley, P., Gunter, B., and Buckle, L. (1987) ' "Reading" television in the classroom: more results from the television literacy project', *Journal of Educational Television* 13: 7–20.

Kent, N., and Facer, K. (2004) 'Different worlds? A comparison of young people's home and school ICT use', *Journal of Computer Assisted Learning* 20: 440–55.

Kenway, J., and Bullen, E. (2001) *Consuming Children: Education – Entertainment – Advertising*. Buckingham: Open University Press.

Kerawalla, L., and Crook, C. (2002) 'Children's computer use at home and at school: context and continuity', *British Educational Research Journal* 28 (6): 751–71.

Kerawalla, L., and Crook, C. (2005) 'From promises to practices: the fate of educational software in the home', *Technology, Pedagogy and Education* 14 (1): 107–25.

Kerr, S. (1996) 'Visions of sugarplums: the future of technology, education and the schools', pp. 1–27 in S. T. Kerr (ed.), *Technology and the Future of Schooling*. Chicago: National Society for the Study of Education.

Kinder, M. (1991) *Playing with Power in Movies, Television and Video Games: From Muppet Babies to Teenage Mutant Ninja Turtles*. Berkeley, University of California Press.

Kirkpatrick, H., and Cuban, L. (1998) 'Computers make kids smarter, right?', *Technos* 7 (2).

Kirriemuir, J., and McFarlane, A. (2004) *Literature Review in Games and Learning*. Bristol: NESTA Futurelab.

Kline, S. (1993) *Out of the Garden: Toys and Children's Culture in the Age of TV Marketing*. London: Verso.

Kline, S., Dyer-Witheford, N., and de Peuter, G. (2003) *Digital Play: The Interaction of Technology, Culture and Marketing*. Montreal: McGill–Queens University Press.

Kress, G. (1997) *Before Writing: Rethinking the Paths to Literacy*. London: Routledge.

Kress, G., and van Leeuwen, T. (2001) *Multimodal Discourse: The Modes and Media of Contemporary Communication*. London: Edward Arnold.

Lachs, V. (2000) *Making Multimedia in the Classroom: A Practical Guide*. London: Routledge.

Laurillard, D. (1987) 'Computers and emancipation of students: giving control to the learner', *Instructional Science* 16 (1): 3–18.

Lawson, T., and Comber, C. (2000a) 'Introducing information and communication technologies into schools: the blurring of boundaries', *British Journal of Sociology of Education* 21 (3): 419–33.

Lawson, T., and Comber, C. (2000b) 'Censorship, the internet and schools: a new moral panic?', *Curriculum Journal* 11 (2): 273–85.

Leadbeater, C. (2004) *Personalisation through Participation: A New Script for Public Services*. London: Demos.

Leavis, F., and Thompson, D. (1933) *Culture and Environment*. London: Chatto & Windus.

Lee, N. (2001) *Childhood and Society*. Buckingham: Open University Press.

Leuven, E., Lindahl, M., Oosterbeek, H., and Webbink, D. (2004) *The Effect of Extra Funding for Disadvantaged Pupils on Achievement*. Bonn: Forschungsinstitut zur Zukunft der Arbeit.

Levene, K. (1986) *The Social Context of Literacy*. London: Routledge & Kegan Paul.

Levin, D., and Arafeh, S. (2002) *The Digital Disconnect: The Widening Gap between Internet-Savvy Students and their Schools*. Washington, DC: Pew Internet and American Life Project, www.pewinternet.org/pdfs/PIP_Schools_Internet_Report.pdf.

Lewin, C. (2004) 'Access and use of technologies in the home in the UK: implications for the curriculum', *Curriculum Journal* 15 (2): 139–54.

Lievrouw, L., and Livingstone, S. (eds) (2002) *Handbook of New Media*. London: Sage.

Livingstone, S. (2002) *Young People and New Media*. London: Sage.

Livingstone, S. (2004) 'The challenge of changing audiences: or, what is the audience researcher to do in the age of the internet?', *European Journal of Communication* 19 (1): 75–86.

Livingstone, S., and Bober, M. (2004) *UK Children Go Online: Surveying the Experiences of Young People and their Parents*. London: London School of Economics and Political Science.

Livingstone, S., and Bovill, M. (1999) *Young People, New Media*. London: London School of Economics and Political Science.

Livingstone, S., Bober, M., and Helsper, E. (2005) 'Active participation or just more information? Young people's take-up of opportunities to act and interact on the internet', *Information, Communication and Society* 8 (3): 287–314.

Livingstone, S., van Couvering, E., and Thumim, N. (2005) *Adult Media Literacy: A Review of the Research Literature*. London: Ofcom.

Lorac, C., and Weiss, M. (1981) *Communication and Social Skills*. Exeter: Wheaton.

Luke, C. (1989) *Pedagogy, Printing and Protestantism: The Discourse on Childhood*. Albany: SUNY Press.

Luke, C. (2000) 'Cyber-schooling and technological change: multiliteracies for new times', pp. 69–91 in B. Cope and M. Kalantzis (eds), *Multiliteracies: Literacy Learning and the Design of Social Futures*. London: Routledge.

McClay, J. K. (2002) 'Hidden "treasure": new genres, new media and the teaching of writing', *English in Education* 36: 46–55.

McDougall, J. (2006) *The Media Teacher's Book*. London: Edward Arnold.

McFarlane, A., Sparrowhawk, A., and Heald, Y. (2002) *Report on the Educational Use of Games*. Cambridge: Teachers Evaluating Educational Media.

Machin, S., McNally, S., and Silva, O. (2005) *Investing in Technology: Is There a Payoff in Schools?* London: Centre for the Economics of Education.

McNeal, J. U. (1999) *The Kids' Market: Myths and Realities*. Ithaca, NY: Paramount Market.

Mackenzie, D., and Wajcman, J. (eds) (1985) *The Social Shaping of Technology*. Milton Keynes: Open University Press.

Mackey, M. (2002) *Literacies across Media: Playing the Text*. London: Routledge.

Marvin, C. (1988) *When Old Technologies Were New*. New York: Oxford University Press.

May, C. (2002) *The Information Society*. Cambridge: Polity.

Melody, W. (1973) *Children's Television: The Economics of Exploitation*. New Haven, CT: Yale University Press.

Menchik, D. (2004) 'Placing cybereducation in the UK classroom', *British Journal of Sociology of Education* 25 (2): 193–213.

Messaris, P. (1994) *Visual 'Literacy': Image, Mind and Reality*. Boulder, CO: Westview Press.

Meyrowitz, J. (1996) 'Taking McLuhan and "medium theory" seriously: technological change and the evolution of education', pp. 73–110 in S. T. Kerr (ed.), *Technology and the Future of Schooling*. Chicago: National Society for the Study of Education.

Miliband, D. (2004) 'Foreword', pp. 11–14 in C. Leadbeater, *Personalisation through Participation: A New Script for Public Services*. London: Demos.

Mitchell, A., and Savill-Smith, C. (2004) *The Use of Computer and Video Games for Learning: A Review of the Literature*. London: Learning and Skills Development Agency.

Moir, G. (ed.) (1967) *Teaching and Television: ETV Explained*. Oxford: Pergamon.

Molnar, A., and Garcia, D. (2005) *Empty Calories: Commercializing Activities in America's Schools*. Tempe: Education Policy Studies Laboratory, Arizona State University.

Moore, D., and Dwyer, F. (1994) *Visual Literacy: A Spectrum of Visual Learning*. Englewood Cliffs, NJ: Educational Technology Publications.

Moran-Ellis, J., and Cooper, G. (2000) 'Making connections: children, technology, and the National Grid for Learning', *Sociological Research Online* 5 (3), www.socresonline.org.uk/5/3/moran-ellis.html.

Mumford, L. (1934) *Technics and Civilization*. New York: Harcourt, Brace.

Mumford, L. (1967, 1970) *The Myth of the Machine*, vols. 1 and 2. New York: Harcourt, Brace.

Mumtaz, S. (2000) 'Factors affecting teachers' use of information and communication technology: a review of the literature', *Journal of Information Technology for Teacher Education* 9 (3): 319–42.

Mumtaz, S. (2001) 'Children's perception and enjoyment of computer use in the home and the school', *Computers and Education* 36 (4): 347–62.

Nadesan, M. H. (2002) 'Engineering the entrepreneurial infant: brain science, infant development toys, and governmentality', *Cultural Studies* 16 (3): 401–32.

Negroponte, N. (1995) *Being Digital*. London: Hodder & Stoughton.

Neuman, S. (1995) *Literacy in the Television Age: The Myth of the Television Effect*. 2nd edn, Norwood, NJ: Ablex.

Newburn, T. (1996) 'Back to the future? Youth crime, youth justice and the rediscovery of "authoritarian populism"', in J. Pilcher and S. Wagg (eds), *Thatcher's Children? Politics, Childhood and Society in the 1980s and 1990s*. London: Falmer.

Newman, J. (2004) *Videogames*. London: Routledge.

Nixon, H. (1998) 'Fun and games are serious business', pp. 21–42 in J. Sefton-Green (ed.), *Digital Diversions: Youth Culture in the Age of Multimedia*. London: UCL Press.

Oblinger, D. G., and Oblinger, J. L. (eds) (2005) *Educating the Net Generation*. Boulder, CO: Educause; www.educatingthenetgen/.

OECD (Organization for Economic Co-operation and Development) (2004) *Completing the Foundation for Lifelong Learning*. Innsbruck: Studien Verlag.

Ofcom (Office of Communications) (2004) *Strategies and Priorities for the Promotion of Media Literacy: A Statement*. London: Ofcom.

Ofcom (2006) *Media Literacy Audit: Report on Media Literacy among Children*. London: Ofcom.

Ofsted (Office for Standards in Education) (2000) *Family Learning: A Survey of Current Practice*. London: Ofsted.

Ofsted (2004) *ICT in Schools: The Impact of Government Initiatives Five Years On*. London: Ofsted.

Ong, W. (1982) *Orality and Literacy*. London: Methuen.

Oppenheimer, T. (2003) *The Flickering Mind: The False Promise of Technology in the Classroom and How Learning Can Be Saved*. New York: Random House.

Oram, B., and Newman, J. (2006) *Teaching Videogames*. London: British Film Institute.

Palmer, R. (1947) *School Broadcasting in Britain*. London: BBC.

Papadakis, M. C. (2001) *The Application and Implications of Information Technologies in the Home: Where Are the Data and What Do They Say?* Arlington, VA: National Science Foundation.

Papert, S. (1980) *Mindstorms: Children, Computers and Powerful Ideas*. New York: Basic Books.

Papert, S. (1984) 'Trying to predict the future', *Popular Computing* (October).

Papert, S. (1993) *The Children's Machine: Rethinking School in the Age of the Computer*. New York: Basic Books.

Papert, S. (1996) *The Connected Family*. Atlanta: Longstreet.

Parker, D. (1999) 'You've read the book, now make the film: moving image media, print literacy and narrative', *English in Education* 33: 24–35.

Passey, D., and Rogers, C., with Machell, J., and McHugh, G. (2004) *The Motivational Effect of ICT on Pupils*. London: DfES.

Pegg, M. (1983) *Broadcasting and Society, 1918–1939*. London: Croom Helm.

Perelman, L. J. (1992) *School's Out: A Radical New Formula for the Revitalization of America's Educational System*. New York: Avon Books.

Plowman, L. (1996a) 'Designing interactive multimedia for schools', *Information Design Journal* 8 (3): 258–66.

Plowman, L. (1996b) 'Narrative, interactivity and the secret world of multimedia', *English and Media Magazine* 35: 44–8.

Postman, N. (1983) *The Disappearance of Childhood*. London: W. H. Allen.

Postman, N. (1992) *Technopoly: The Surrender of Culture to Technology*. New York: Knopf.

Potter, J. (2005) ' "This brings back a lot of memories": a case study in the analysis of digital video production by young learners', *Education, Communication and Information* 5 (1): 5–23.

Prensky, M. (2001a) 'Digital natives, digital immigrants', www.marcprensky.com [accessed March 2006].

Prensky, M. (2001b) 'Digital natives, digital immigrants, Part II: do they really *think* differently?', www.marcprensky.com [accessed March 2006].

Prensky, M. (2003) 'Escape from Planet Jar-Gon: or what video games have to teach academics about teaching and writing', www.marcprensky.com/writing [accessed May 2006].

Prensky, M. (2006) *'Don't Bother Me, Mom – I'm Learning!'* St Paul, MN: Paragon House.

Propp, V. (1970) *Morphology of the Folktale*. Austin: University of Texas Press.

PWC (PricewaterhouseCoopers) (2002) *Market Assessment of the BBC's Digital Curriculum Proposition*. London: PWC.

Reay, D. (1998) *Class Work: Mothers' Involvement in their Children's Primary Schooling*. London: UCL Press.

Reid, M., Parker, D., and Burn, A. (2002) *Evaluation Report of the BECTA Digital Video Pilot Project*, www.becta.org.uk/research/reports/digitalvideo/index.html.

Reynolds, D., Treharne, D., and Tripp, H. (2003) 'ICT – the hopes and the reality', *British Journal of Educational Technology* 34 (2): 151–67.

Roberts, D., Foehr, U., Rideout, V., and Brodie, M. (2003) *Kids and Media in America*. New York: Cambridge University Press.

Robertson, J. (1998) 'Paradise lost: children, multimedia and the myth of interactivity', *Journal of Computer Assisted Learning* 14: 31–9.

Robins, K., and Webster, F. (1999) *Times of the Technoculture*. London: Routledge.

Robinson, J. (1982) *Learning over the Air*. London: BBC.

Roe, K., and Broos, A. (2005) 'Marginality in the information age: the socio-demographics of computer disquietude', *Communications* 30 (1): 91–6.

Roe, K., and Muijs, D. (1998) 'Children and computer games: a profile of the heavy user', *European Journal of Communication* 13 (2): 181–200.

Roszak, T. (1986) *The Cult of Information*. New York: Pantheon.

Roszak, T. (1999) 'Shakespeare never lost a document to a computer crash', *New York Times* (11 March).

Salen, K., and Zimmerman, E. (2003) *Rules of Play: Game Design Fundamentals*. Cambridge, MA: MIT Press.

Salomon, G., and Perkins, D. (1996) 'Learning in wonderland: what do computers really offer education?', pp. 111–30 in S. T. Kerr (ed.), *Technology and the Future of Schooling*. Chicago: National Society for the Study of Education.

Scanlon, M., and Buckingham, D. (2003) 'Debating the digital curriculum: intersections of the public and the private in educational and cultural policy', *London Review of Education* 1 (3): 191–205.

Scanlon, M., Buckingham, D., and Burn, A. (2005) 'Motivating maths? Digital games and mathematical learning', *Technology, Pedagogy and Education* 14 (1): 127–39.

Schofield, J. W. (1995) *Computers and Classroom Culture*. Cambridge: Cambridge University Press.

Schofield, J. W., and Davidson, A. L. (2002) *Bringing the Internet to School: Lessons from an Urban District*. San Francisco: Jossey-Bass.

Schools Broadcasting Council (1962) *After Five Years: A Report on BBC School Television Broadcasting*. London: BBC.

Scupham, J. (1964) *Broadcasting and Education*. London: BBC.

Scupham, J. (1967) *Broadcasting and the Community*. London: Watts.

Seetharaman, S. (2006) ' "Bad Mums Watch Telly": Lay Theories Surrounding Pre-School Children's Television', MA dissertation, Institute of Education, University of London.

Sefton-Green, J. (1990) 'Teaching and learning about representation: culture and *The Cosby Show* in a North London comprehensive', pp. 127–50 in D. Buckingham (ed.), *Watching Media Learning: Making Sense of Media Education*. London: Falmer.

Sefton-Green, J. (ed.) (1999a) *Young People, Creativity and New Technologies*. London: Routledge.

Sefton-Green, J. (1999b) 'Media education, but not as we know it: digital technology and the end of media studies?', *English and Media Magazine* 40: 28–34.

Sefton-Green, J. (2003) 'Informal learning: substance or style?', *Teaching Education* 14 (1): 37–51.

Sefton-Green, J. (2004) *Literature Review in Informal Learning with Technology Outside School*. Bristol, NESTA Futurelab.

Sefton-Green, J., and Buckingham, D. (1996) 'Digital visions: young people's "creative" uses of multimedia technologies in the home', *Convergence* 2 (2): 47–79.

Seiter, E. (1993) *Sold Separately: Parents and Children in Consumer Culture*. New Brunswick, NJ: Rutgers University Press.

Seiter, E. (2005) *The Internet Playground: Children's Access, Entertainment, and Mis-Education*. New York: Peter Lang.

Selwyn, N. (1998a) 'The effect of using a home computer on students' educational use of IT', *Computers and Education* 31: 211–27.

Selwyn, N. (1998b) 'What's in the box? Exploring learners' rejection of educational computing', *Educational Research and Evaluation* 4 (3): 193–212.

Selwyn, N. (1999) 'Gilding the grid: the marketing of the National Grid for Learning', *British Journal of Sociology of Education* 20 (1): 59–72.

Selwyn, N. (2002) 'Learning to love the micro: the discursive construction of "educational" computing in the UK, 1979–1989', *British Journal of Sociology of Education* 23 (3): 427–43.

Selwyn, N. (2003) ' "Doing IT for the kids": re-examining children, computers and the "information society" ', *Media, Culture and Society* 25: 351–78.

Selwyn, N. (2005) 'Online/of-course: exploring the political and social construction of digital learning', paper presented at the Centre for the Study of Children, Youth and Media, Institute of Education, University of London, 7 June.

Selwyn, N. (2006) 'Exploring the "digital disconnect" between net-savvy students and their schools', *Learning, Media and Technology* 31 (1): 5–18.

Selwyn, N., and Brown, P. (2000) 'Education, nation states and the globalization of information networks', *Journal of Education Policy* 15 (6): 661–82.

Sims, R. (1997) 'Interactivity: a forgotten art?', *Computers in Human Behavior* 13 (2): 157–80.

Sinker, R. (1999) 'The Rosendale Odyssey: multimedia memoirs and digital journeys', pp. 22–31 in J. Sefton-Green (ed.), *Young People, Creativity and New Technologies*. London: Routledge.

Sinker, R. (2000) 'Making multimedia: evaluating young people's creative multimedia production', pp. 187–215 in J. Sefton-Green and R. Sinker (eds), *Evaluating Creativity: Making and Learning by Young People*. London: Routledge.

Skinner, B. F. (1954) 'The science of learning and the art of teaching', *Harvard Educational Review* 24 (2): 86–97.

Skinner, B. F. (1958) 'Teaching machines', *Science* 128 (3330): 969–77.

Solomon, C. (1986) *Computer Environments for Children: A Reflection on Theories of Learning and Education*. Cambridge, MA: MIT Press.

Somekh, B. (2004) 'Taking the sociological imagination to school: an analysis of the (lack of) impact of information and communication technologies on education systems', *Technology, Pedagogy and Education* 13 (2): 163–79.

Spector, J. M. (2001) 'An overview of progress and problems in educational technology', *Interactive Educational Multimedia* 3: 27–37.

Spencer, M. (1986) 'Emergent literacies: a site for analysis', *Language Arts* 63 (5): 442–53.

Squire, K. (2002) 'Cultural framing of computer/video games', *Game Studies* 2 (1), www.gamestudies.org.

Stephen, C., and Plowman, L. (2003) *Come Back in Two Years: A Study of the Use of ICT in Pre-School Settings during Spring and Summer 2002*. Dundee: Learning and Teaching Scotland.

Stoll, C. (1999) *High-Tech Heretic: Reflections of a Computer Contrarian*. New York: Doubleday.

Street, B. (1984) *Literacy in Theory and Practice*. Cambridge: Cambridge University Press.

Sutherland, R. et al. (2005) *InterActive Education: Teaching and Learning in the Information Age*. Swindon: ESRC.

Sutherland-Smith, W., Snyder, I., and Angus, L. (2003) 'The digital divide: differences in computer use between home and school in low socio-economic households', *L1 – Educational Studies in Language and Literature* 3: 5–19.

Sutton-Smith, B. (1998) *The Ambiguity of Play*. Cambridge, MA: Harvard University Press.

Tapscott, D. (1998) *Growing up Digital: The Rise of the Net Generation*. New York: McGraw Hill.

Taylor, T. L. (2003) 'Multiple pleasures: women and online gaming', *Convergence* 9 (1): 21–46.

Tearle, P. (2003) 'ICT implementation: what makes the difference?', *British Journal of Educational Technology* 34 (5): 567–83.

Tingstad, V. (2003) 'Children's Chat on the Net: A Study of Social Encounters in Two Norwegian Chat Rooms', PhD thesis, NTNU Trondheim.

Triggs, P., and John, P. (2004) 'From transaction to transformation: information and communication technology, professional development and the formation of communities of practice', *Journal of Computer Assisted Learning* 20: 426–39.

Turnbull, S. (1998) 'Dealing with feeling: why girl number twenty still doesn't answer', pp. 88–106 in D. Buckingham (ed.), *Teaching Popular Culture: Beyond Radical Pedagogy*. London: UCL Press.

Tyack, D., and Cuban, L. (1995) *Tinkering Toward Utopia: A Century of Public School Reform*. Cambridge, MA: Harvard University Press.

Tyner, K. (1998) *Literacy in a Digital World*. Mahwah, NJ: Lawrence Erlbaum.

Urwin, C. (1985) 'Constructing motherhood: the persuasion of normal development', pp. 164–202 in C. Steedman, C. Urwin and V. Walkerdine (eds), *Language, Gender and Childhood*. London: Routledge & Kegan Paul.

Valentine, G., Marsh, J., Pattie, C., and BMRB (2005) *Children and Young People's Home Use of ICT for Educational Purposes: The Impact on Attainment at Key Stages 1–4*. London: DfES.

Wade, B., and Moore, M. (2000) *Baby Power: Give your Child Real Learning Power*. London: Egmont.

Wagg, S. (1992) 'One I made earlier: media, popular culture and the politics of childhood', pp. 150–78 in D. Strinati and S. Wagg (eds), *Come on Down? Popular Media Culture in Post-War Britain*. London: Routledge.

Walkerdine, V. (1999) 'Violent boys and precocious girls: regulating childhood at the end of the millennium', *Contemporary Issues in Early Childhood* 1 (1): 3–23.

Walkerdine, V., and Lucey, H. (1989) *Democracy in the Kitchen*. London: Virago.

Waltermann, J., and Machill, M. (eds) (2000) *Protecting our Children on the Internet*. Gutersloh: Bertelsmann Foundation.

Warlick, D. (2005) *Raw Materials for the Mind: A Teacher's Guide to Digital Literacy*. 4th edn, Raleigh, NC: Landmark Project.

Warschauer, M. (2003) *Technology and Social Inclusion: Rethinking the Digital Divide*. Cambridge, MA: MIT Press.

Watson, D. (1998) 'The reality behind the rhetoric of information technology policy for schools', *Policy Options* (July/August): 71–5.

Watson, D. (2001) 'Pedagogy before technology: re-thinking the relationship between ICT and teaching', *Information and Communication Technologies* 6 (4): 251–66.

Webster, F. (1995) *Theories of the Information Society*. London: Routledge.

Wellington, J. (2001) 'Exploring the secret garden: the growing importance of ICT in the home', *British Journal of Educational Technology* 32 (2): 233–44.

Westbrook, K. C., and Kerr, S. (1996) 'Funding educational technology: patterns, plans and models', pp. 49–72 in S. T. Kerr (ed.), *Technology and the Future of Schooling*. Chicago: National Society for the Study of Education.

White, J. (2004) 'Howard Gardner: the myth of multiple intelligences', public lecture, Institute of Education, University of London, 17 November.

Williams, J., Clemens, S., Oleinikova, K., and Tarvin, K. (2003) *The Skills for Life Survey: A National Needs and Impact Survey of Literacy, Numeracy and ICT Skills.* London: DfES.

Williams, R. (1974) *Television: Technology and Cultural Form.* Glasgow: Fontana.

Wolf, M. J. P. (2002) *The Medium of the Video Game.* Austin: University of Texas Press.

Wolf, M. J. P., and Perron, B. (eds) (2003) *The Video Game Theory Reader.* London: Routledge.

Woolgar, S. (ed.) (2002) *Virtual Society? Technology, Cyberbole, Reality.* Oxford: Oxford University Press.

Index